John McHugh
Travel Sketches

John McHugh Travel Sketches

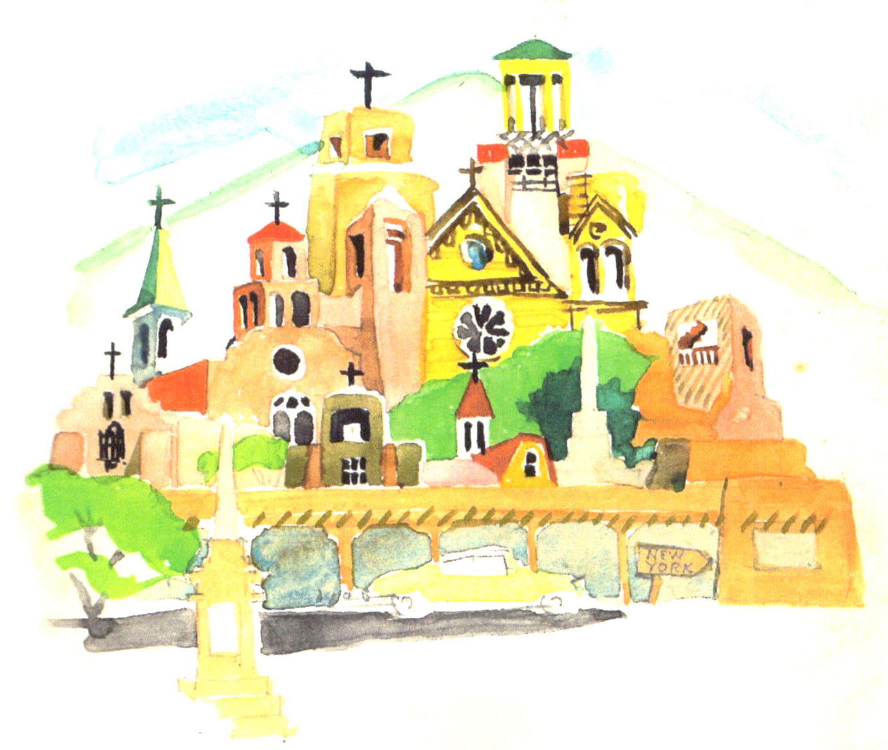

A Record of His Travels and Observations and a Guide to Sketching in the Field

Norman Crowe

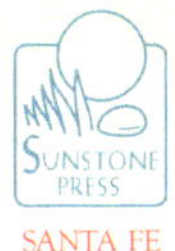

SANTA FE

Front cover: Collage of images from Santa Fe from a sketchbook by John McHugh, September 10, 1959. Back cover: European street scene.

Sunstone books may be purchased for educational, business, or sales promotional use. For information please write: Special Markets Department, Sunstone Press, P.O. Box 2321, Santa Fe, New Mexico 87504-2321.

Book and Cover design › Vicki Ahl
Body typeface › Goudy Old Style ‹› Display typeface › Monotype Corvisa
Printed on acid-free paper

Library of Congress Cataloging-in-Publication Data

John McHugh travel sketches : a record of his travels and observations and a guide to sketching in the field / Norman Crowe, editor.
pages cm
Includes bibliographical references.
ISBN 978-0-86534-895-0 (softcover : alk. paper)
1. McHugh, John, 1918-1995--Notebooks, sketchbooks, etc.
2. McHugh, John, 1918-1995--Travel. I. Crowe, Norman, editor of compilation.
II. McHugh, John, 1918-1995. Works. Selections. 2012.
NA737.M4365A4 2012
741.973--dc23

2012024536

WWW.SUNSTONEPRESS.COM
SUNSTONE PRESS / POST OFFICE BOX 2321 / SANTA FE, NM 87504-2321 /USA
(505) 988-4418 / ORDERS ONLY (800) 243-5644 / FAX (505) 988-1025

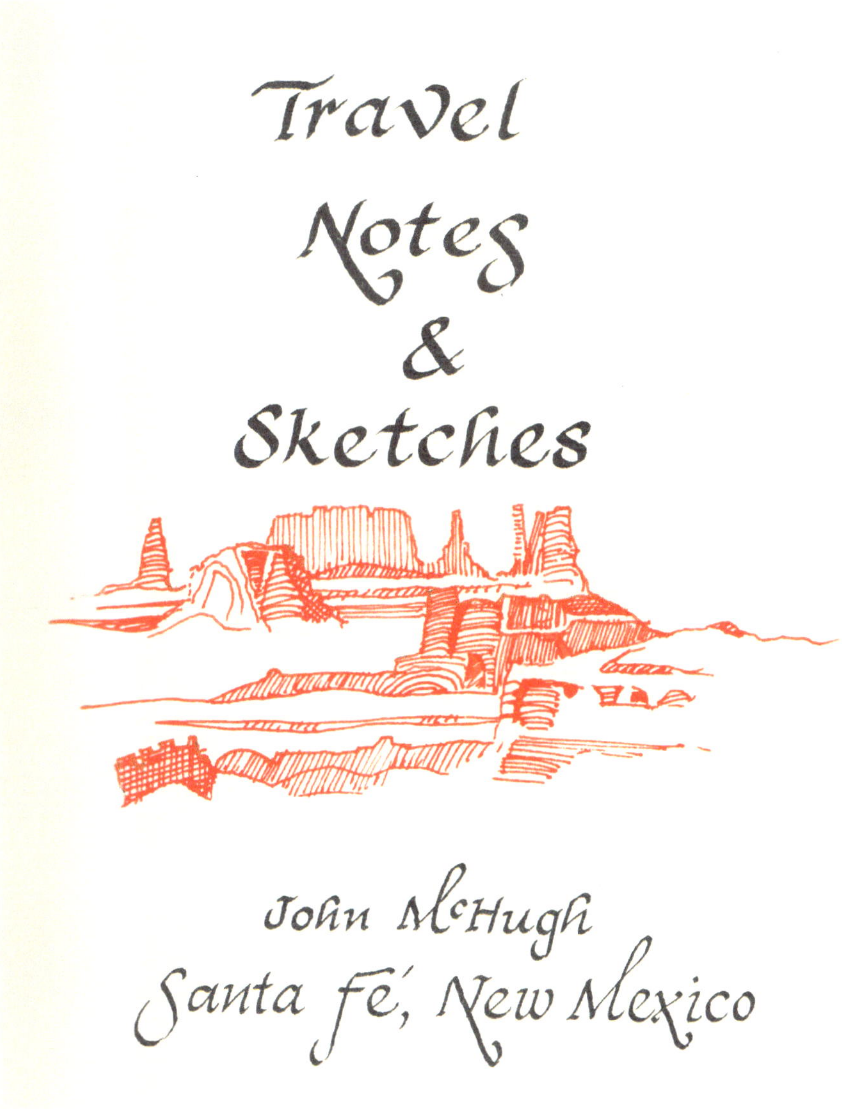

Travel

Notes

&

Sketches

John McHugh

Santa Fé, New Mexico

1. First page of a sketchbook by John McHugh, begun in the early 1980s.

Contents

Note: All sketches included here, unless otherwise noted, are reproduced from the eight travel sketchbooks of John McHugh, made available to the editor for reproduction by Gillian Wethey McHugh.

Preface

The intent of this publication is to balance two objectives. One is the presentation of a tapestry of travel sketches by an architect of note, to be thumbed through for enjoyment by anyone who may wish to travel with him on quiet journeys of exploration. The other is to encourage architects and others who themselves wish to grasp the richness of places more fully, to embark on the enjoyable lifelong habit of sketching. Whether or not we are successful—and I speak for myself as well as for John McHugh's widow, Gillian McHugh, and for his friend and business partner Van Dorn Hooker, both of whom wanted these two objectives for this collection of sketches—will ultimately be up to the reader.

While John McHugh's travel sketches are beautiful depictions in themselves, it is important to point out that the act of recording special places by means of sketching need not be considered the exclusive domain of artists. Sometimes beautiful drawings and watercolors, like those you will find in this volume, may inspire others to try their hand at sketching, but also there is the danger that a presentation of the work of an especially skillful draftsperson might discourage. Some might say apologetically, "Why, I could never draw like that! I'm not an artist." It is our hope that the effect of what follows here is the former response, not the latter. Sketching should be considered like handwriting: Some may write beautifully while others may scrawl only for the record, but it is the essence of what is written that is important. Visual notes, like written ones, have a double purpose. Taking notes helps to organize one's thoughts about a place or thing, while the act of sketching leads to discoveries otherwise overlooked. Sketches made on the spot serve from the time of their inception to enhance the memory of what is important and therefore worthy of remembering thereafter.

Further, sketching may be seen as something that amplifies written notes. Being too self critical of what the sketches look like on the page tends to discourage continuing on. But if the objective is to capture information, as with travel notes written in longhand, the habit soon takes hold, and the interplay between hand, eye, and mind in the process of sketching becomes itself an enjoyable part of travel.

We believe this book may be approached in a number of ways. One is to simply thumb through these pages from time to time to get a sense of John McHugh's travels and interests, stopping here and there to look more intently at something that catches the eye. At other times, one or another category of subjects depicted on these pages may be of interest, to be studied closely to learn more about places or ways of capturing their essence with pen, pencil, or watercolor on pages of a sketchbook. Especially we hope the reader comes to enjoy the sense of discovery the author of these sketches felt as he created them.

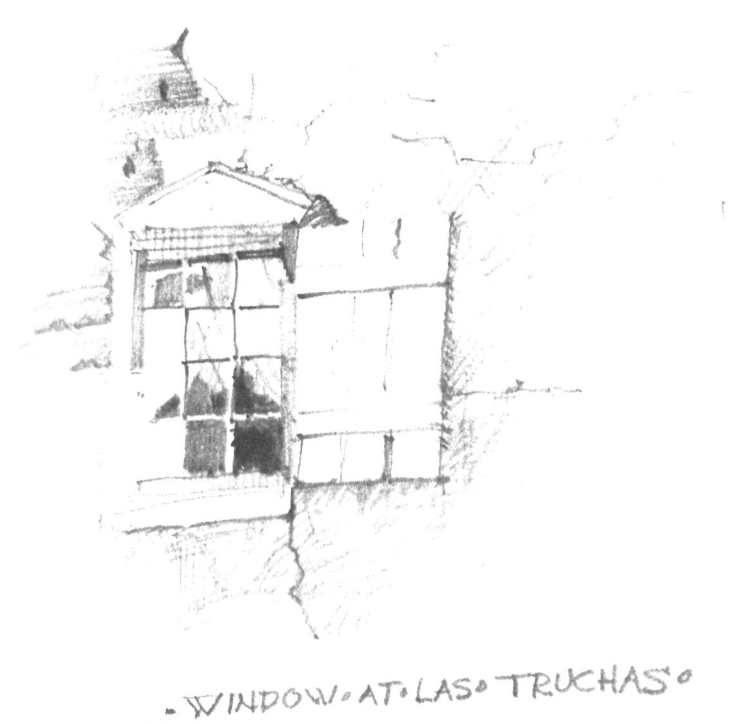

2. "Window at Las Truchas." Sketch by John McHugh in a sketchbook that he titled, "Northern New Mexico Architectural Details."

Acknowledgements

Two individuals initiated this project. This project owes its existence to John McHugh's widow, Gillian Wethey McHugh, whose idea it was from the onset. She made her husband's sketchbooks and other artistic materials available for study and reproduction and she cheerfully discussed his approach to traveling and sketching. Of special assistance was Van Dorn Hooker, John McHugh's longtime friend and partner in the Santa Fe architectural firm of McHugh, Hooker, Bradley P. Kidder and Associates-Architects. Van Dorn's recognition of the importance of sketching to the life and work of an architect gave meaning and purpose to the task of assembling these otherwise private sketches and watercolors for publication. Further, this project is indebted to monetary contributions from Van Dorn Hooker and from the New Mexico Architectural Foundation. Without the generosity of both, this project would not have become a reality.

Sketching, Memory, and Discovery

1

This is a collection of sketches by an architect who loved to travel and to sketch. For John McHugh, sketching while traveling provided the best means to absorb the scenes before him. As the reader will discover by thumbing through the sketches that follow, this is an account of his explorations, recorded in visual images. His evolving skill, the variety of subjects and media employed in their execution—graphite pencil, colored pencil, pen, Conté crayon, and watercolor—are the substance and focus of this volume.

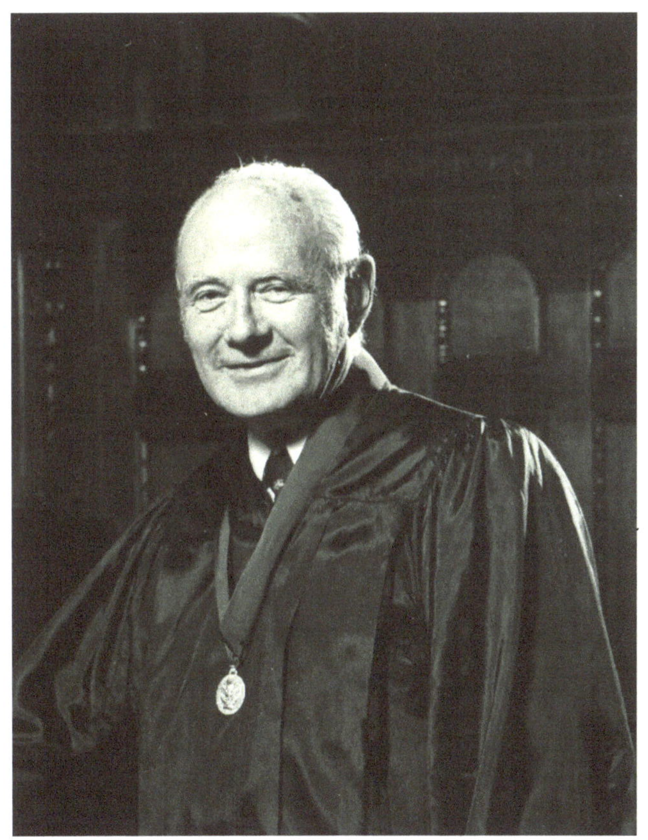

John McHugh

John McHugh provides us with a superb example of an old and venerable tradition. Throughout his life he maintained the custom of freehand sketching, both as he traveled and in the conduct of his work as an architect. The sketches presented on these pages begin with his journeys in New Mexico and they continue with trips across the U.S. and to Europe. They comprise a record of his lifelong love of traveling and of sketching. Maintaining a sketchbook was once common to just about all who traveled and took their journeys seriously. Today, however, the practice is largely limited to architects and artists, and fewer and fewer of them pursue that custom with the passing of time. Now most everyone presumes cameras have replaced the need to develop the sketcher's skill as well as the need to spend the quiet time it takes to stand before the subject of a sketch—a scene, a building, a place to be remembered—pen or pencil in one hand, sketchbook in the other. But does the camera actually replace all of what sketching once accomplished?

Why Sketch?

I am reminded of an amusing story told to me by a friend who to this day engages in the tradition of sketching while traveling. On a sunny morning while sketching in the Piazza San Marco in Venice, he noticed several young Greek sailors looking over his shoulder. When they realized he was aware of their presence, they smiled and gestured broadly without speaking to show they meant no harm, as people often do when they believe the person they are addressing is either deaf or does not understand their language. The sketcher, however, speaks fluent Greek and could not suppress his amusement when he heard one of them exclaim to the others, "Poor fellow! He must not be able to afford a camera." Like those sailors, many assume that sketching is an archaic practice now fully replaced by the miracle of point-and-shoot digital photography.

Recording visual information alongside verbal notes was once simply a part of how one took in the salient qualities of a place, as well as reinforced the memory of that place for a later time. The custom of quick sketches, especially by architects, has ancient roots. Their sketches were often both diagrammatic and realistic, sometimes cluttered with notes while at other times, pristine depictions of iconic scenes.

While it is our tendency to think of travel sketches as simply a way of recording scenes we would like to remember–which for the most part can be done more efficiently with a camera–we tend to forget that an important part of sketching, as noted above, is that it leads to a greater depth of understanding. It is in the act of sketching a scene or a thing such as a building that what would otherwise be overlooked is discovered—the relationship between things in an urban or natural setting, or the many complex and ephemeral qualities of a place that make it important—proportions, colors, subtleties of light and shade, and the role of shadows in alternately revealing and obscuring form. Unlike the point and shoot habit of photography where we shoot and move on, drawing leads to increasing discernment, thought, and understanding. The Swiss-French architect known as Le Corbusier, whose extensive sketchbooks from the teens and twenties of the last century are revered today, said it simply: "Cameras get in the way of seeing."

We inevitably lose something when we completely surrender past custom to a new technological development. Of course every shift in direction within the continuous evolution in a culture loses something when it gains something new. There is always a compromise of some sort. The loss is not always to be lamented, but it is a loss nonetheless. It is said that when the dark ages of ancient Greece began to wane and written language throughout the Greek speaking world slowly re-emerged, there were those who lamented the eventual demise of the bard and his practice of memorizing and reciting long and beautiful passages of epic poetry and life affirming myths. It was not only the professional bard that faded into the mysteries of time like the poems he recited, but the practice of memorizing epic stories and poetry as well. Threatened was the custom of passing on the poetry and myths of their people by elders of the clan to generations of wide-eyed youth by the fireside. With the demise of the practice of storytelling, we may wonder too if some of the traditional ties between youth and their elders also began to fade. Something gained, but something certainly lost.

The habit of sketching, however, need not necessarily be abandoned to photography any more than the recitation of poetry must yield exclusively to the written verse, silently read. Because it is a shortcut, photography does not train our minds to decipher the information before us in the way that sketching can do. That is what Le Corbusier meant when he said "cameras get in the way of seeing." For instance, research has revealed that taking photographs engages a different part of the brain than sketching. Parallel to that, is research published in 2003, conducted by neuroscientist Eleanor Maguire of University College London. She discovered that spatial understanding is enhanced by direct experience with something in its true three-dimensional state versus seeing it in a two-dimensional abstraction such as a photograph, a hard copy map, or a map on a global positioning device. In her research she studied London cabdrivers who, it turns out, develop a larger posterior hippocampus—the region of the brain that files spatial memories—than that of the average Londoner. Of course today, one could negotiate London's complex street network with a GPS navigational aid. However, using a GPS navigational device reduces or supplants using one's mind for understanding the spatial organization of streets and landmarks. Consequently, it appears relying on a GPS device may deprive the brain of developing more subtle and refined spatial understanding of a place.

If this is the case, it would follow that, like negotiating the streets of London with a GPS device, operating computer graphics such as computer aided design, short circuits the fuller neuronal involvement of drawing by hand. This effect was illustrated by a recent inadvertent discovery involving the application of computer graphics versus hand drawing in the School of Architecture at the University of Notre Dame. Initially it was decided that students would be prohibited from using computer graphics in the design process until they had reached their fourth year of architectural studies. The reason had to do with the observation that hand drawing required a much greater conscious understanding of how things go together in architectural, material, and general spatial terms—as opposed to simply selecting a detail or element from a digitized plan file in a computer aided design (CAD) program. But it turned out that there was an unexpected additional advantage to learning to draw by hand before coming to rely on a CAD or other computer graphics program. When the architecture students who had begun with hand drawing finally transitioned to computer graphics, their computer drawings were noticeably superior to the drawings by students who had begun with computer graphics at the onset. The use of line weight, perspective devices, color and the like, which clarify formal understanding and convey it effectively to others, was more refined among students who had begun with hand drawing before they turned to using the computer.

A recent publication of scientific field notes reiterates the point. The book is entitled, *Field Notes on Science and Nature*, and was edited by Michael Canfield, a biologist at Harvard. Canfield speaks of the importance of hand written and hand drawn field notes for the scientist because, "Good scientific documentation captures the development of the thinking, methods, and even the peregrinations that go into the particular work." He goes on to ask, "Does a technological application lend itself to substantial observation or is it simply designed to gather data? Capturing data is not the same thing as observation. A good example of this is comparing the process of taking a digital photograph with making a sketch." It should be clear that what applies to the scientist and his or her scientific field notes, applies to architectural field notes in the very same way.

All of this reveals a parallel between the abstract understanding of spatial form as reproduced in computer graphics and the situation of photography-versus-sketching. Something is gained while something else is lost, of course. But, if both photography and sketching are employed, each for its own advantage, a greater breadth of useful understanding is the result. Now we can have our cake and eat it too.

Field Sketches: An Ancient Practice

The practice of sketching by architects has traditionally played a special role in their education. In the West, as far as we know, the practice may be seen to date from the time of medieval masons who pursued the custom of compiling travel sketches in their guild books. Guild books, which spanned generations, held the best and most useful sketches accomplished by astute apprentices, during their mandatory one-year journeys between the completion of their apprenticeship and their advancement in their guild. They were required to travel across the continent of Europe to search for exemplary buildings and ongoing construction projects, and subsequently record them in their sketchbooks. Once they returned to their own guild, their sketchbooks would be scrutinized by the master masons, and those sketches that were judged to hold useful information for the guild would then be incorporated into the composite guild book for the benefit of future generations of apprentices as well as for general use among all members of the guild.

Unfortunately, no complete medieval guild books survive today. However, a beautiful example of a sketchbook from the 15th century and undoubtedly inspired by practices of the then waning guilds, is a travel sketchbook by the Italian architect, Francesco di Giorgio Martini. The pages of his sketchbook are parchment, it is bound in leather and has pewter hinges and clasp. He likely carried it in a leather pouch attached to a belt around his waist. The sketches were necessarily tiny, but they ranged from buildings and construction details to machinery for hoisting stone into place on construction projects, to ideas that occurred to him while traveling—ideas set in motion by things he observed and wanted to understand and remember. The precious character of the sketchbook itself—pewter, leather, and parchment—was consistent with the presumed importance of the thoughts and scenes recorded within.

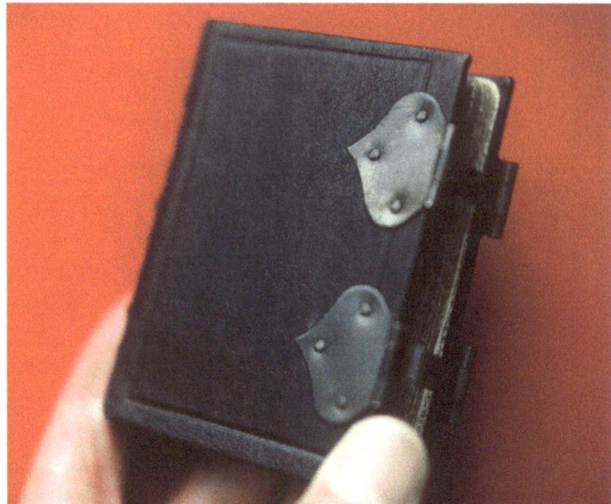

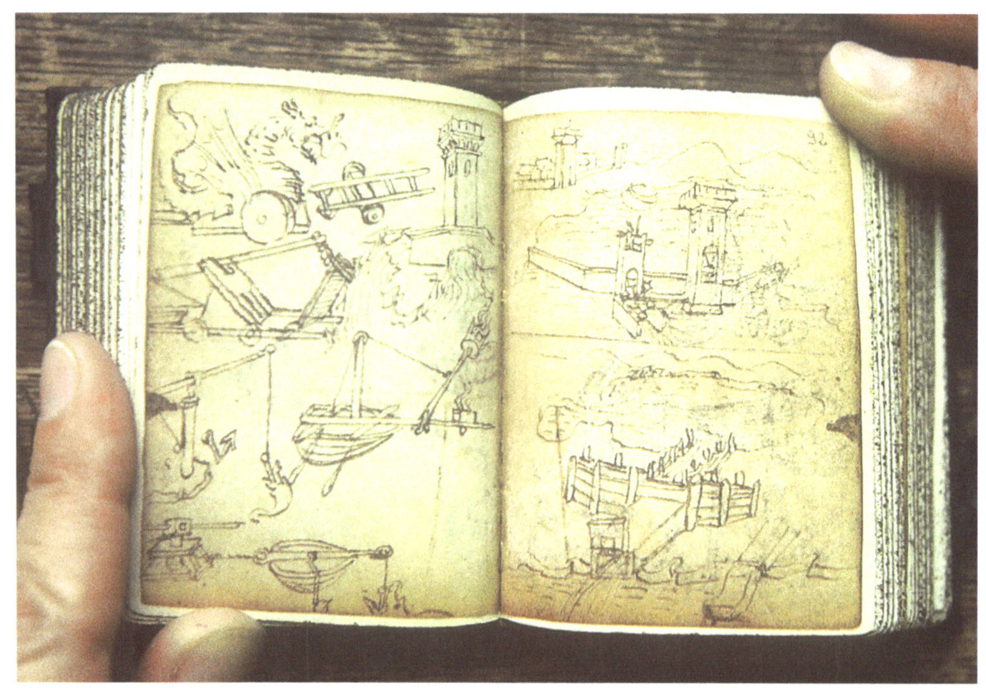

3. Facsimile of 16th century sketchbook of architect Francesco di Giorgio Martini, Urbino, Italy.

John McHugh's Travel Sketches and His Architecture

Like architects before him, John McHugh's travel sketches informed his architecture. His early mentor for sketching was Francesco (Frank) Montana, who was the director of the program in architectural education at the University of Notre Dame when McHugh studied there. Montana's sketching abilities are legendary among his students. He was so completely ambidextrous that he could sketch and paint with equal skill using either hand. When one hand or arm tired, he simply switched to the other. But most of all, his sketching served to entice students to follow the example of his observational skills, and consequently, to discover how his practice of sketching informed his architecture. I worked with Frank Montana when we taught Notre Dame architecture students in the School of Architecture's Rome Program in the 1970's. Frank was semi-retired then, his teaching activities limited to sketching and watercolor instruction while he conducted professional architectural commissions in the Middle East from his small professional office in Rome. Sketching to Montana was an integral part of life, and so it was for his student John McHugh.

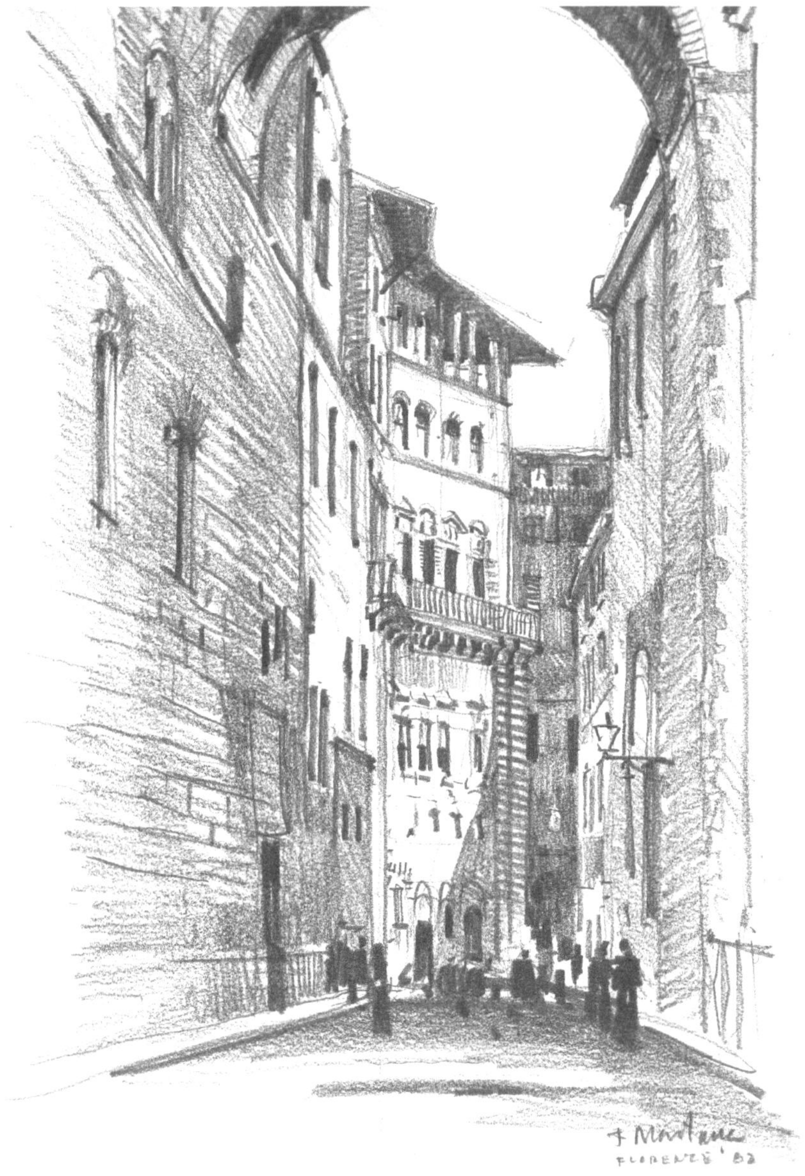

4. A typical Francesco Montana sketch in soft pencil, created on-site, on paper attached to an easel. Florence, Italy. (Courtesy of the Montana Drawing and Watercolor Collection, School of Architecture, University of Notre Dame.)

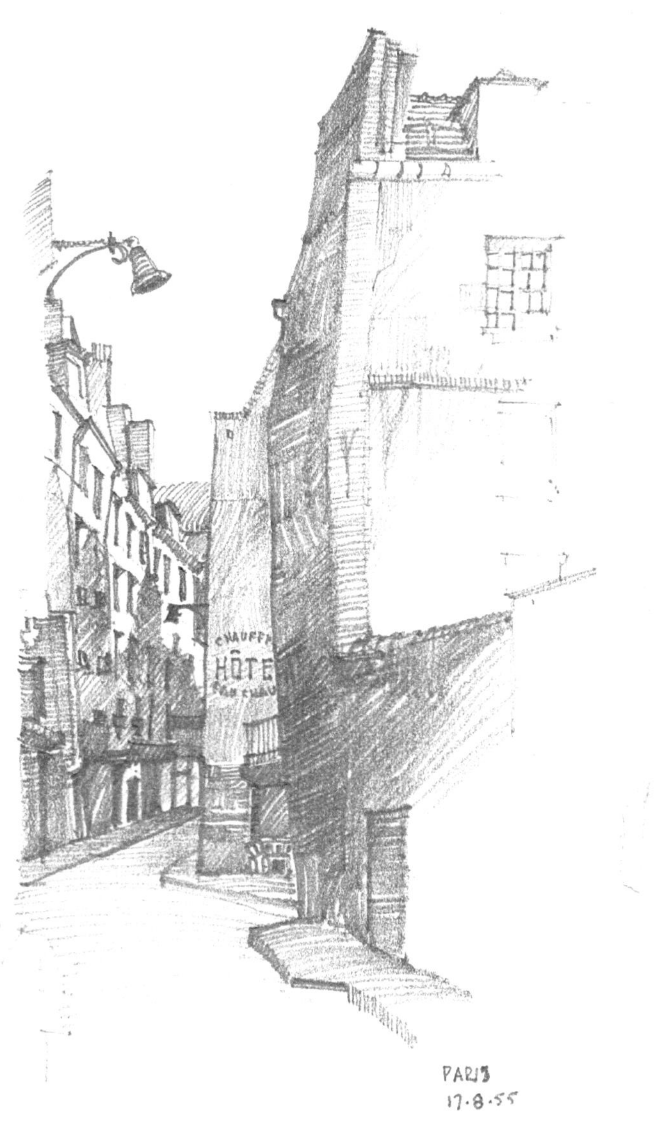

5. “Paris. 17-8-55.” A sketch by John McHugh, in soft pencil on a sketchbook page. Paris, France.

The connection between the travel sketches of an architect and his or her designs may not always be obvious. This is especially true when the sketches stretch across a broad range of subjects and techniques, as do John McHugh's. However, form, color, shadow, composition, as well as observations about ways of living that buildings and cities foster, once absorbed, are soon committed to an intuitive understanding and thereby inform subsequent designs.

Following are examples of presentation drawings by John McHugh. They are of buildings that he designed during his career as an architect. Following these drawings is an aerial photograph of the complex for which he is perhaps best known to Santa Feans, the first Santa Fe Opera Pavilion. These drawings and the photograph are included here as reminders of the intricate and important relationship between sketching, observation, and design.

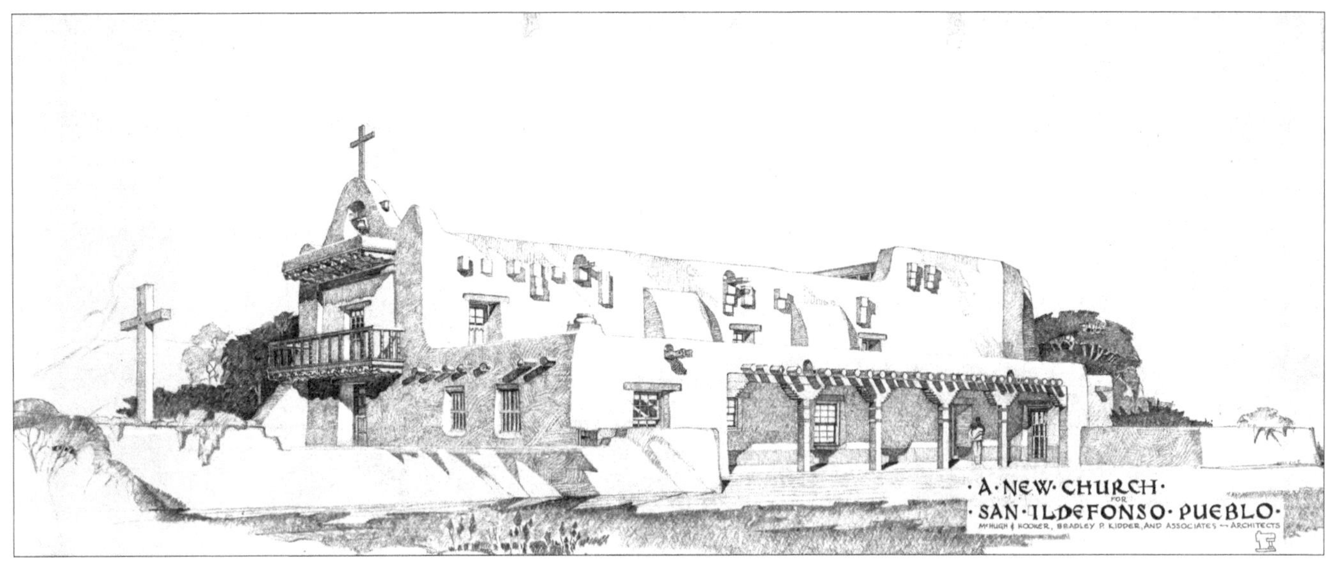

6. “A New Church, San Ildefonso Pueblo,” McHugh & Hooker, Bradley P. Kidder, and Associates–Architects. (Courtesy of the John W. McHugh Architectural Drawings Collection, Center for Southwest Research, General Library, University of New Mexico.)

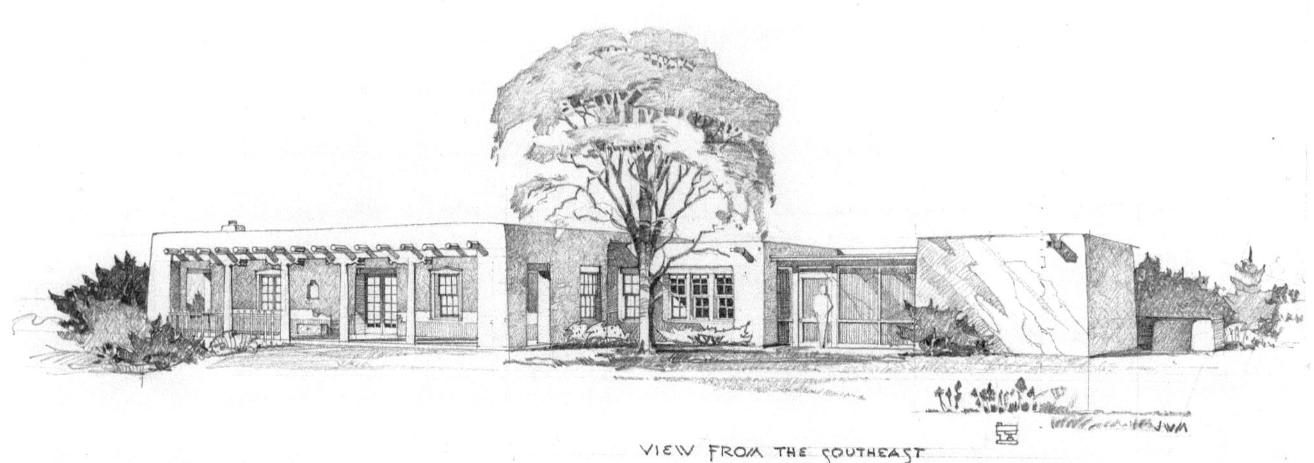

7. "Preliminary Plans of a Residence for Mrs. Elizabeth Proctor, Old Pecos Road, Santa Fe, New Mexico," McHugh & Hooker–Architects, Santa Fe. (Reproduced from John W. McHugh Architectural Drawings, Courtesy of The Center for Southwest Research, General Library, University of New Mexico.)

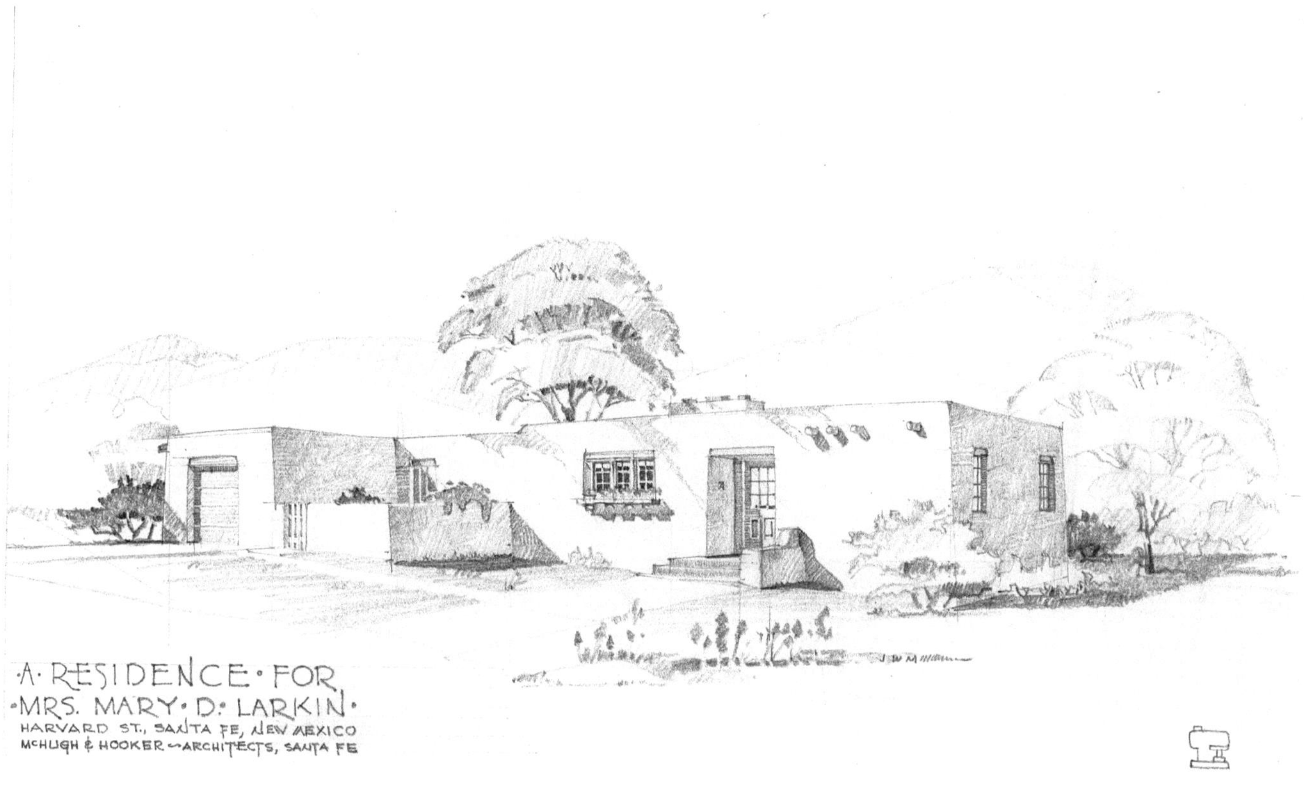

8. "A Residence for Mrs. Mary D. Larkin, Harvard St. Santa Fe, New Mexico," McHugh & Hooker—Architects, Santa Fe. (Courtesy of the John W. McHugh Architectural Drawings Collection, The Center for Southwest Research, General Library, University of New Mexico.)

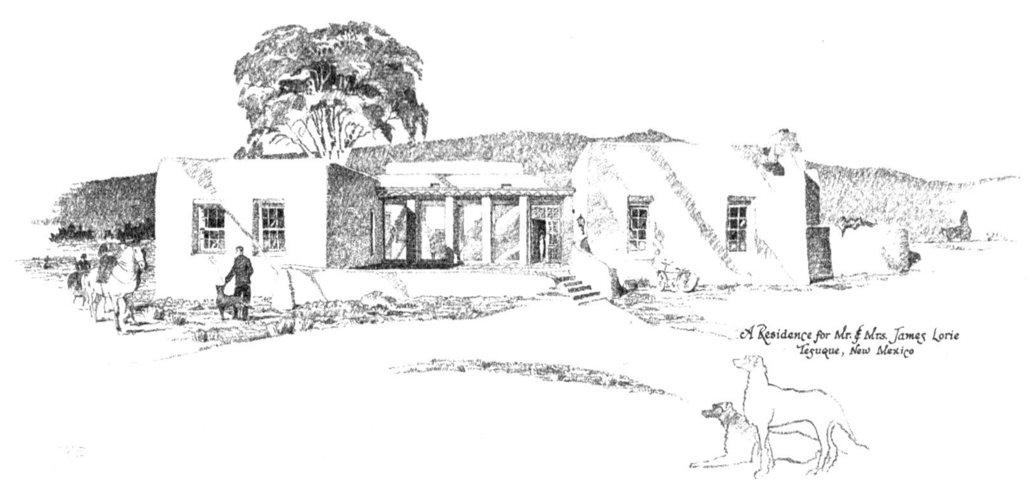

9. "A Residence for Mr. & Mrs. James Lorie, Tesuque, New Mexico," McHugh & Hooker–Architects. (Courtesy of the John W. McHugh Architectural Drawings Collection, The Center for Southwest Research, General Library, University of New Mexico.)

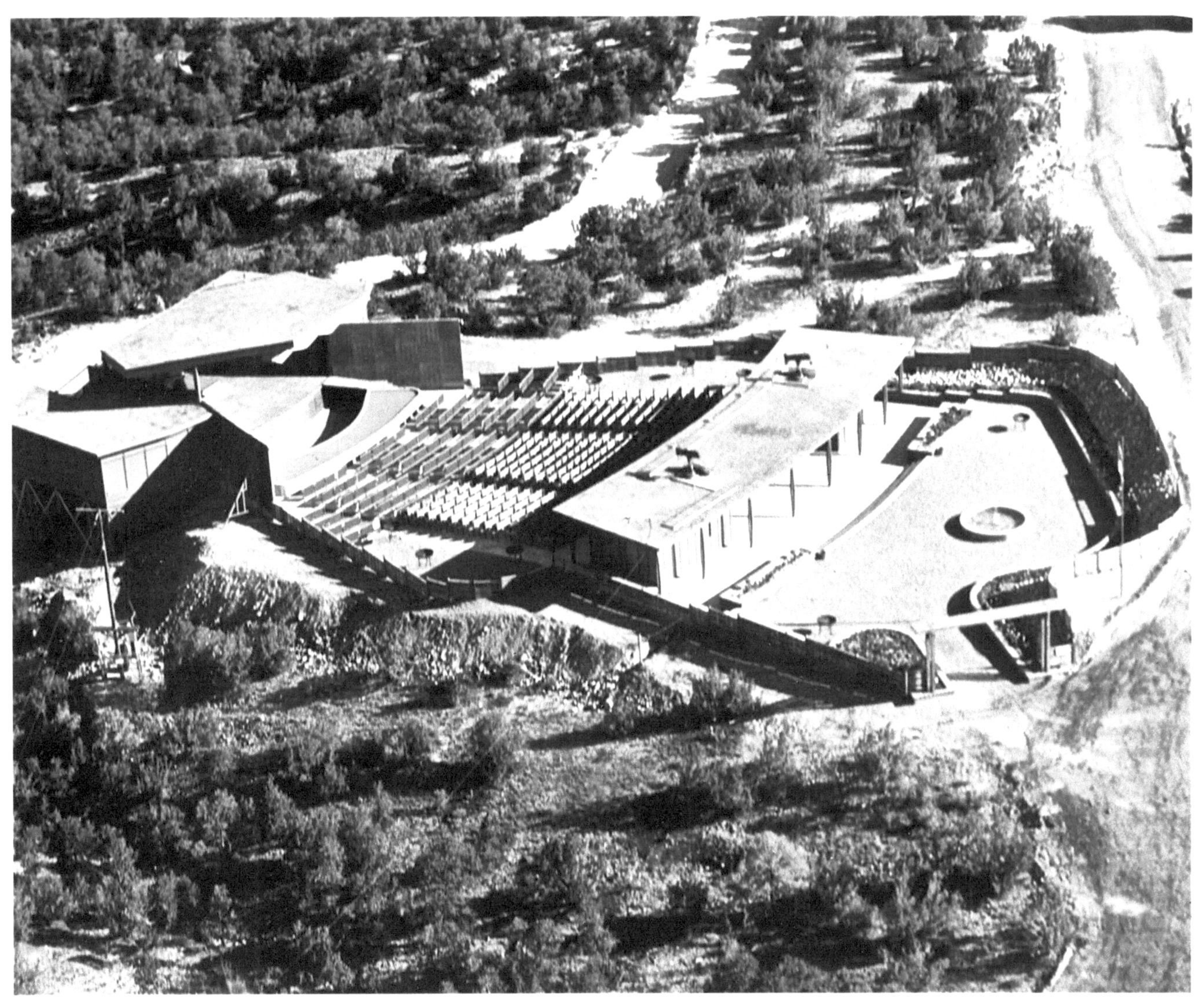

10. Aerial View, first Santa Fe Opera Pavilion. McHugh, Hooker–Architects.
(Courtesy of the John W. McHugh Architectural Drawings Collection,
The Center for Southwest Research, General Library, University of New Mexico.)

A note about John McHugh's travel sketches as presented in the chapters that follow: McHugh did not necessarily fill one sketchbook before beginning another. Instead, sketches from various periods are interspersed within most of his sketchbooks. The reason is most likely that he switched back and forth between sketchbooks, depending on which sketchbook provided the most appropriate paper or the appropriate page size or texture of paper for a given technique and subject.

We trust these sketches, drawings, and paintings by John McHugh will inspire as well as provide the reader with an enjoyable collection of lively, sensitive, and frequently beautiful examples. Especially, they may be seen to represent journeys—journeys across lands and oceans, journeys of discovery, and journeys of understanding in the pursuit of architectural knowledge—and finally, the journey of life itself.

Journeys 2

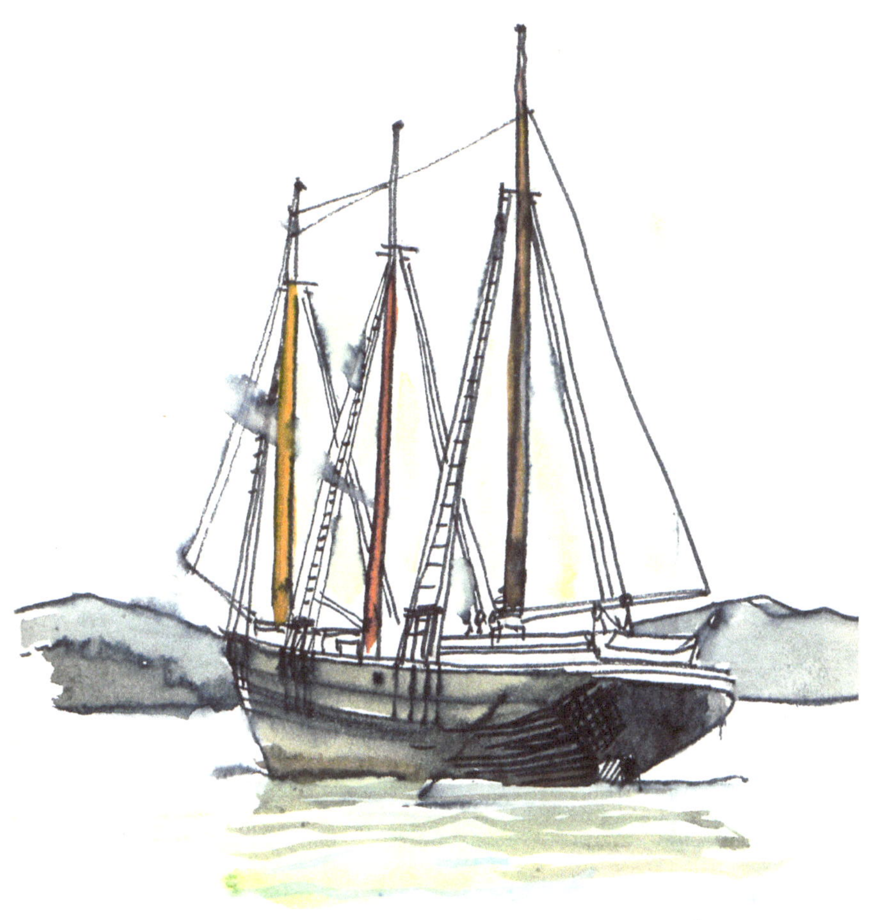

11. "G. A. Thayer." Undated sketch, ink and watercolor on sketchbook page.

John McHugh's travel sketches may be seen to chronicle his journeys of exploration within the larger journey of life itself. After graduating cum laude in architecture from the University of Notre Dame in 1941, he entered military service in WWII, after which he returned to Notre Dame to join its faculty following the war. After a brief teaching stint at Notre Dame, he began a trip across the country, stopping in Santa Fe for car repairs, after which he intended to continue on to California. He applied for short-term employment in the office of Santa Fe architect John Gaw Meem, who was rapidly becoming New Mexico's most celebrated architect. That "brief time" with Meem lasted until McHugh began his own firm in Santa Fe with partner and friend Van Dorn Hooker in 1956. John McHugh remained a Santa Fean until his death in 1995.

The establishment of an architectural firm with Van Dorn Hooker began what is perhaps the most productive part of McHugh's professional career as an architect. The work of the firm included private residences, commercial establishments and institutional designs, as well as the restoration of venerable adobe churches and the project for which the firm was best known in Santa Fe, the design of the first Santa Fe Opera Pavilion.

While many architectural firms engaged professional architectural renderers to do drawings for presentation to clients to inform them how their buildings would look once completed, John McHugh took care of that task himself. (Illustrations 6 through 10). The approach to an architectural rendering of a proposed work is, of course, much more formal than sketchbook entries. For professional renderings, the drawings are adjusted to perspective lines laid out mechanically with drafting instruments in accordance with the rules of optical perspective.

The renderings of architectural designs by John McHugh may be seen in contrast to his sketches of existing architecture and urbanism throughout the remainder of this book, sketches made in the field during his travels. This is to say that architectural renderings are created in lockstep as part of the production of a professional firm, while in-the-field sketches typically follow a more serendipitous and relaxed mode. The eight sketchbooks, from which drawings here have been reproduced, represent vacations and trips of personal exploration. In effect they present us with the quiet thoughts of one whose interests range across architecture, urbanism, and nature, revealing personal reflections on what is of interest to capture, to learn from and to remember. From these drawings we may sense something of the journeys they chronicle.

Perhaps the most trying event in John McHugh's life was a stroke that he suffered at age sixty-nine and which seriously impaired his visual acuity as well as motor skills necessary for sketching. Simply put, he could no longer draw. He had to teach himself to sketch all over again. Sketching soon became a kind of self directed therapy, a challenge to return his life to what it had been before. However, because sketching demands more precision and control than creating a painting with broad strokes and bold colors, he turned to painting for awhile. Once he had restored the coordination of hand and eye to a satisfactory minimum level, he returned to sketching. He carefully lettered his intents into a new sketchbook. "Good sketching demands manual dexterity," he wrote, "the ability to see both at a distance and up close. The need to design the page [and] organize the composition ... should be good therapy for me. I begin with high hopes [and] the confidence I'll be able to summon up the patience [and] persistence necessary." This statement, lettered in a now shaky architectural lettering, demonstrates that the act of lettering itself, a necessary skill for all architects of his generation and before, became an exercise in regaining confidence.

THIS IS A BOOK OF THERAPUTIC EXERCISES - SKETCHES -
MADE FOR THE PURPOSE OF LEARNING - ALL OVER AGAIN -
HOW TO SKETCH. BEGINNING IN THE EARLY 1930'S, I HAVE
SKETCHED AND PAINTED IN CRAYONS, PENCIL,
CHARCOAL, WATER COLOUR, AND OILS. AS I GREW OLDER,
MY EYESIGHT GRADUALLY DETERIORATED; BUT THE
STROK I HAD IN 1987 ALMOST WIPED OUT THESE ABILITIES &
SKILLS: ABILITY TO SEE DECREASED DRAMATICALLY, AND
THE ABILITY TO PERCEIVE, TO "TAKE IN" WHAT I AM
SEEING, HAS ALMOST GONE. MANUAL DEXTERITY -
MAKING THE PENCIL, PEN, OR BRUSH DO WHAT I WANT
THEM TO - IS GREATLY REDUCED ALONG WITH MEMORY AND
THE ABILITY TO THINK COHERENTLY SO THAT I KNOW
WHAT I WANT MY HANDS TO DO. SO I BEGIN THESE
EXERCISES WITH SOME OF THE ABILITIES I HAD 50 YEARS
AGO (BUT NOT ALL OF THEM: FOR ENCOURAGEMENT, I HAVE
THE EXPERIENCE OF THE PAST 12 MONTHS OF SLOW BUT
STEADY IMPROVEMENT PHYSICALLY TOGETHER WITH A
MUCH SLOWER IMPROVEMENT IN MEMORY, IN BEGINNING
TO PLAN SMALL ACTIVITES, AND EVEN TO THINK CON-
STRUCTIVELY. SINCE GOOD SKETCHING DEMANDS
MANUAL DEXTERITY, THE ABILITY TO SEE BOTH AT A DISTANCE
AND UP CLOSE, THE NEED TO DESIGN THE PAGE & ORGANIZE
THE COMPOSITION, IT SHOULD BE GOOD THERAPY FOR ME.
I BEGIN WITH HIGH HOPES & THE CONFIDENCE TAT I'LL
BE ABLE TO SUMMON UP THE PATIENCE & PERSISTENCE
NECESSARY. BEGUN IN SANTA FE JUNE 26, 1988

12. "This is a book of therapeutic exercises ... June 26, 1988." Hand lettered page in a sketchbook.

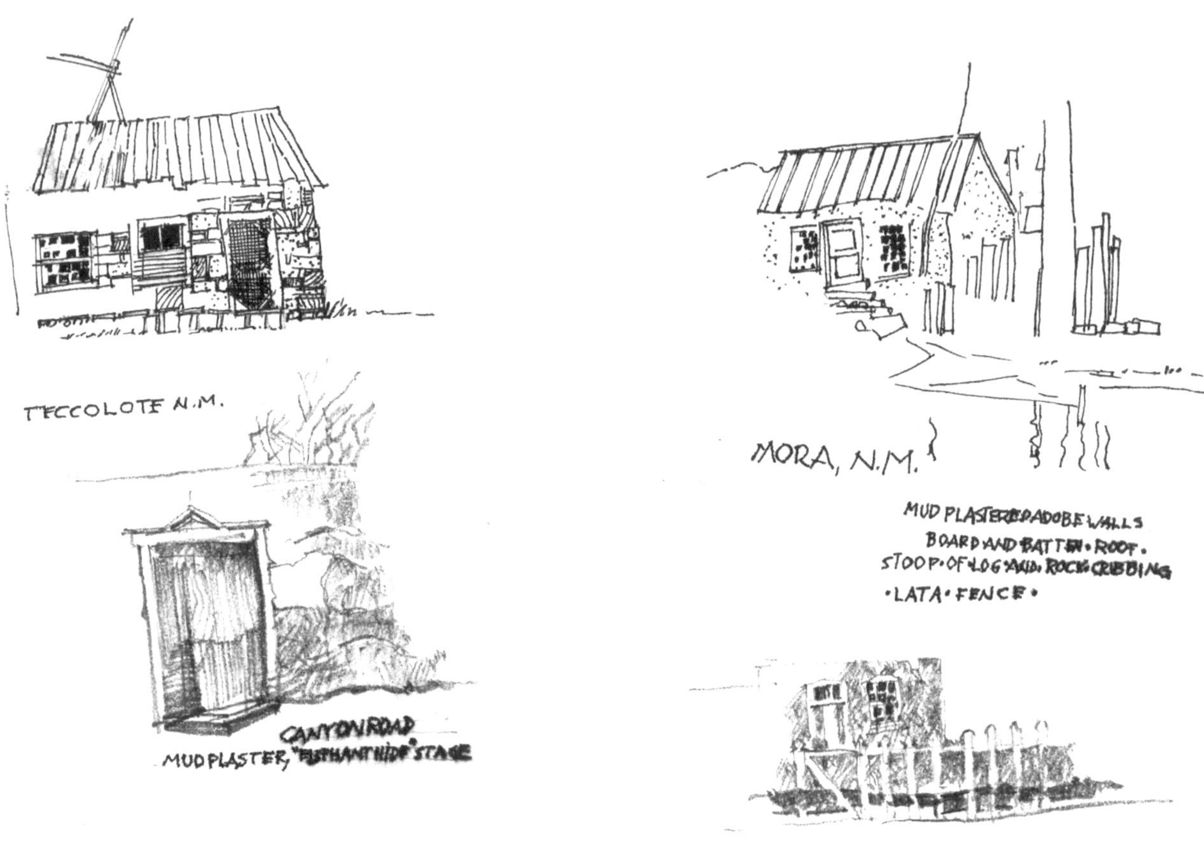

13. A series of four modest sketches accomplished when John McHugh began to regain his ability to sketch after having suffered a stroke in 1987.

New Mexico

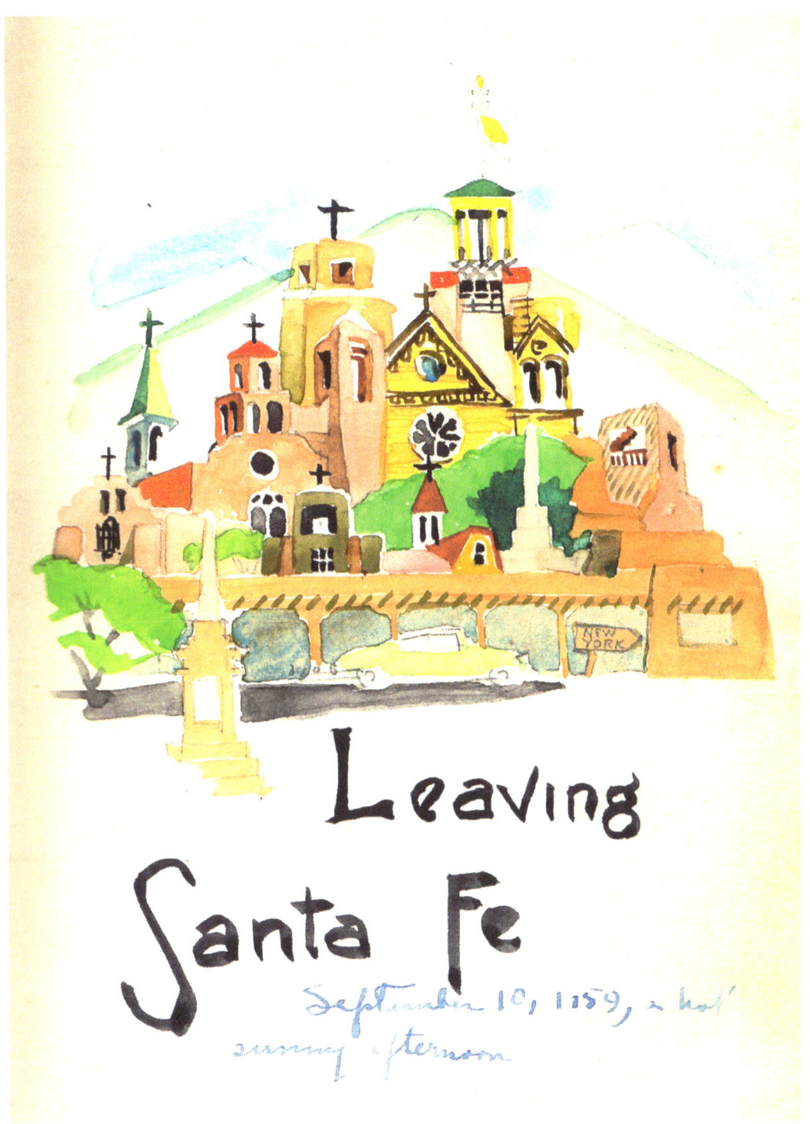

14. "Leaving Santa Fe, September 10, 1959, a hot sunny afternoon." From the first page of a sketchbook.

Most of McHugh's sketches involve exploration of New Mexico, John McHugh's and his wife's adopted home. John grew up in the Midwest and his wife Gillian, in England and Switzerland. At first New Mexico's landscape and architecture must have been distinctly exotic to them both. Its architectural richness involves multiple dimensions of its own combination of time and culture. Early Pueblo Culture ruins in New Mexico date back to the ninth century and before, while still occupied pueblos in Northern New Mexico are as old as a thousand years themselves, each with its own language or dialect of a common indigenous language. As for post-native cultures, Spanish architecture and urbanism arrived in the northern frontier of New Spain in the sixteenth century and American architecture and urbanism after 1848. And then there is the land. The northern high desert and mountains, the hot deserts of the south, and isolated landscape anomalies dotted throughout the varied landscape of New Mexico, offer the sketcher and watercolorist plenty of inspiration for recording on site those special moments in journeys across the state.

Sketches 14 and 15 reflect the excitement and anticipation of beginning a journey. They are followed by sketches of New Mexico taken from several of McHugh's sketchbooks. His travels within New Mexico were interspersed with trips abroad and across the U.S. The sketches included in this volume do not necessarily follow the order in which they were drawn, but rather are arranged by subject and style of drawing. As mentioned earlier, McHugh's sketches do not always follow in chronological order in a given sketchbook but, instead, relate to the array of page sizes and paper types among the eight sketchbooks he filled during his lifetime.

The sketches in this section are all of New Mexico. Soft pencil and watercolor used on its own, or more often in combination with graphite and colored pencil, are the favored media throughout most of McHugh's sketchbooks. The soft pencil techniques are especially effective in capturing softly modeled adobe forms, while the occasional watercolor brings out various colors of raw and painted adobe against the skies and natural landscapes of New Mexico. Note that the final two sketches in this series are different than the others in the following way: While the composition of other objects and scenes reflect a harmonious blend of geometry and nature, the last two sketches capture the happenstance and abrupt juxtaposition of colors and forms that were beginning to change the townscapes of New Mexico and elsewhere in the 1950s. It was the all-pervasive use of the automobile along with rapid change, often characterized as "progress," that began to alter the cultural landscape–compared to the gentle, slow evolution of architecture and urbanism that went before.

This little book begins on a Greyhound bus leaving Santa Fe New Mexico on a glorious sunny-cloudy day in December, 1952 — and who knows where it will end...

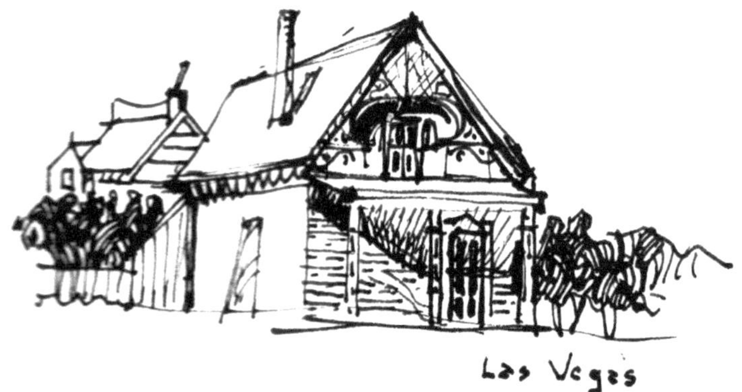

15. "This little book begins on a Greyhound bus ... Las Vegas." This drawing is from the first page of a sketchbook begun in 1952.

The following examples (16 through 45) are sketches of indigenous and vernacular architecture of New Mexico. Also included are architect-designed buildings such as Cristo Rey (28) and the Park Service Building (34). These are modern buildings that accurately reflect vernacular and indigenous architecture and therefore have been included with other vernacular examples. What I have termed as vernacular here may be seen to characterize the pre-modernist architecture of New Mexico. This includes what came to be called the pueblo style as well as buildings in "the territorial style" that were built without the involvement of professional designers. And of course, included are permutations of both in combination with one another in detail, overall form, or constituent elements. Near the end of the following series (44 and 45) are examples of what may be referred to as the new vernacular, coming after the preponderance of the automobile and associated with commercialization that is national in scope, and represents architectural and urban expressions that are no longer unique to New Mexico.

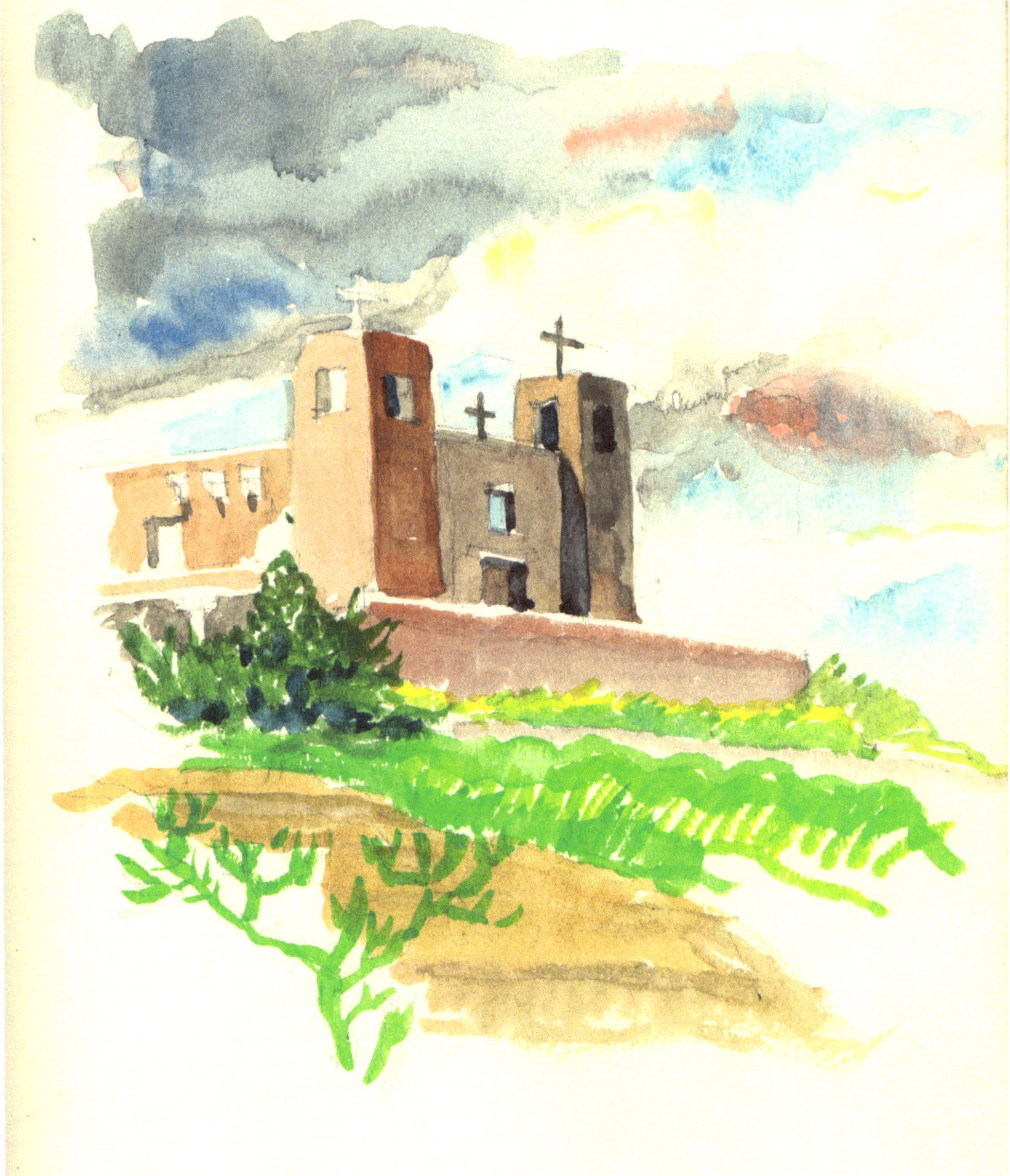

16. New Mexico Mission Church. Watercolor on sketchbook pages.

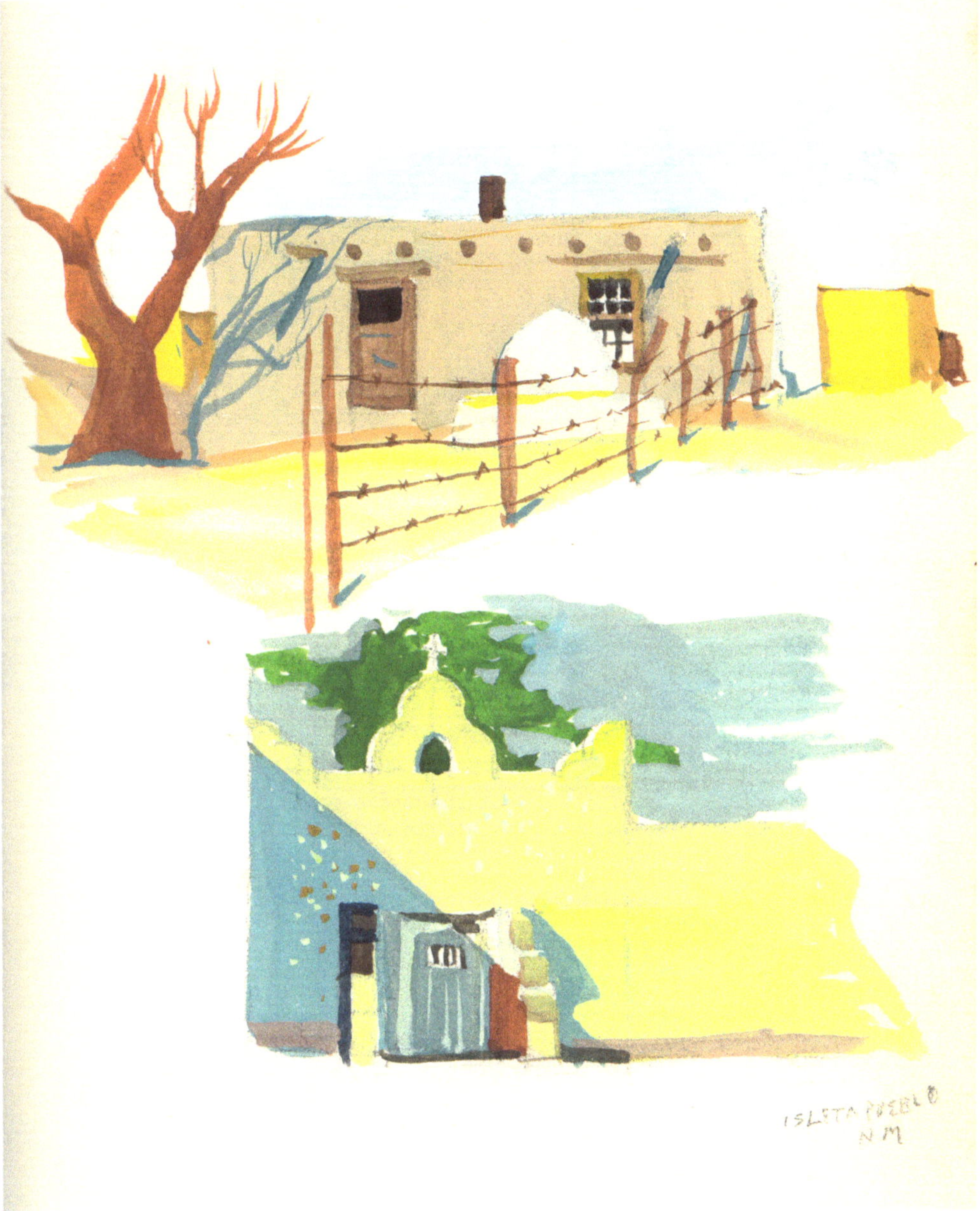

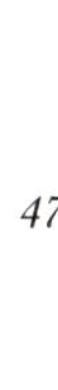

17. "Isleta Pueblo." House and mission church. Watercolor on sketchbook page.

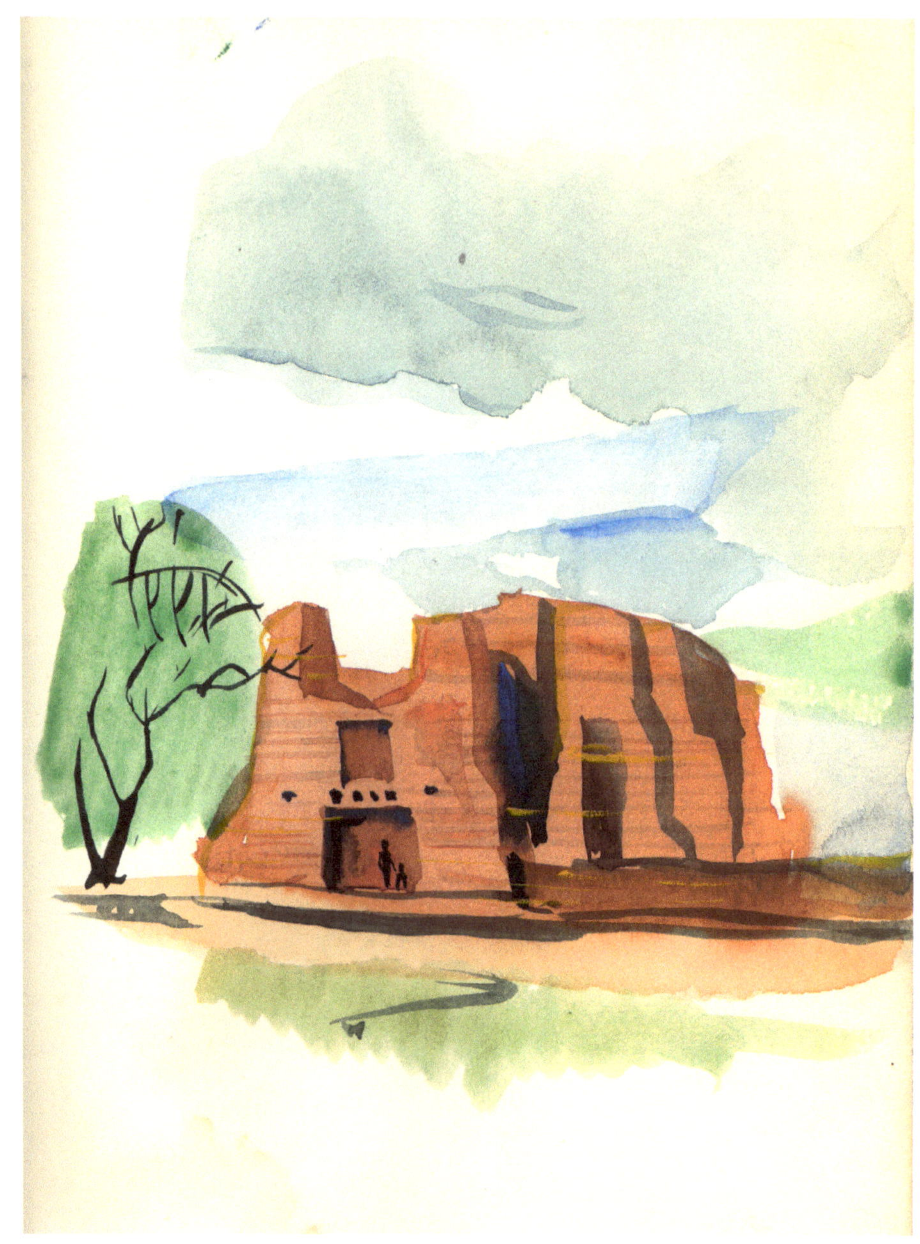

18. Ruin, New Mexico Mission Church, Salinas Pueblo. Watercolor on sketchbook page.

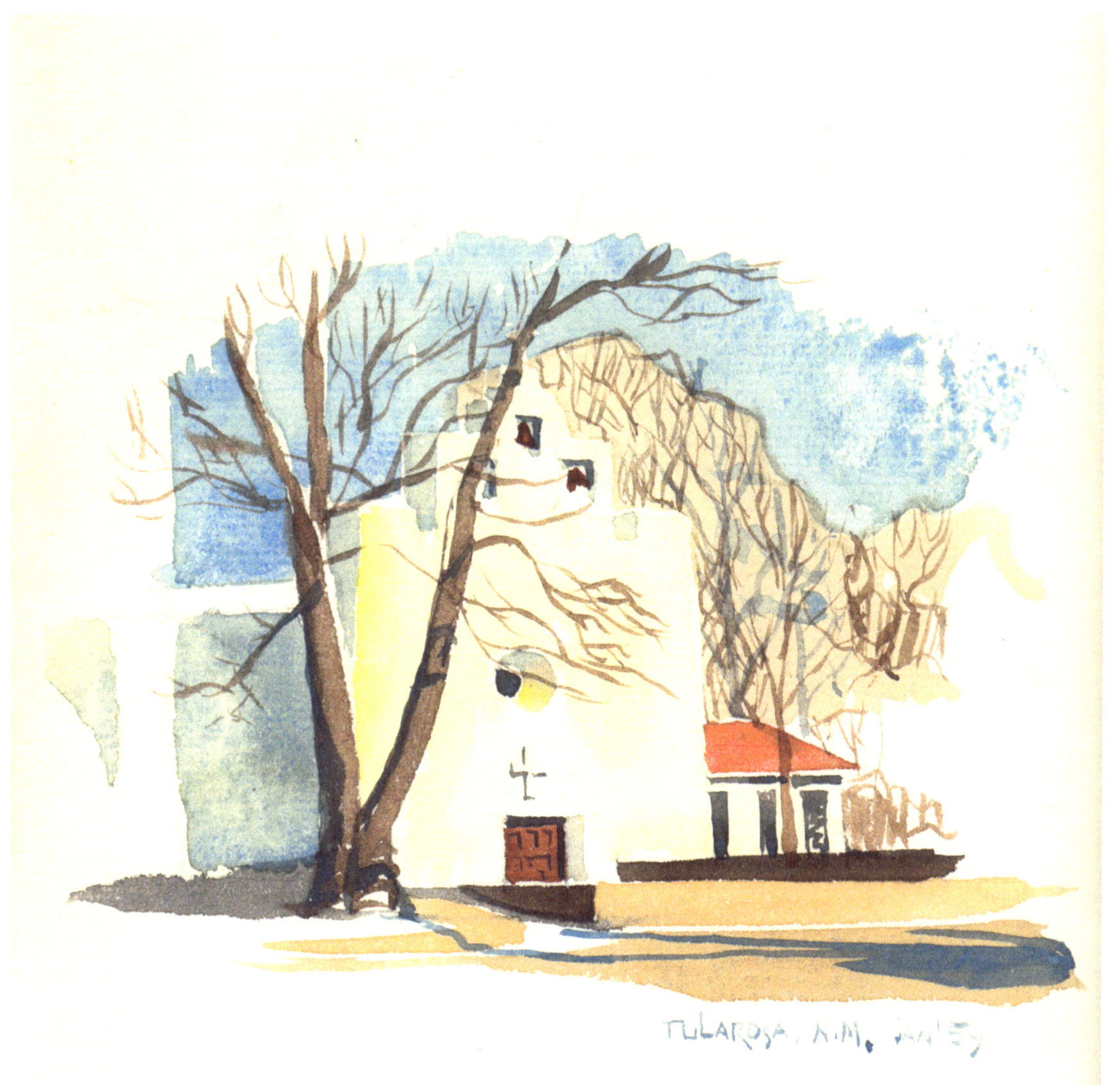

19. “Tularosa, N.M. Jan. ’59.” Church. Watercolor on sketchbook page.

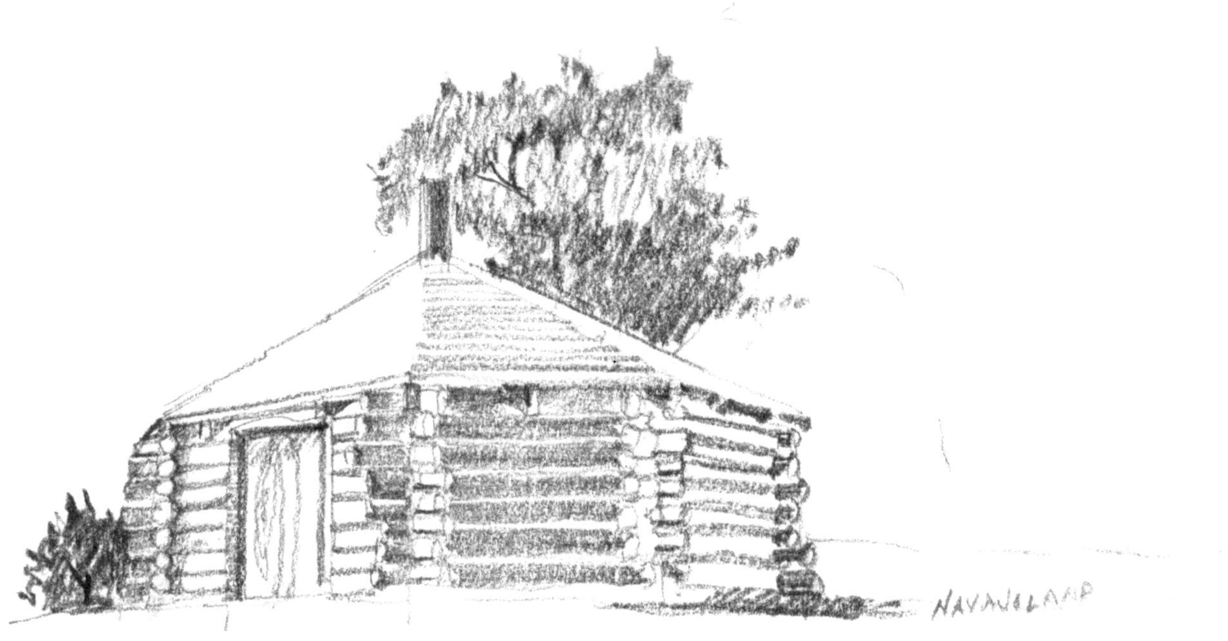

20. “Navajoland” Hogan. Soft pencil on sketchbook page.

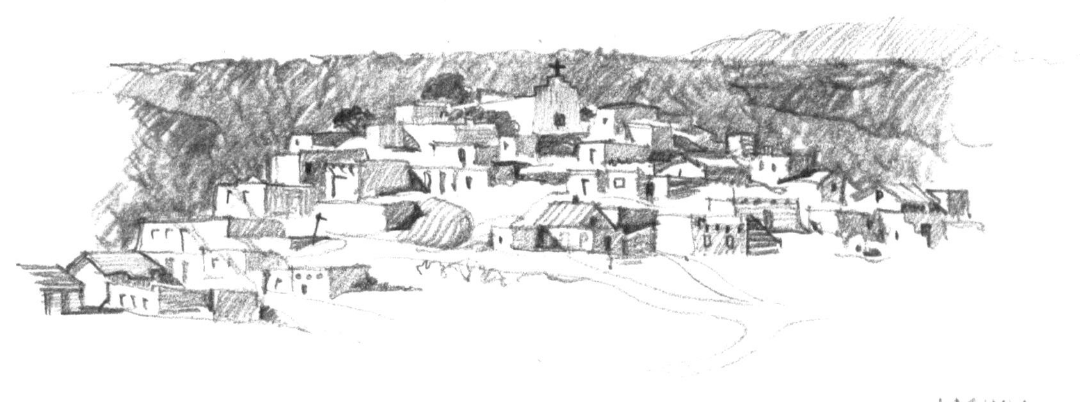

21. "Laguna Pueblo, N.M." Soft pencil on sketchbook page.

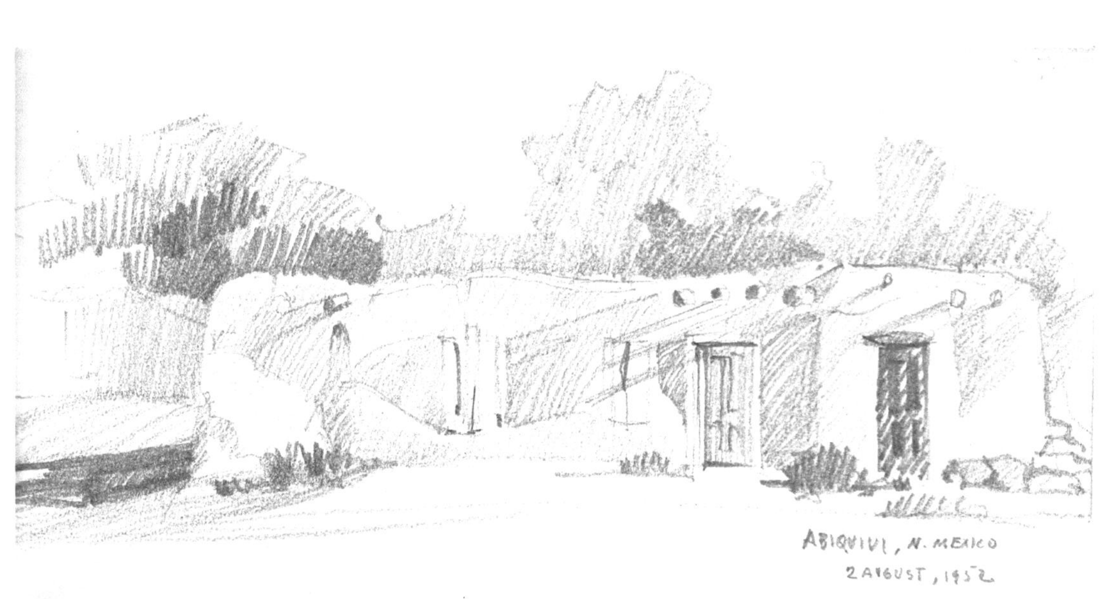

22. "Abiquiqu N. Mexico. 2 August, 1952." Vernacular house. Soft pencil on sketchbook page.

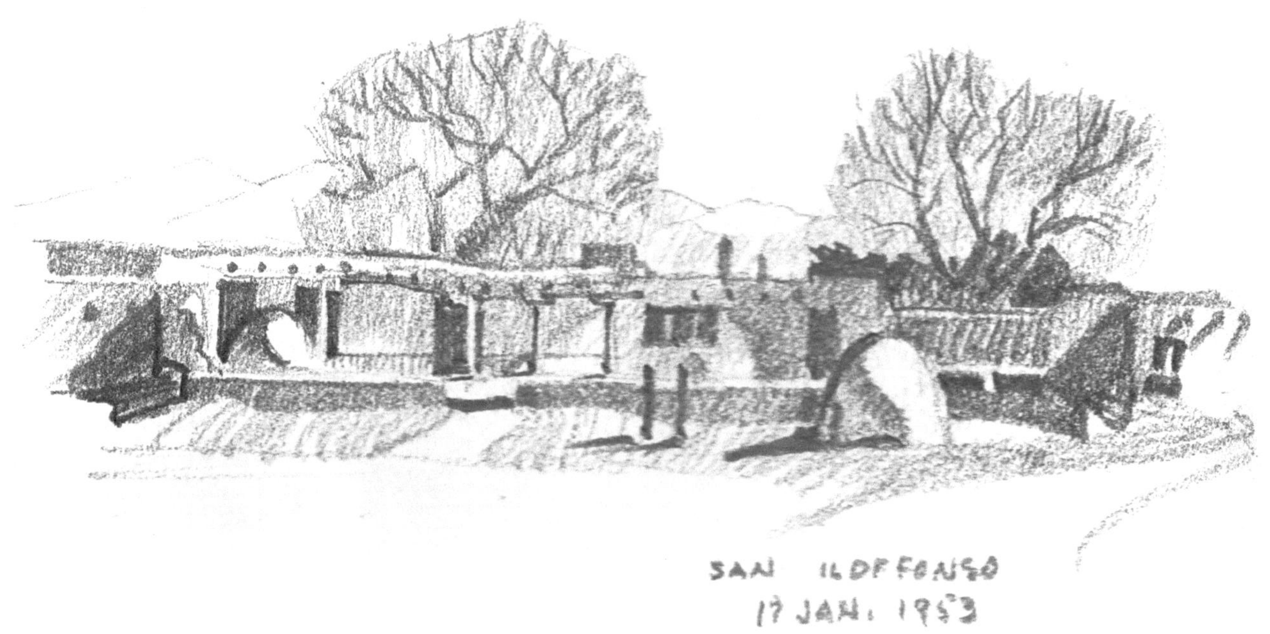

23. "San Ildefonso. 17 Jan. 1953." Soft pencil on sketchbook page.

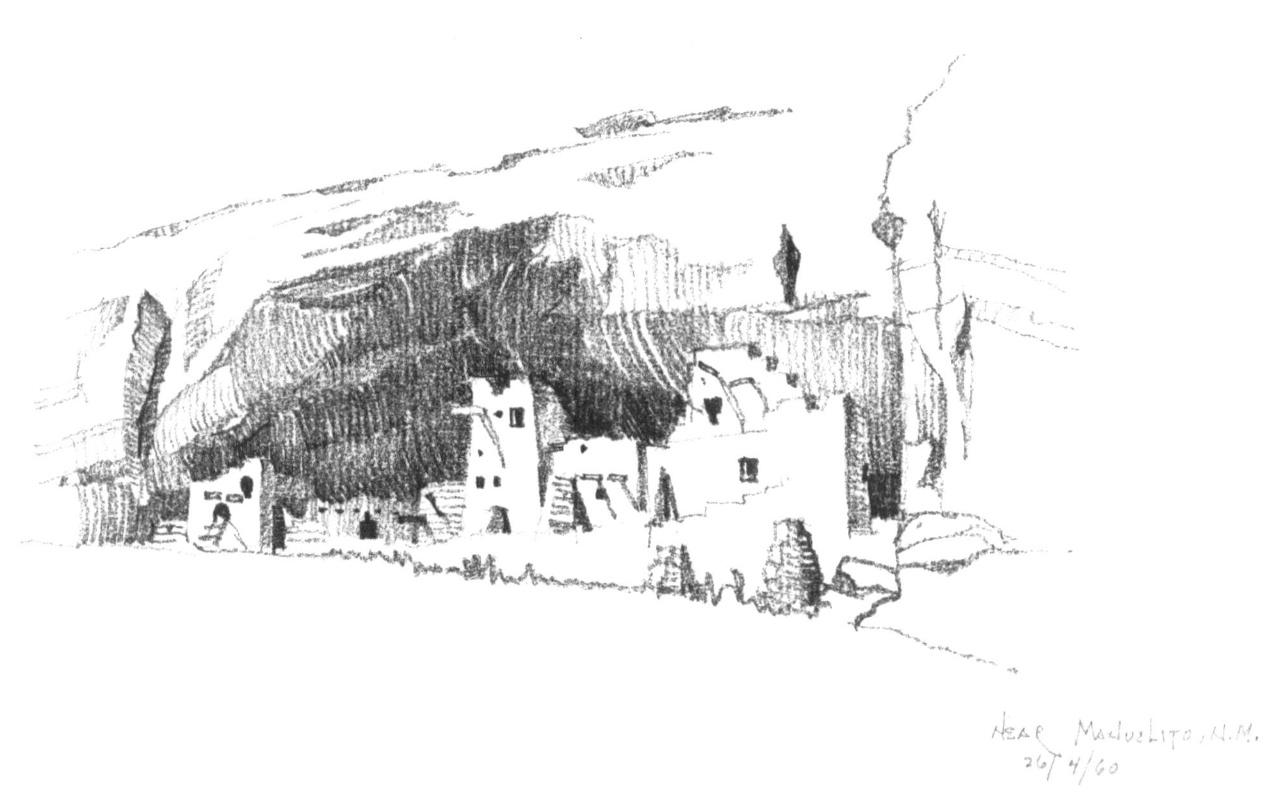

24. "Near Manuelito, N.M. 26/4/60." Early Pueblo Culture ruins. Soft pencil on sketchbook page.

54

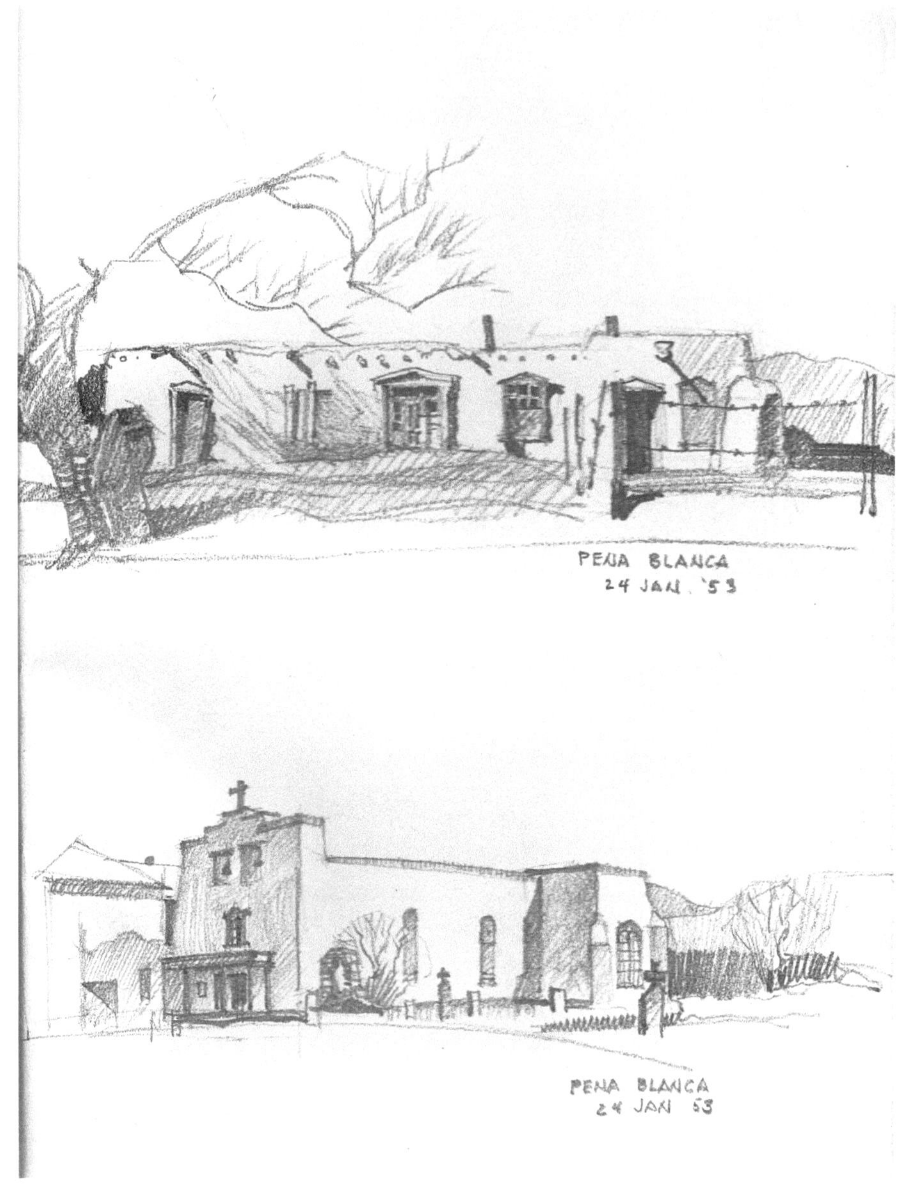

25. "Pena Blanca. 24 Jan. 53." Vernacular house and church. Soft pencil on sketchbook page.

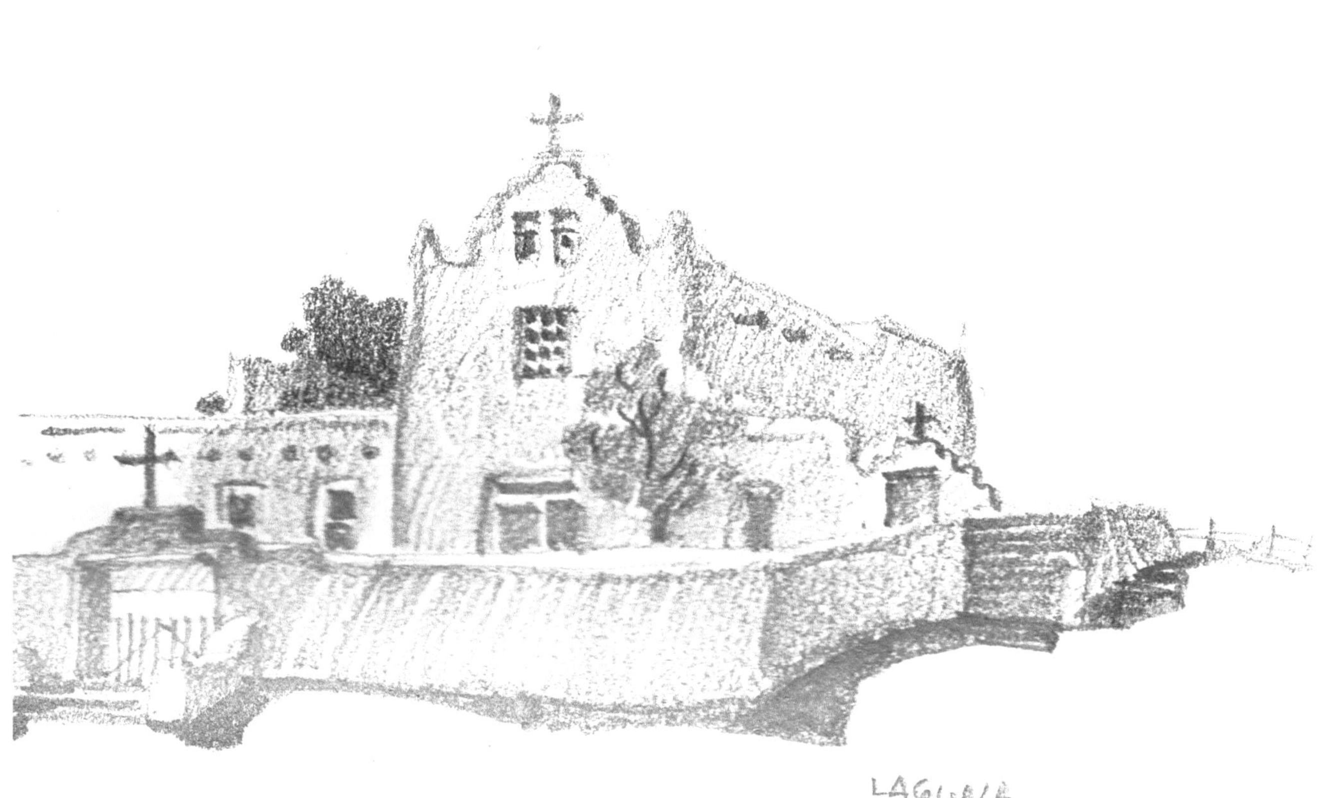

26. “Laguna. 5/10/57.” Mission Church, Laguna Pueblo. Soft pencil on sketchbook page.

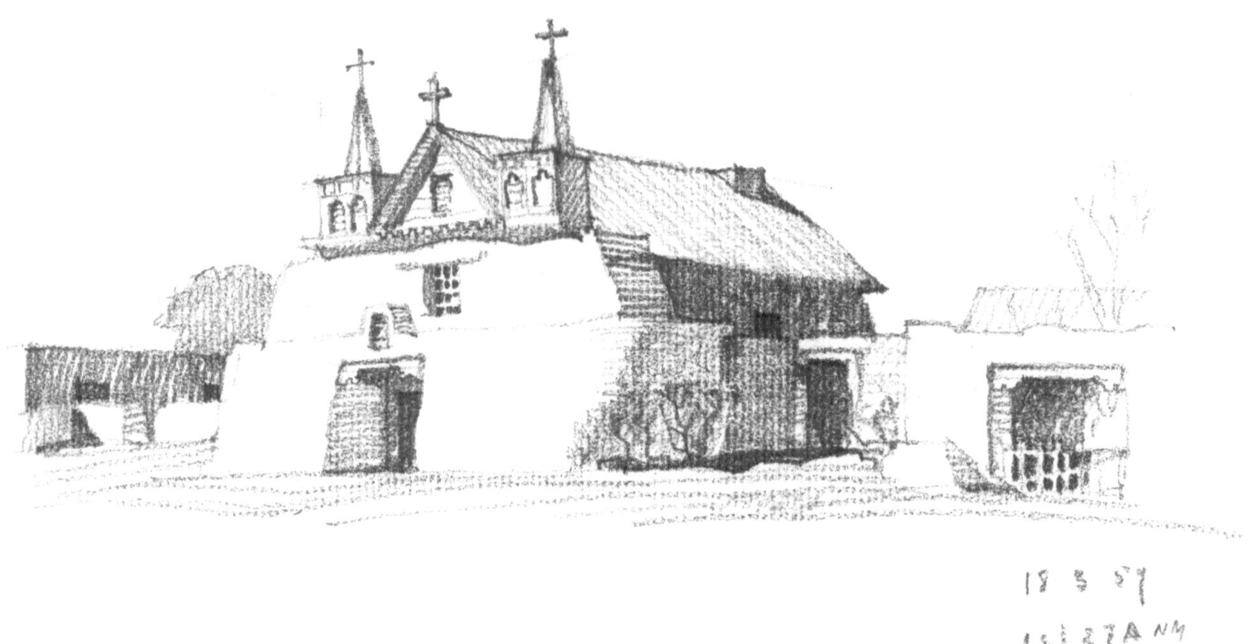

27. "Isleta, N.M. 18/3/57." Mission Church, Isleta Pueblo. Soft pencil on sketchbook page.

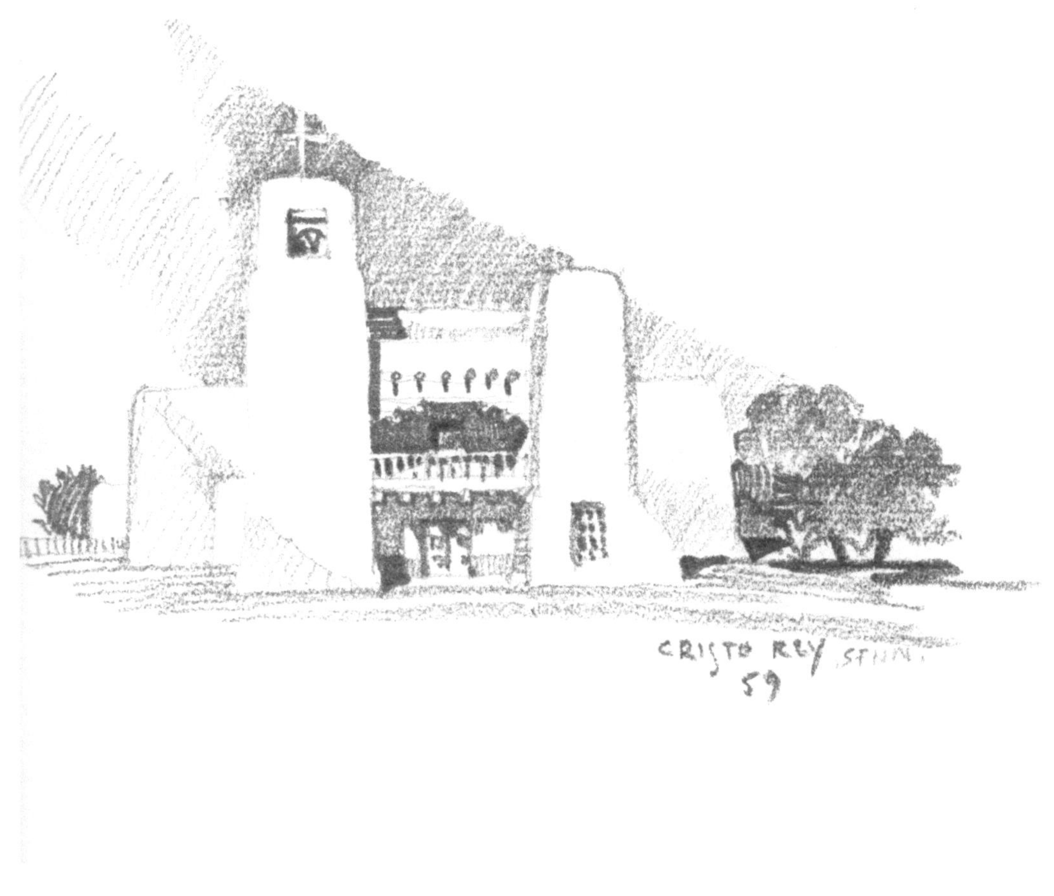

28. "Cristo Rey. 59." Modern vernacular (or "pueblo style") Church, Santa Fe, by architect John Gaw Meem, John McHugh's first employer after his arrival in New Mexico. Soft pencil on sketchbook page.

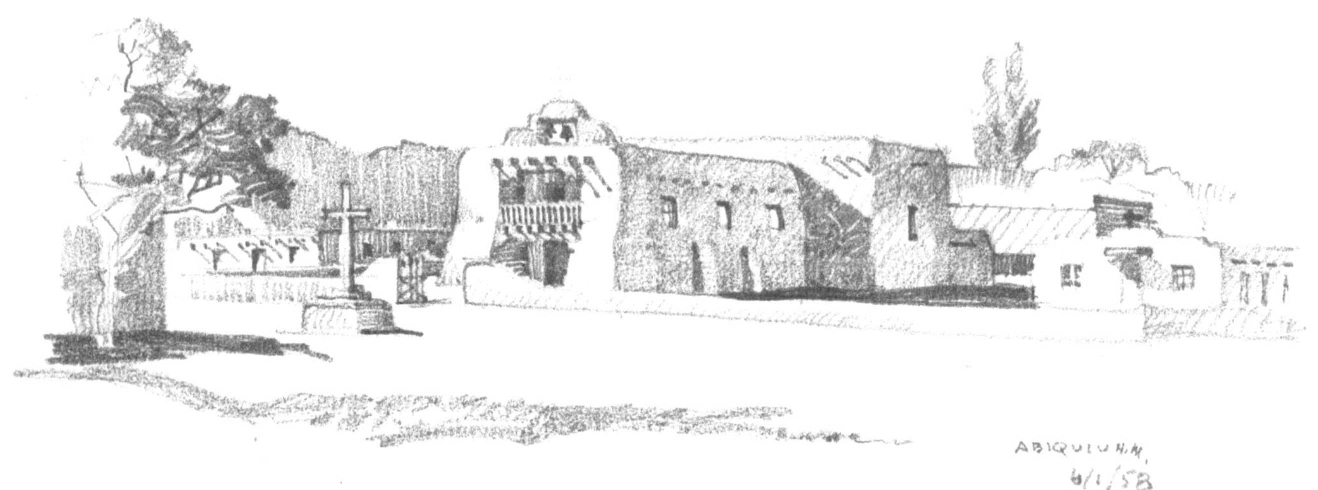

29. "Abiquiu, N.M. 6/1/58." Church complex and plaza. Soft pencil on sketchbook page.

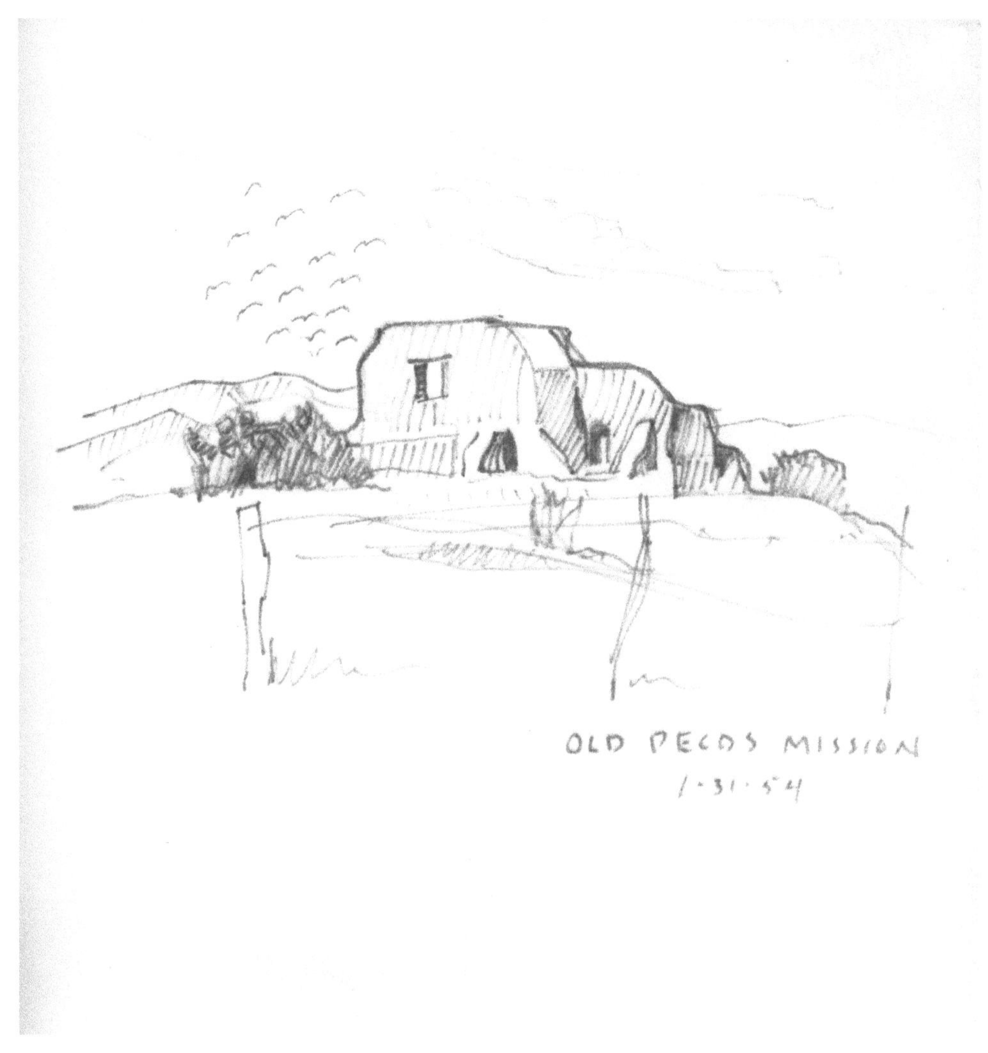

30. "Old Pecos Mission. 1-31-54." Soft pencil on sketchbook page.

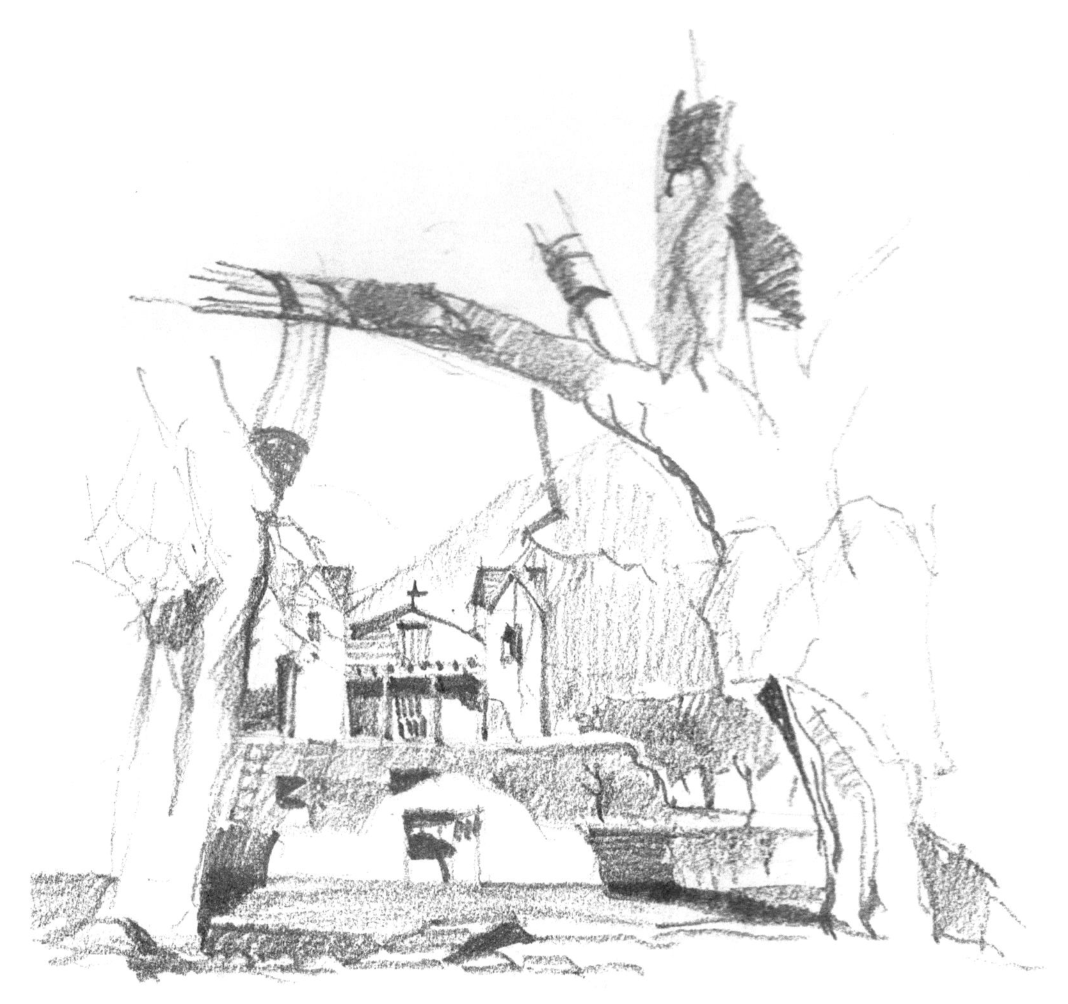

31. Vernacular church. Soft pencil on sketchbook page.

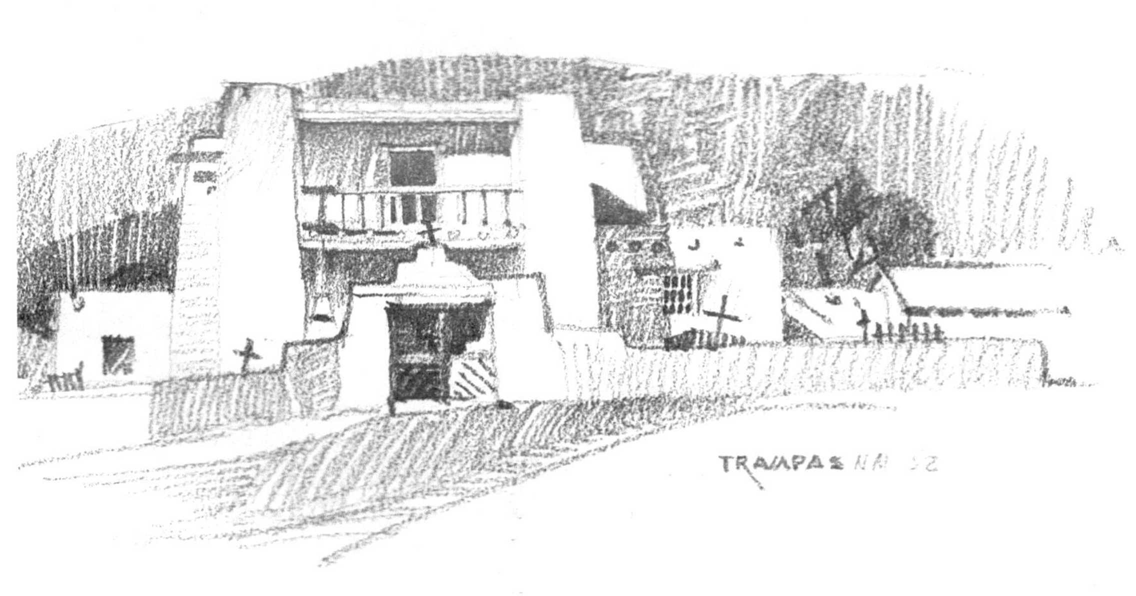

32. “Trampas N.M. ’52.” Mission church. Soft pencil on sketchbook page.

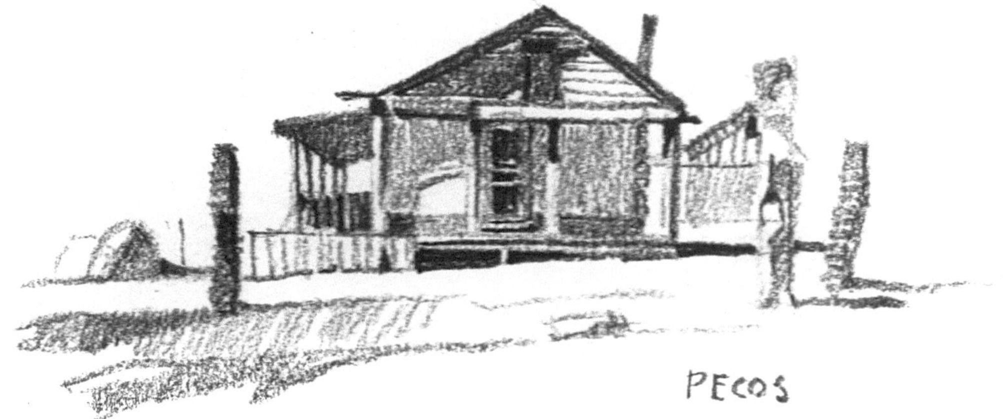

33. "Pecos." Soft pencil on sketchbook page.

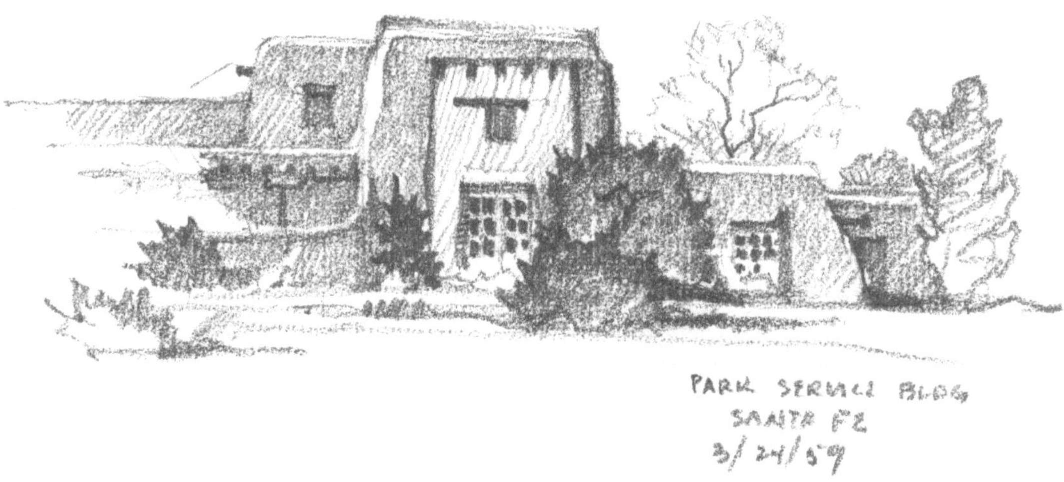

34. "Park Service Building, Santa Fe. 3/24/59." Modern design in vernacular (pueblo) style. Soft pencil on sketchbook page.

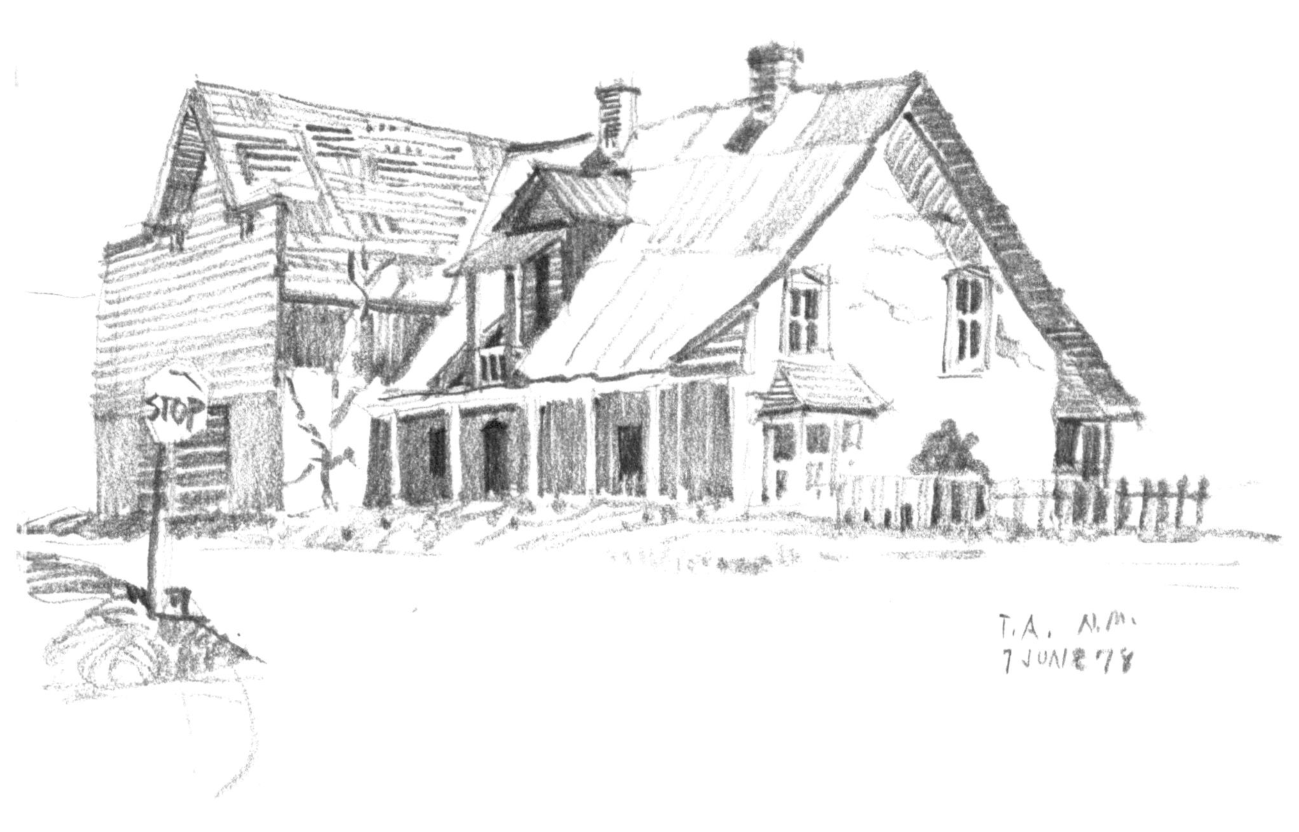

35. "T.A. N.M. 7 June 78." Vernacular adobe and wood structures. Soft pencil on sketchbook page.

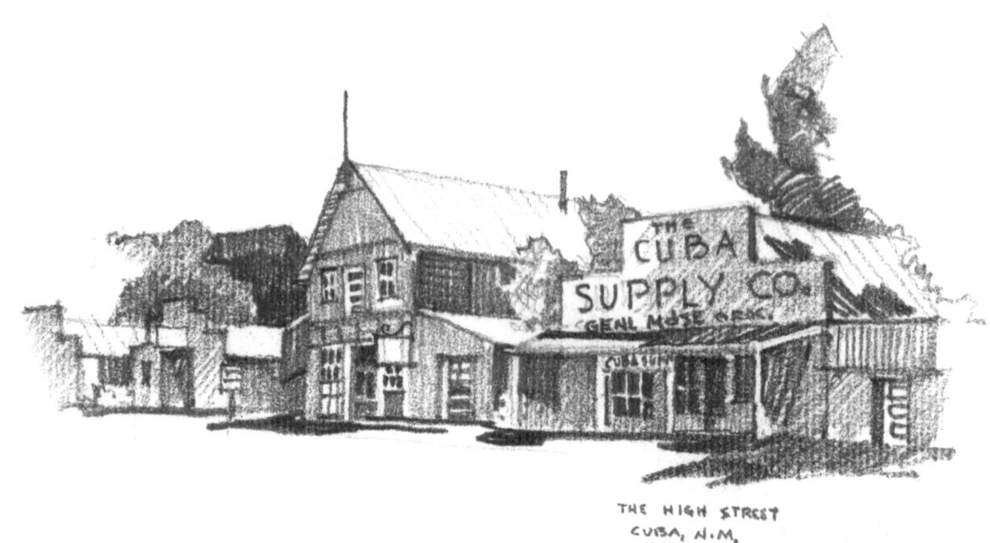

36. “The High Street, Cuba, New Mexico. 31/7/57.” Soft pencil on sketchbook page.

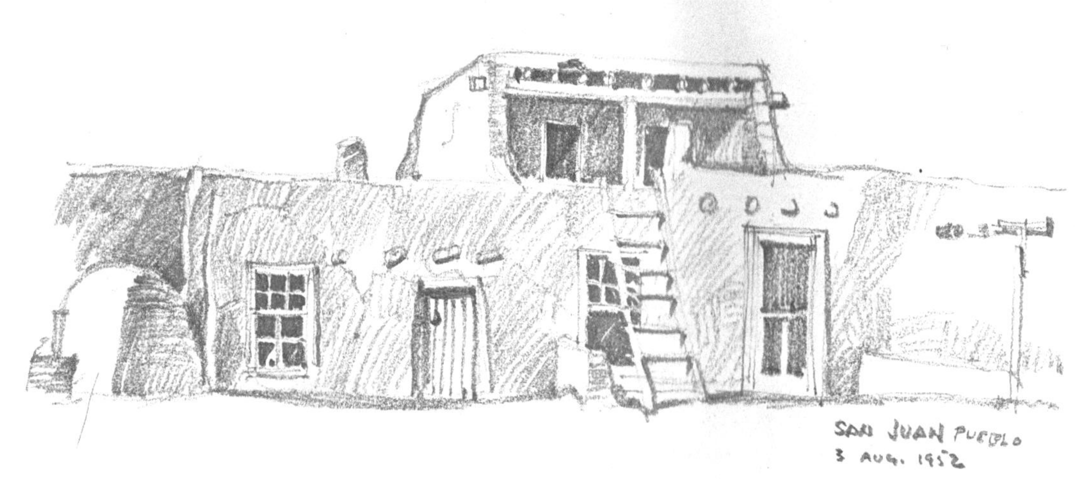

37. “San Juan Pueblo. 3 Aug. 1952.” Soft pencil on sketchbook page.

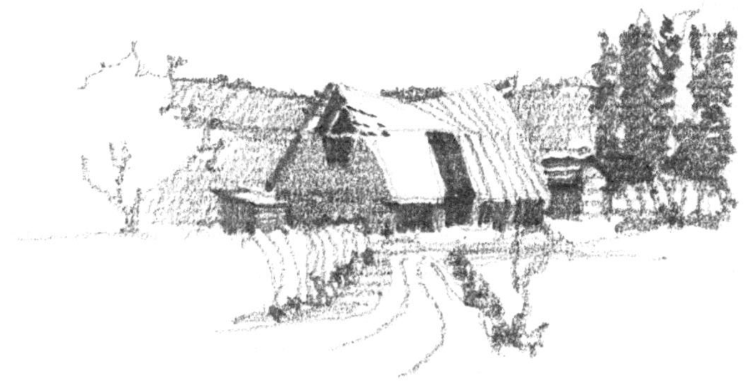

38. Tired Barn. Soft pencil on sketchbook page.

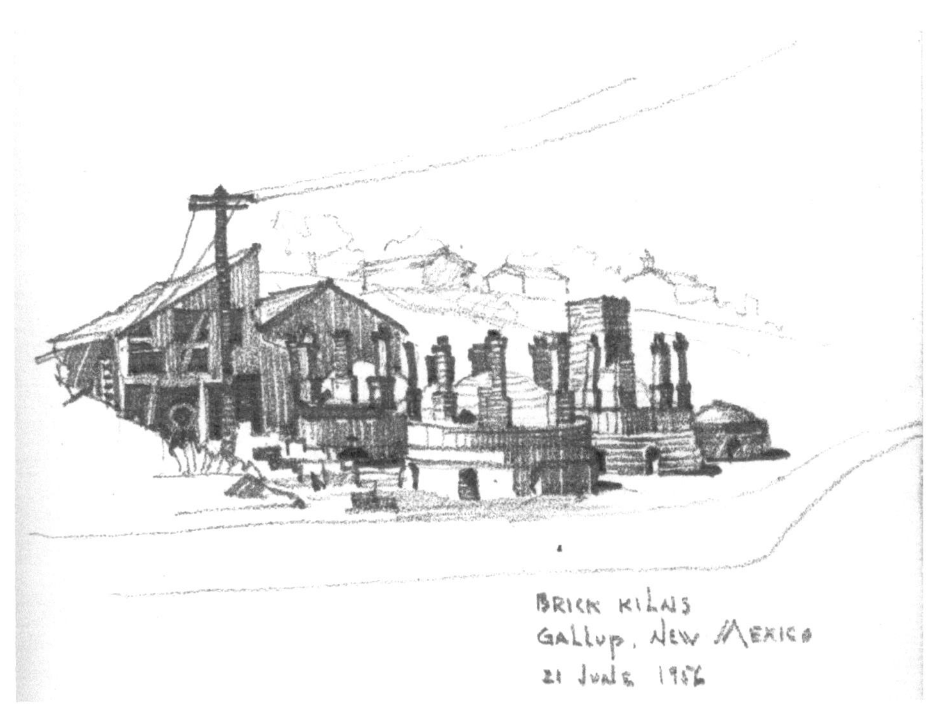

39. "Brick Kilns, Gallup, New Mexico. 21 June 1956." Soft pencil on textured sketchbook page.

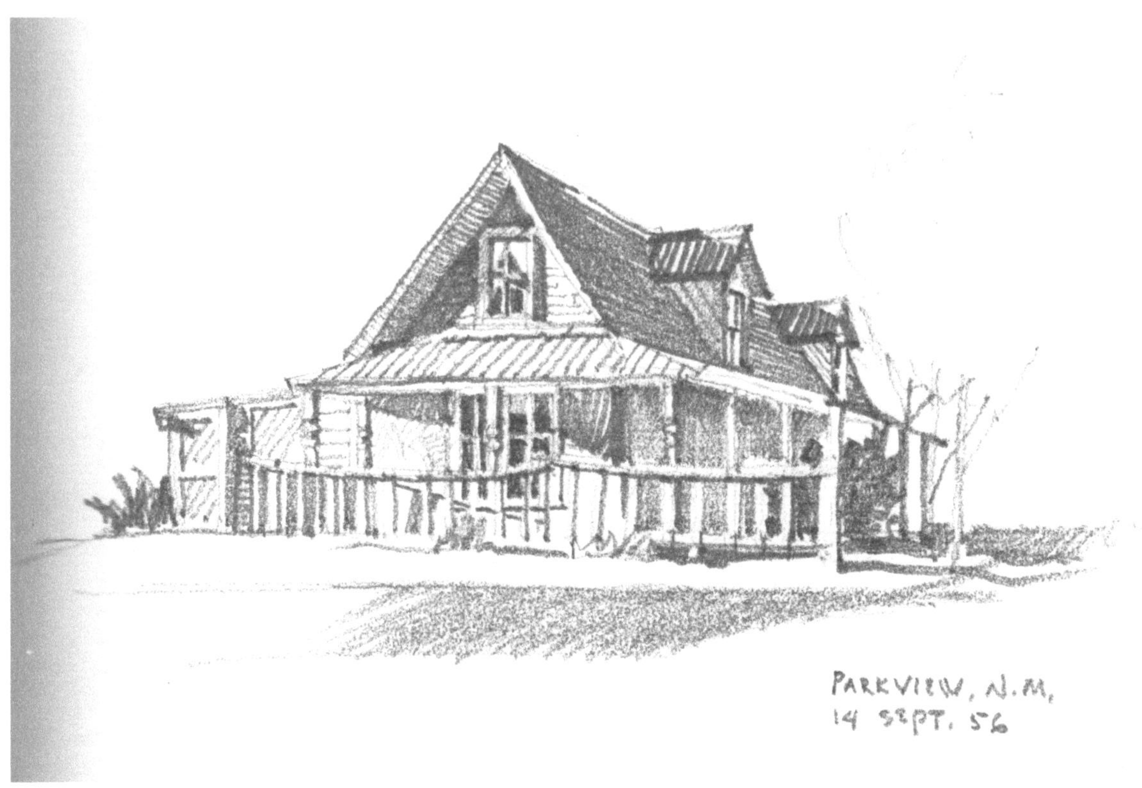

40. “Parkview, N.M. 14 Sept. 56.” Soft pencil on sketchbook page.

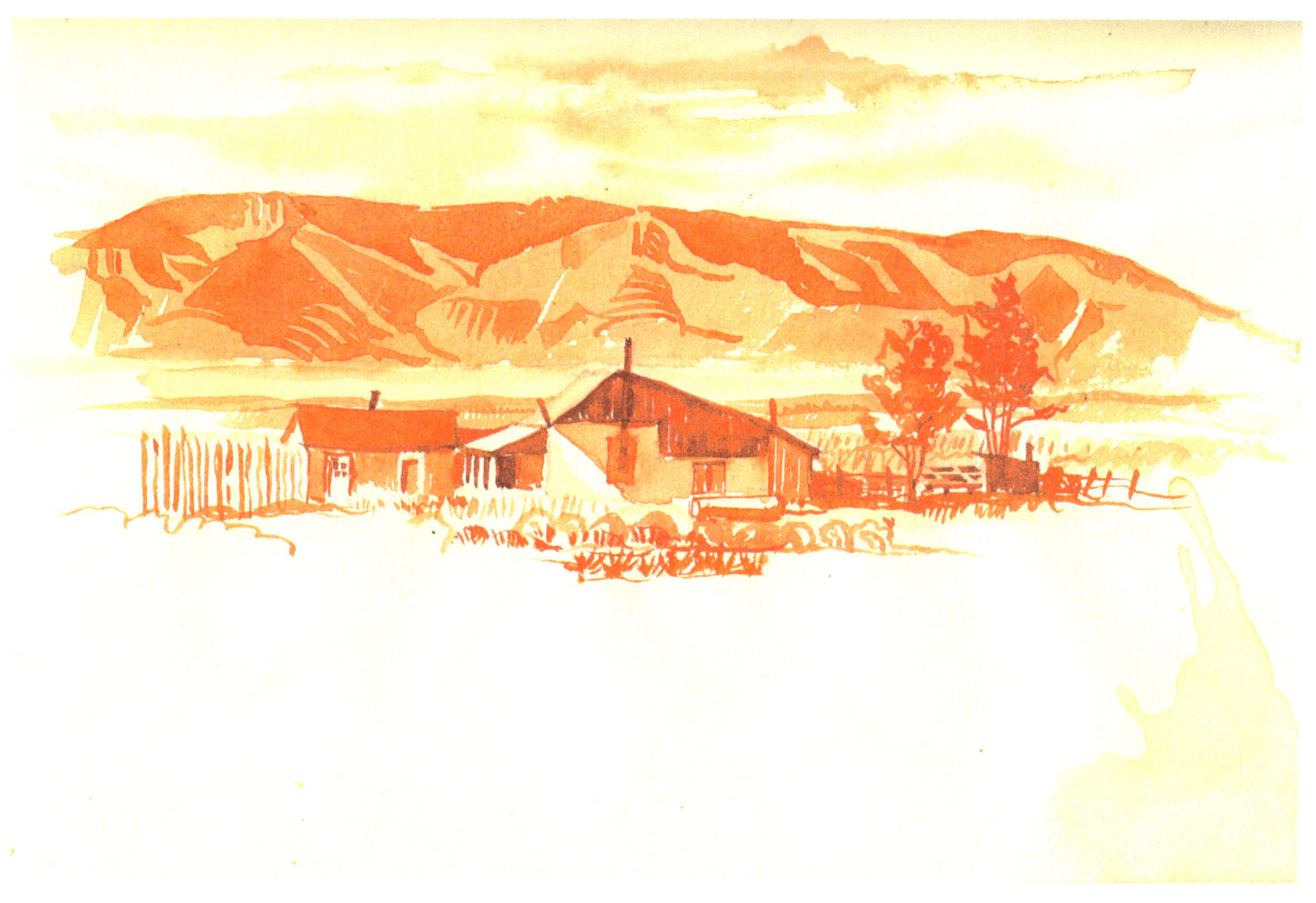

41. Ranch buildings. Monotone watercolor (or red ink wash?) on sketchbook page.

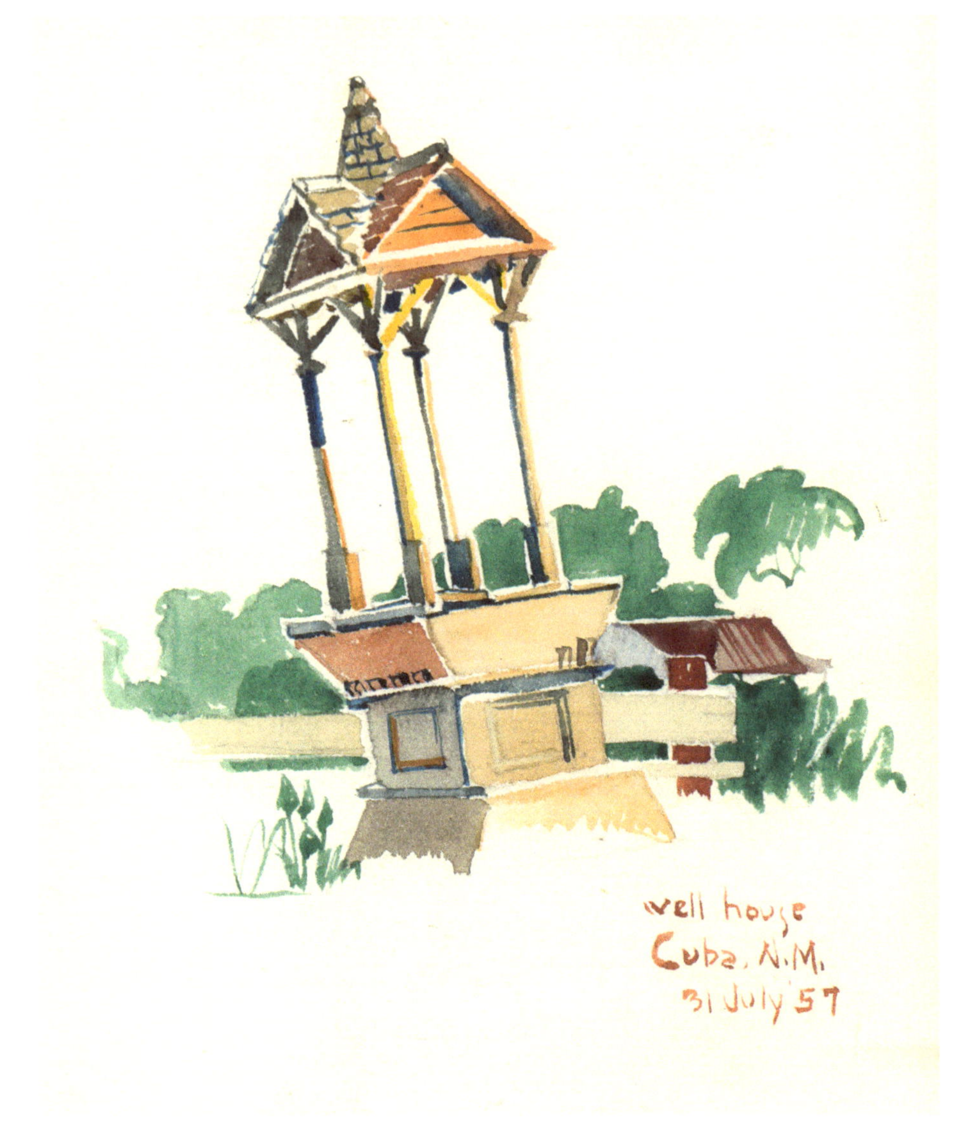

42. “Well house, Cuba, N.M. 31 July 57.” Watercolor on sketchbook page.

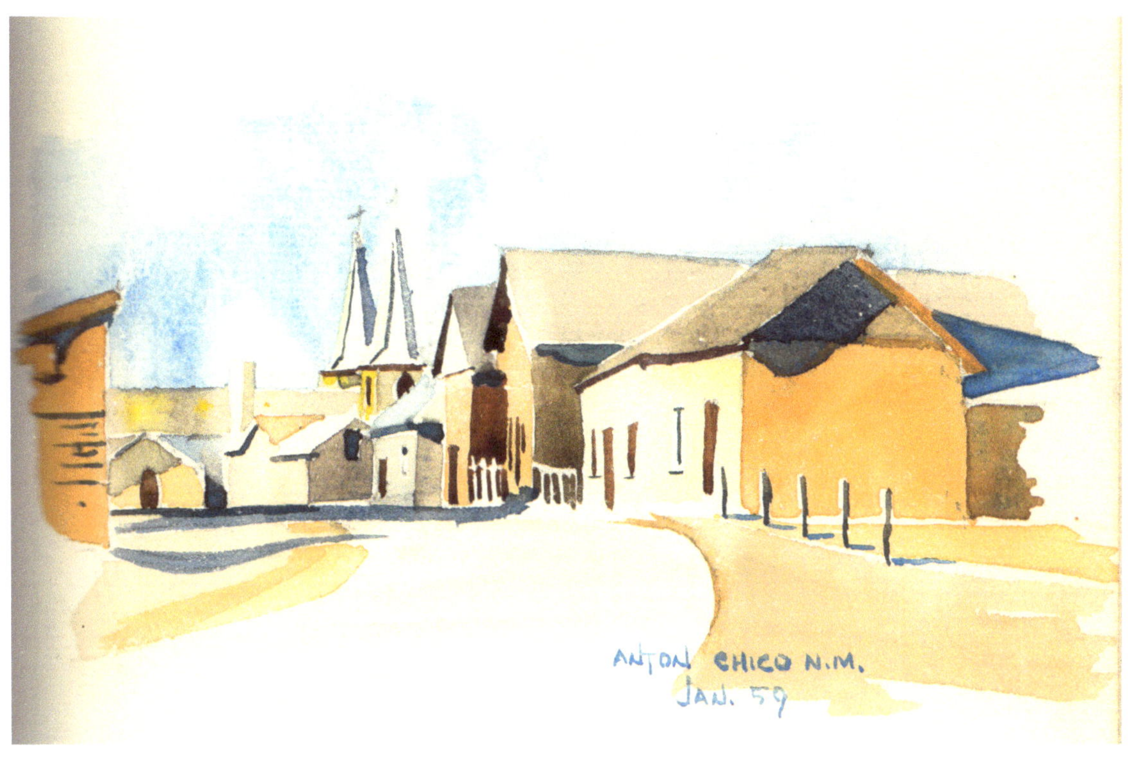

43. "Anton Chico, N.M. Jan 59." Typical town scene before the predominance of the automobile. Watercolor on sketchbook page.

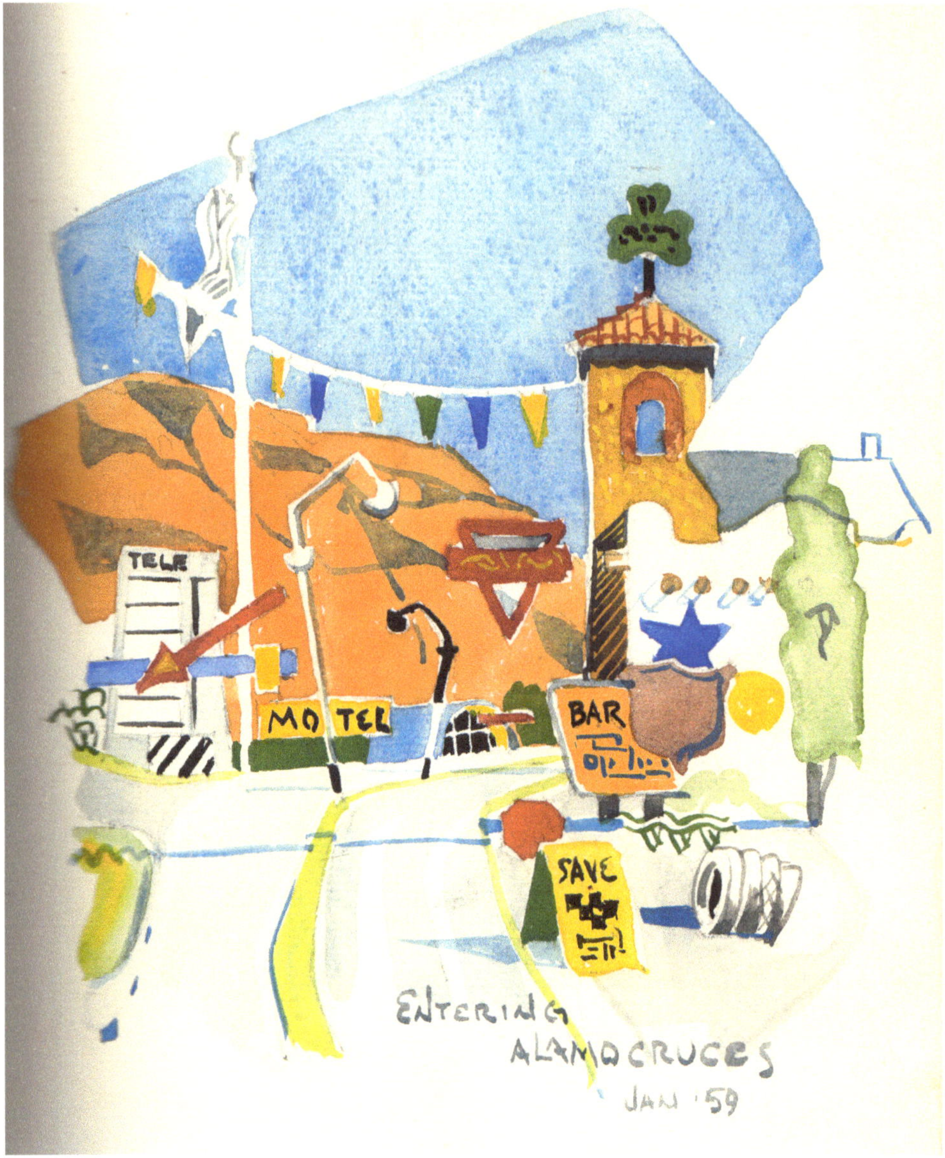

44. "Entering Almo Cruces. Jan. 59." Town scene influenced by the predominance of the automobile. Watercolor on sketchbook page.

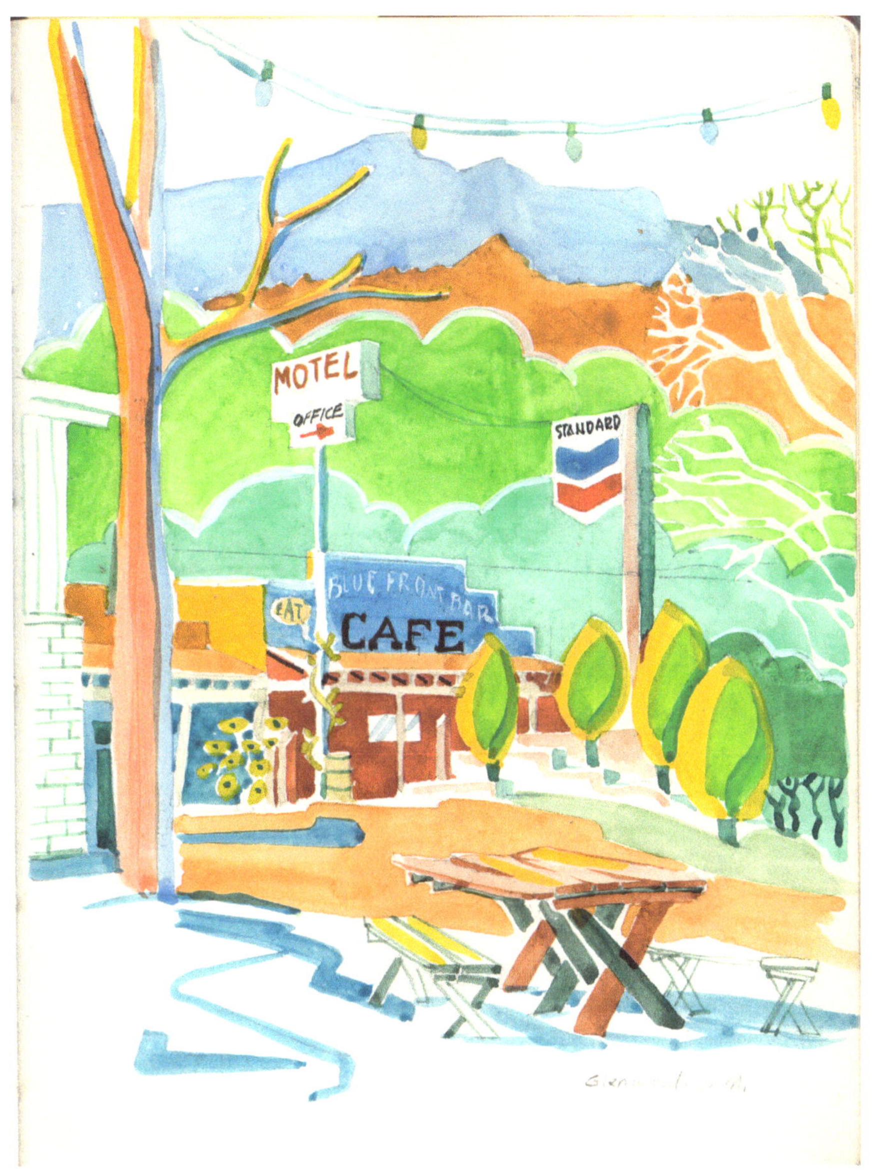

45. "Glenwood, N.M." Town scene influenced by the predominance of the automobile. Watercolor on sketchbook page.

Across the U.S.

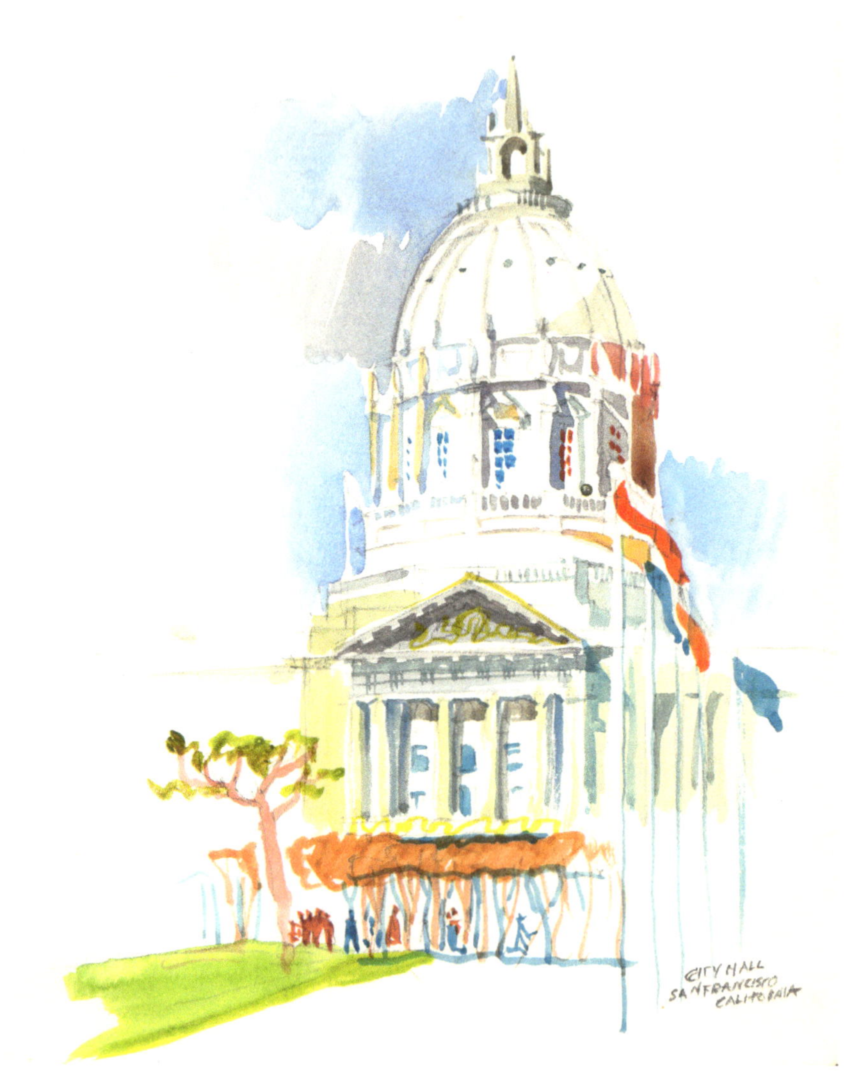

46. "City Hall, San Francisco, California." Watercolor on sketchbook page.

These sketches, in contrast to those of New Mexico, occur in McHugh's sketchbooks somewhat more randomly; that is, they are not necessarily grouped by particular geographic areas. Further, they sometimes show that he was experimenting with techniques appropriate to the subjects drawn. Examples of this are the techniques used for a rainy scene in New York, illus. 47, in contrast to the sharp linear pencil technique, more like an ink drawing, used for another New York City scene, illus. 51. Another experiment with technique emphasizes the color and discordance of particular urban settings such as in illus. 48. This is a technique that McHugh started to use in New Mexico after New Mexican towns began to change into a jangle of bright signage, fast food joints and gas stations as towns began to defer to the rising dominance of automobiles (illus. 44 and 45 for instance).

Some of the "Across the U.S." sketches are from other parts of the Southwest and therefore very much like the sketches in the previous chapter. Political boundaries do not necessarily divide cultural, climatic, and topological regions from one another. Some New Mexicans and Southern Coloradoans for instance cheerfully regard southern Colorado as occupied territory that should really be part of New Mexico because of its cultural, climatic, and topographic similarity with Northern New Mexico! Nonetheless, it is convenient here to group the sketches by politically defined areas because trips outside of New Mexico were seen as journeys away from home.

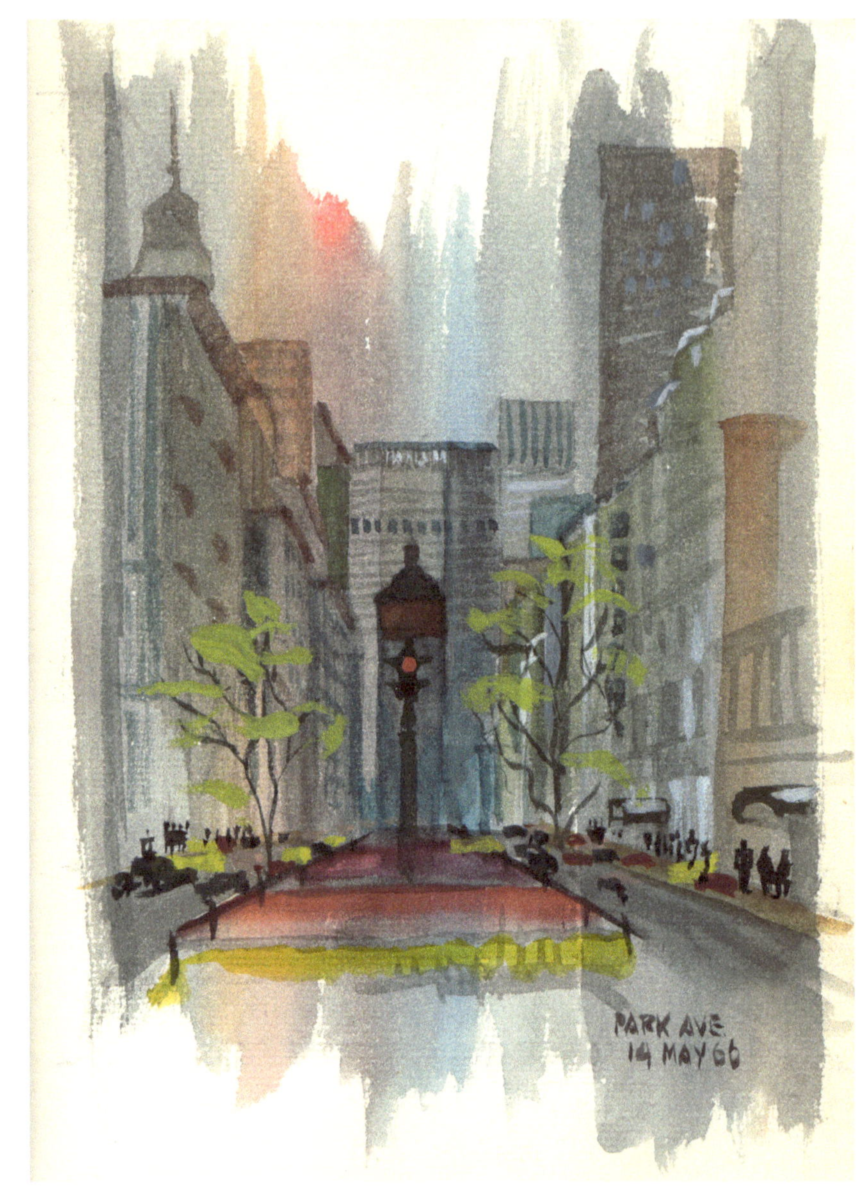

47. "Park Ave. New York City. 14 May 66." Watercolor on sketchbook page.

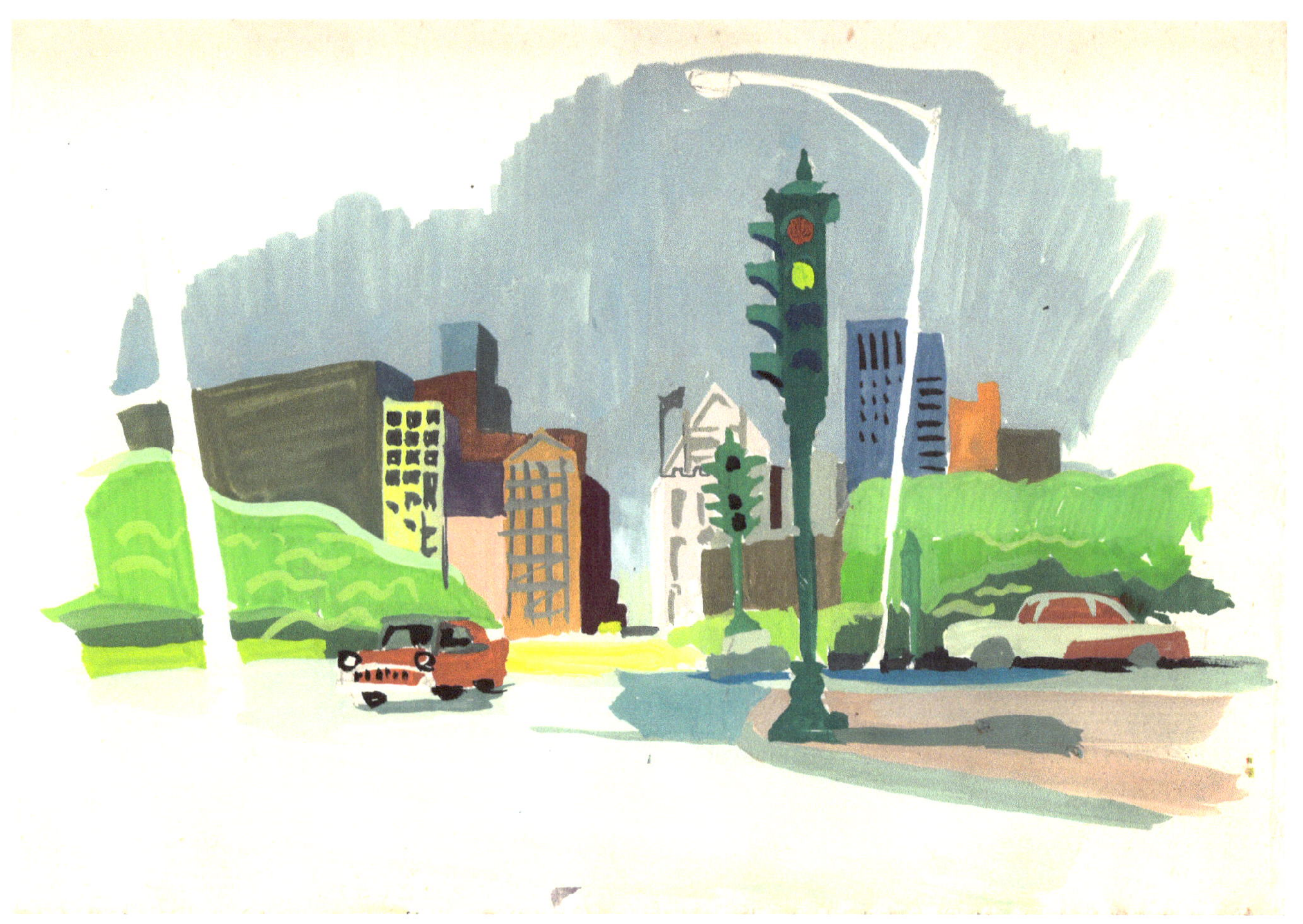

48. U.S. city scene. Opaque media on sketchbook page.

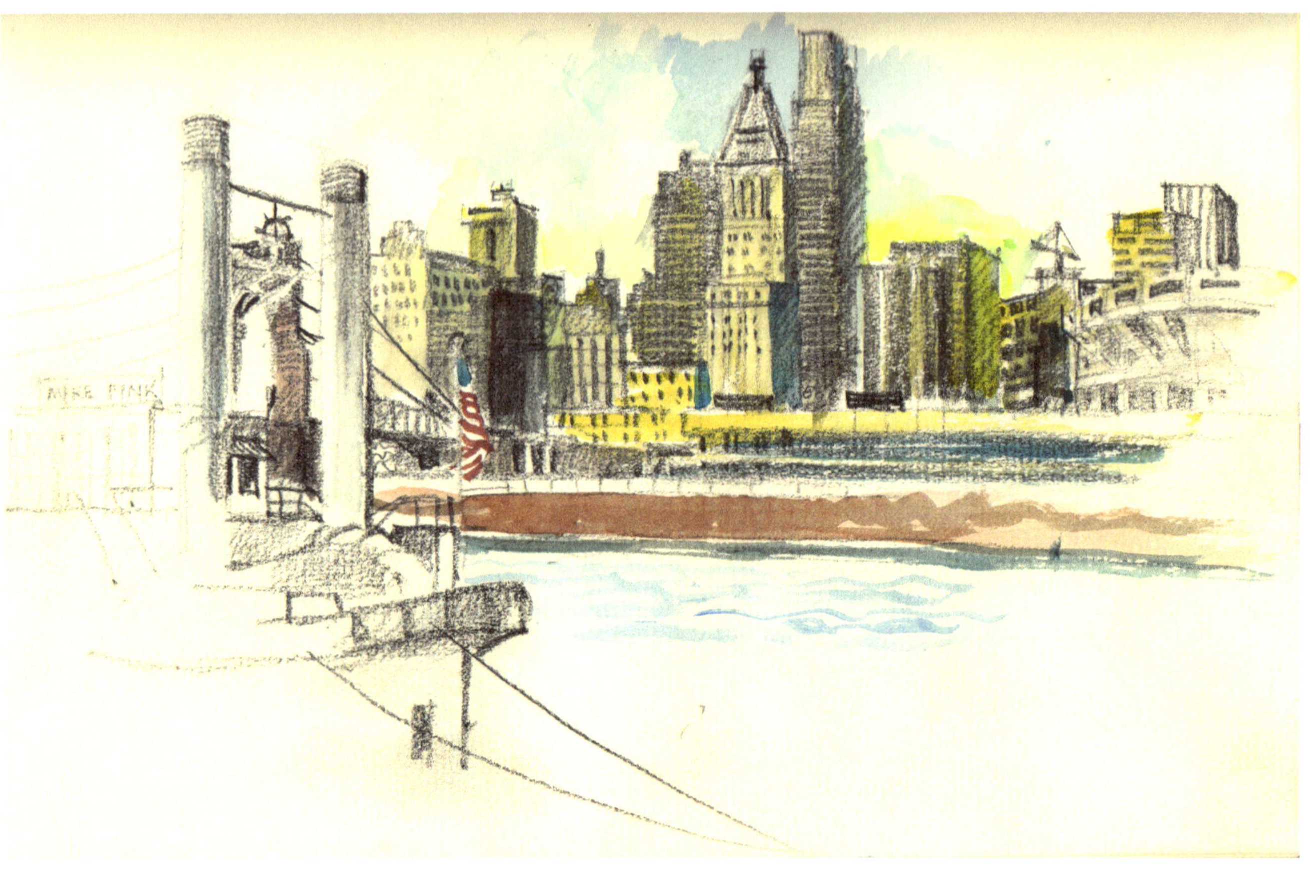

49. Watercolor and soft graphite pencil (or charcoal?) on sketchbook page.

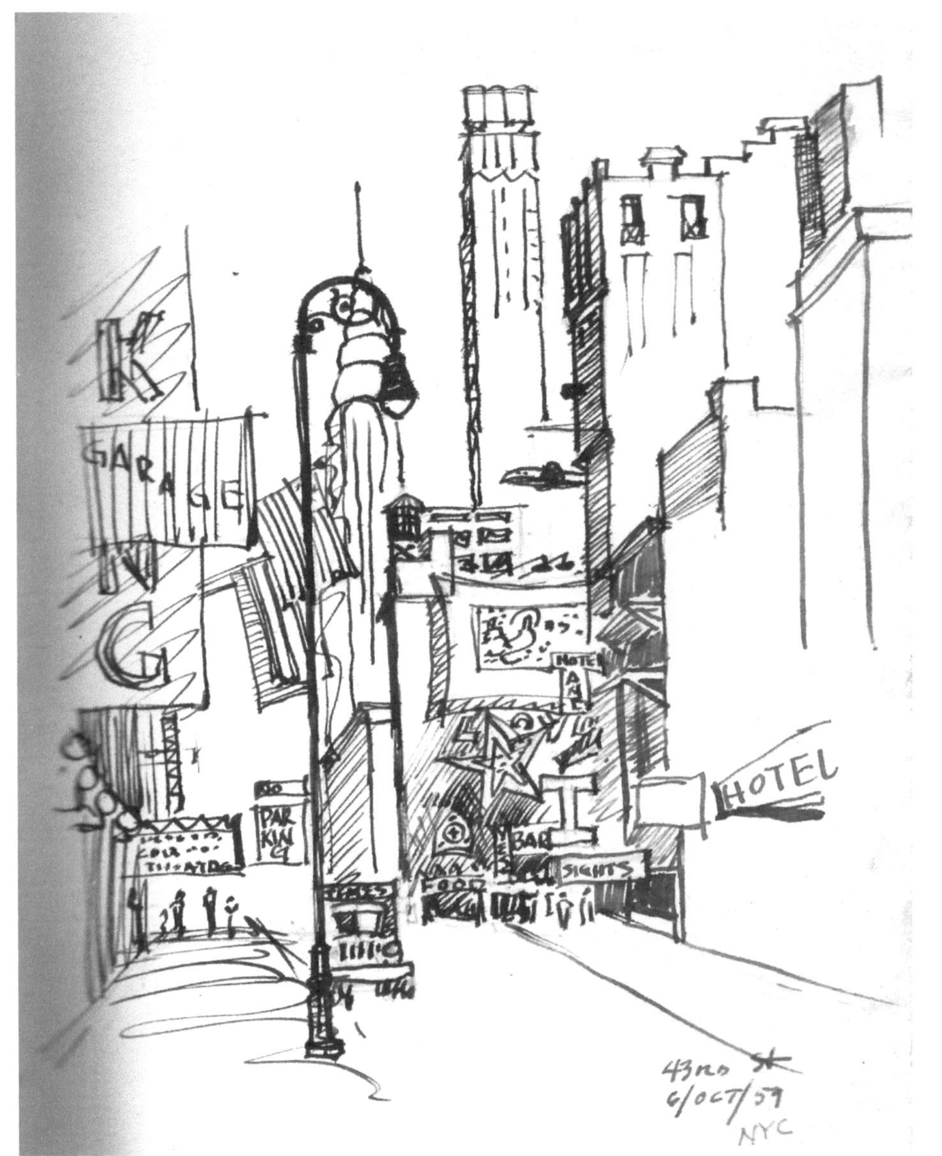

50. "43rd St. NYC. 6 Oct. 59." New York scene.
Black ink (fountain pen or combination of fountain pen and felt tip pen?) on sketchbook page.

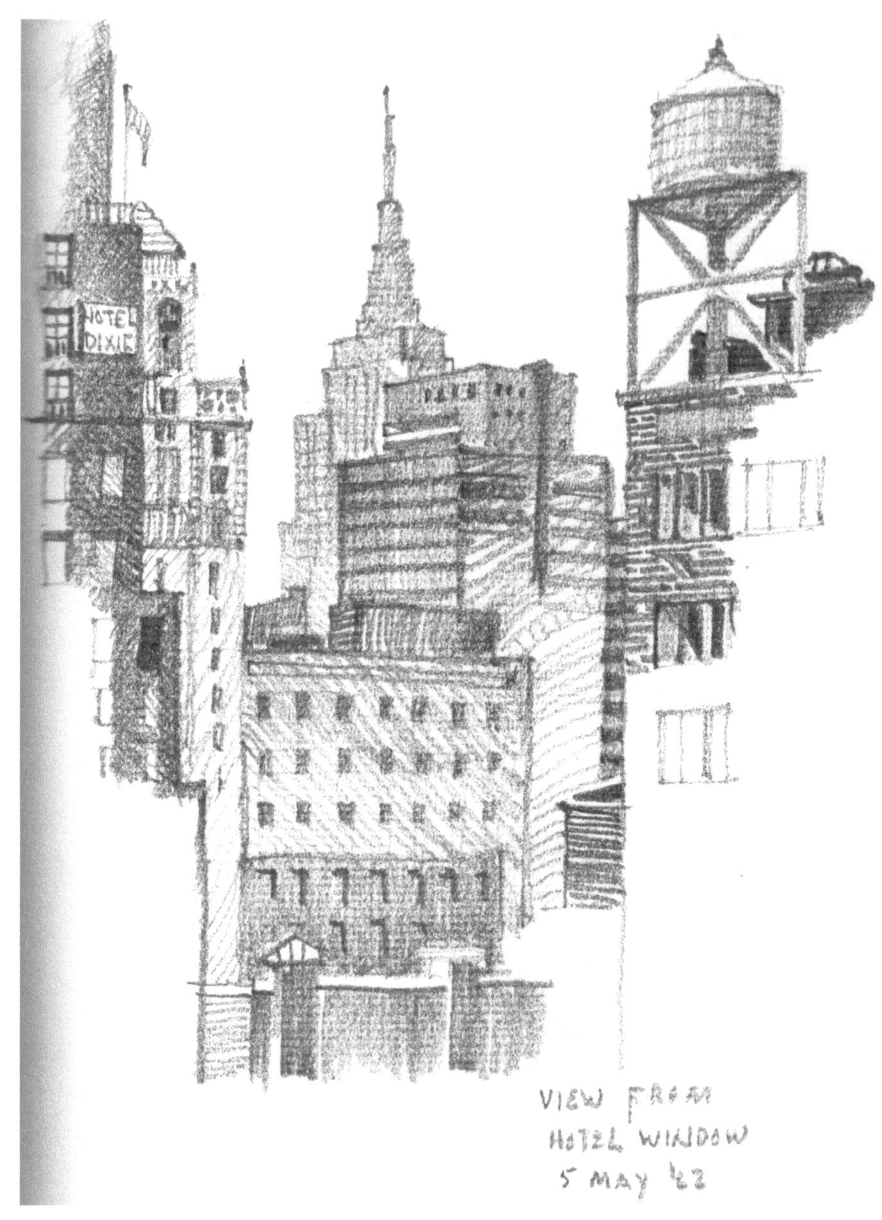

51. "View from Hotel Window. 5 May '62." Soft pencil on sketchbook page.

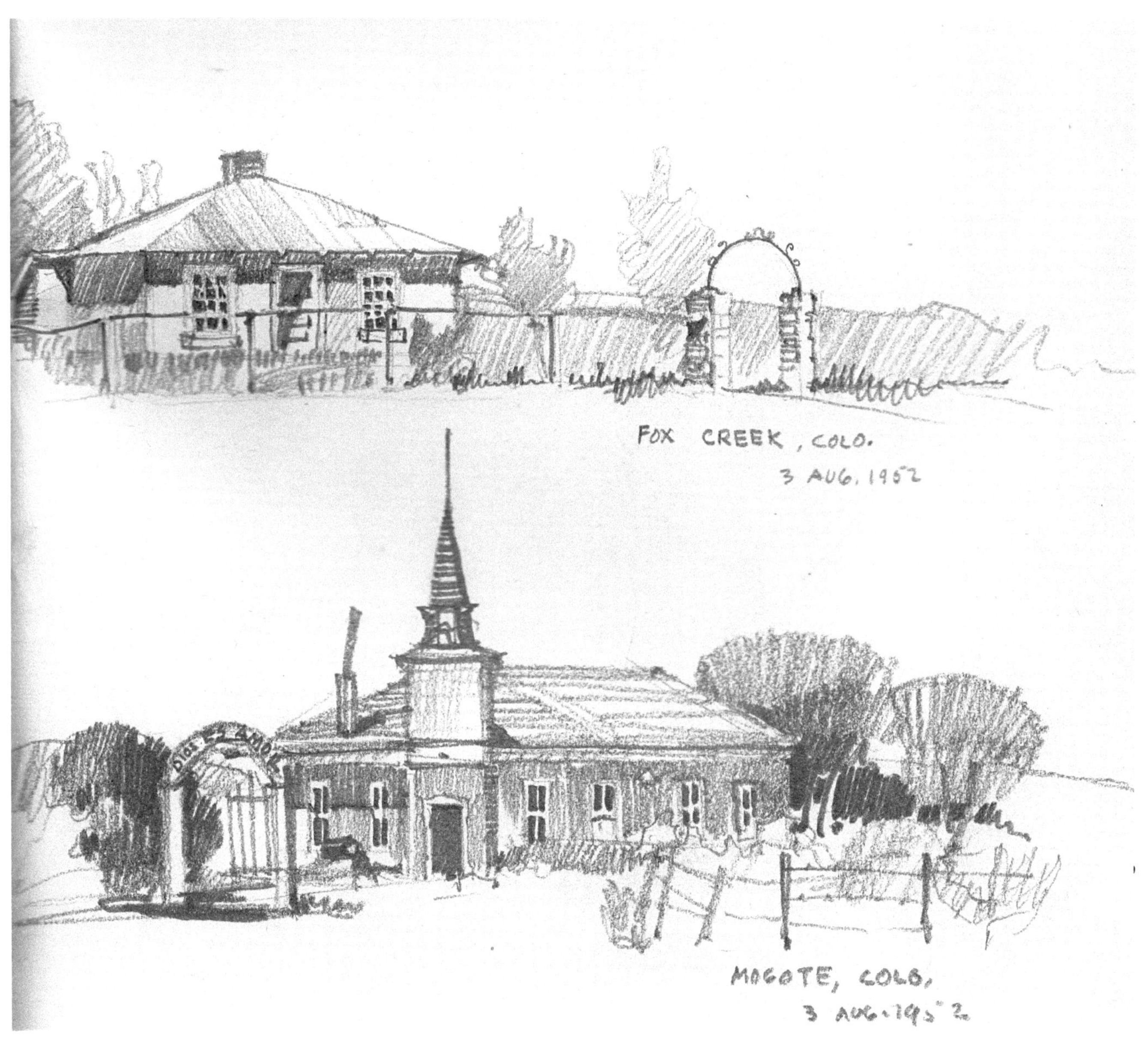

52. "Fox Creek, Colo. 3 Aug. 1952." and "Mocote, Colo." Soft pencil on sketchbook page.

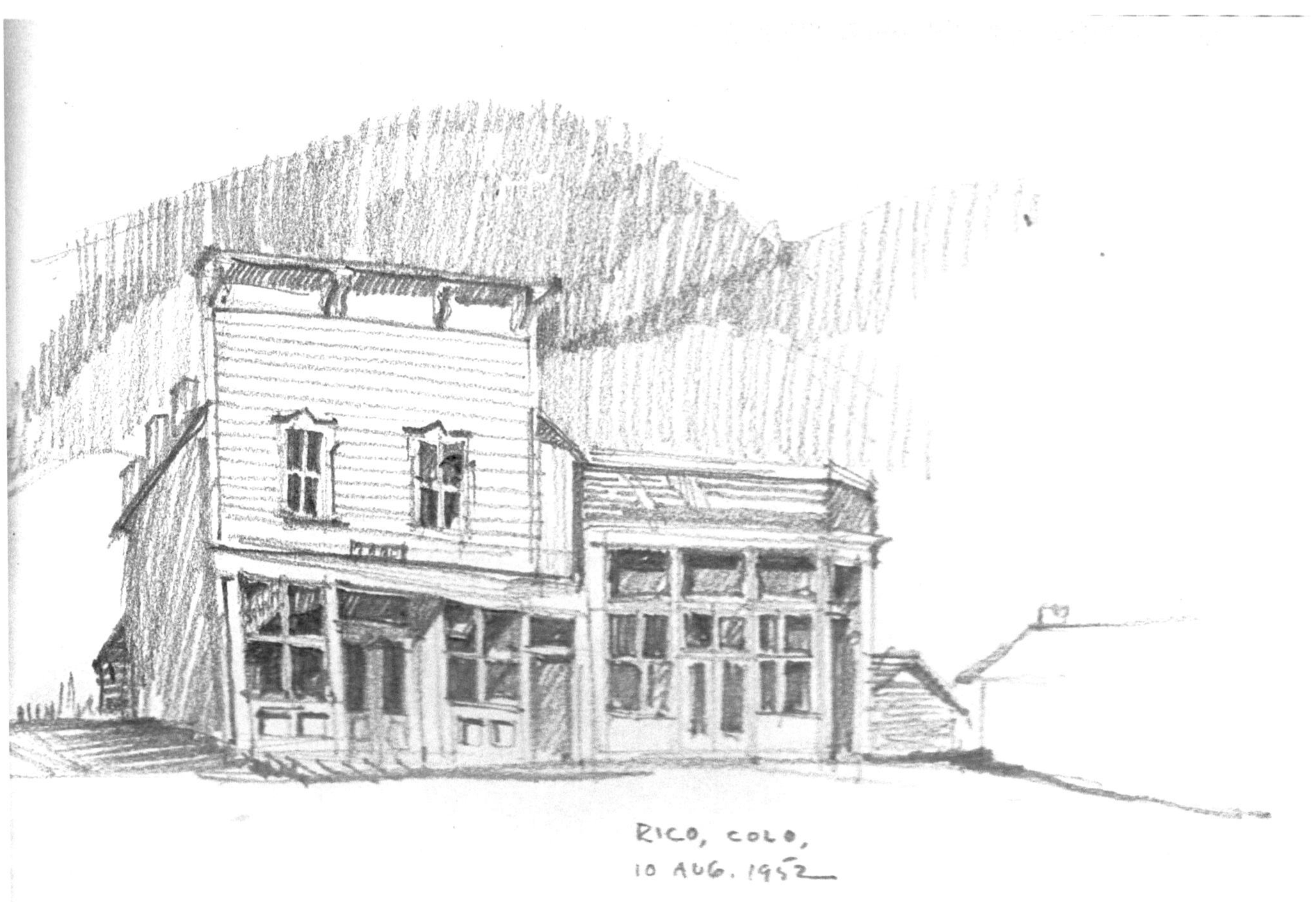

53. “Rico, Colo. 10 Aug. 1952.” Soft pencil on sketchbook page.

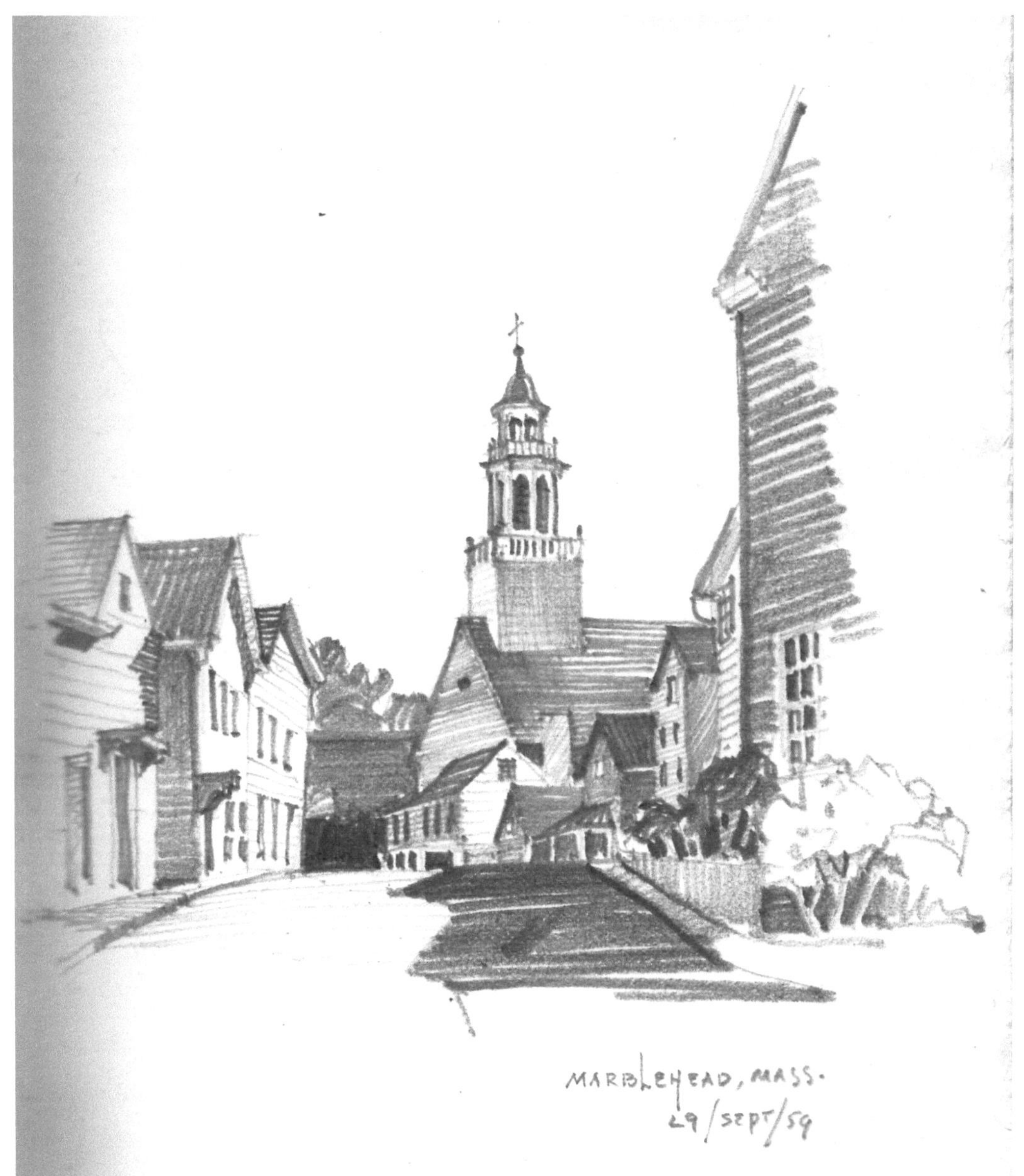

54. "Marblehead, Mass. 29 Sept. 59." Soft pencil on sketchbook page.

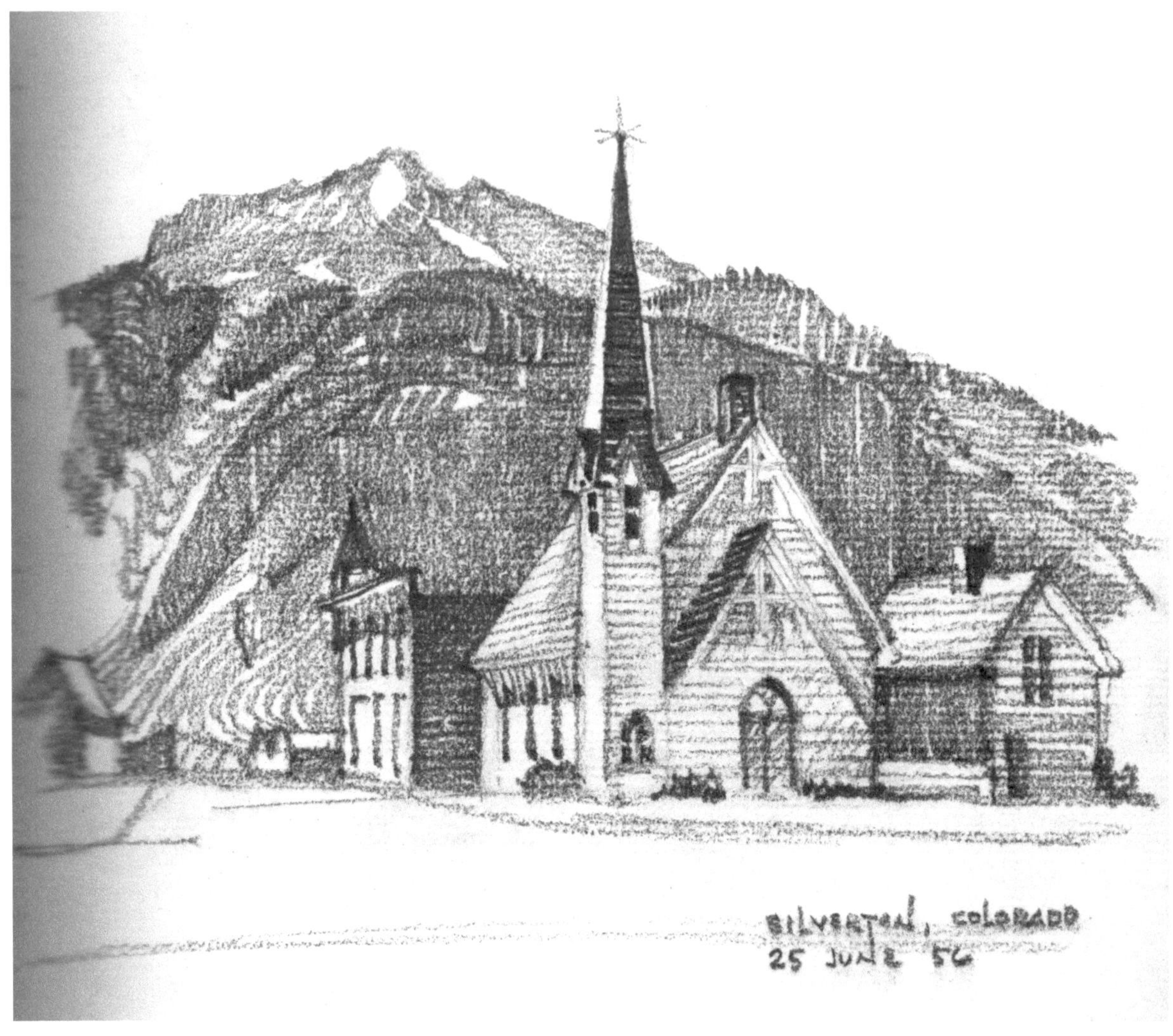

55. "Silverton, Colorado. 25 June 56." Soft pencil on sketchbook page.

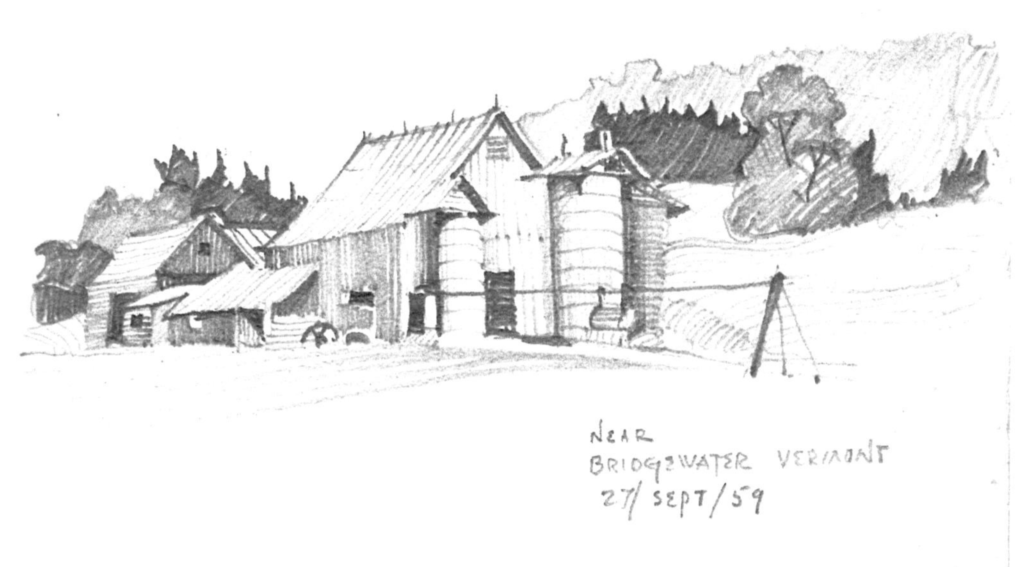

56. "Near Bridgewater, Vermont. 27 Sept. 59." Soft pencil on sketchbook page.

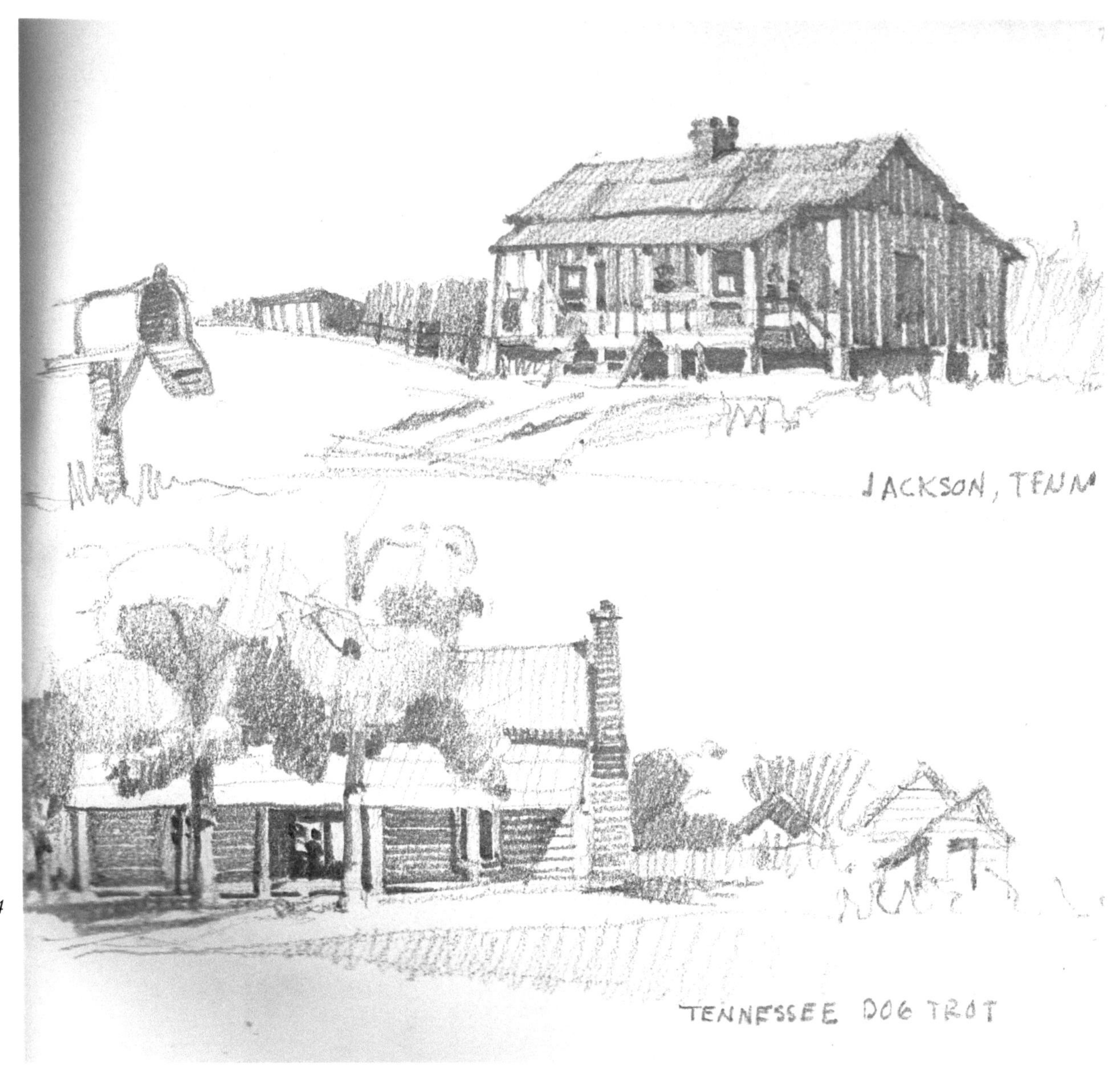

57. “Jackson, Tennessee.” and “Tennessee Dog Trot.” Soft pencil on sketchbook page.

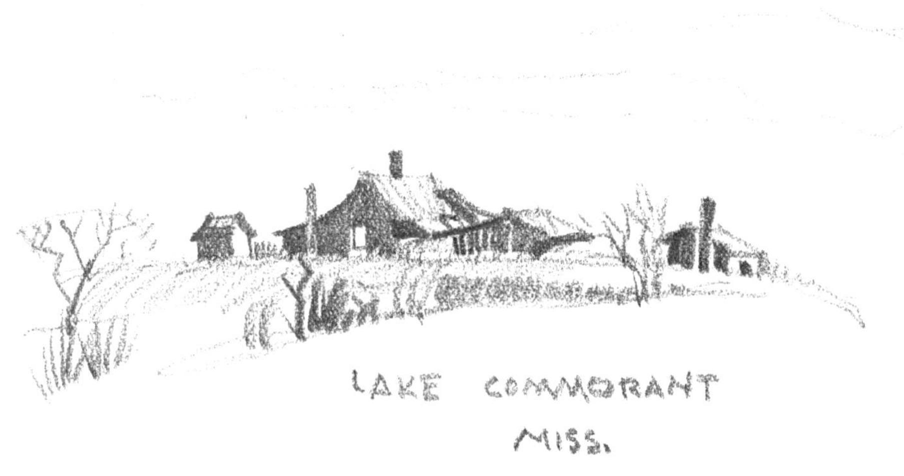

58. "Lake Commorant, Miss." Soft pencil on sketchbook page.

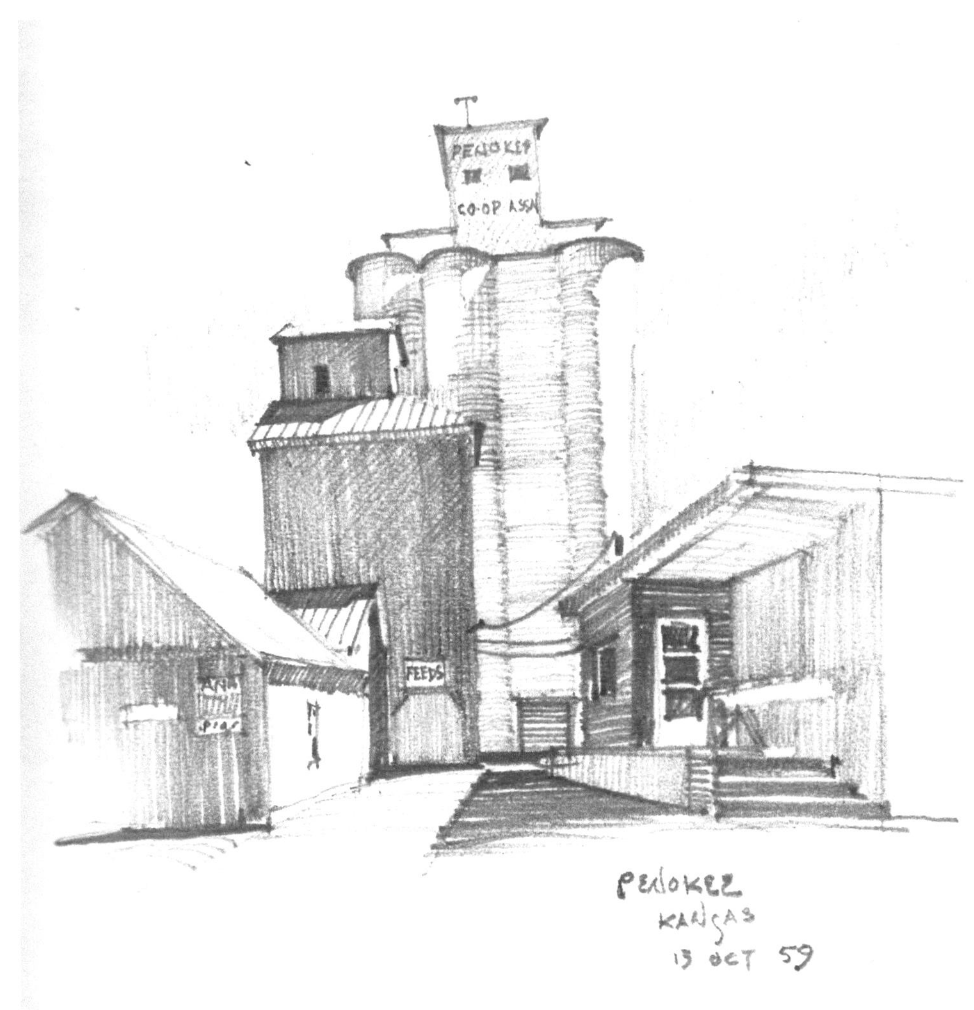

59. “Penokee, Kansas. 13 Oct. 59.” Soft pencil on sketchbook page.

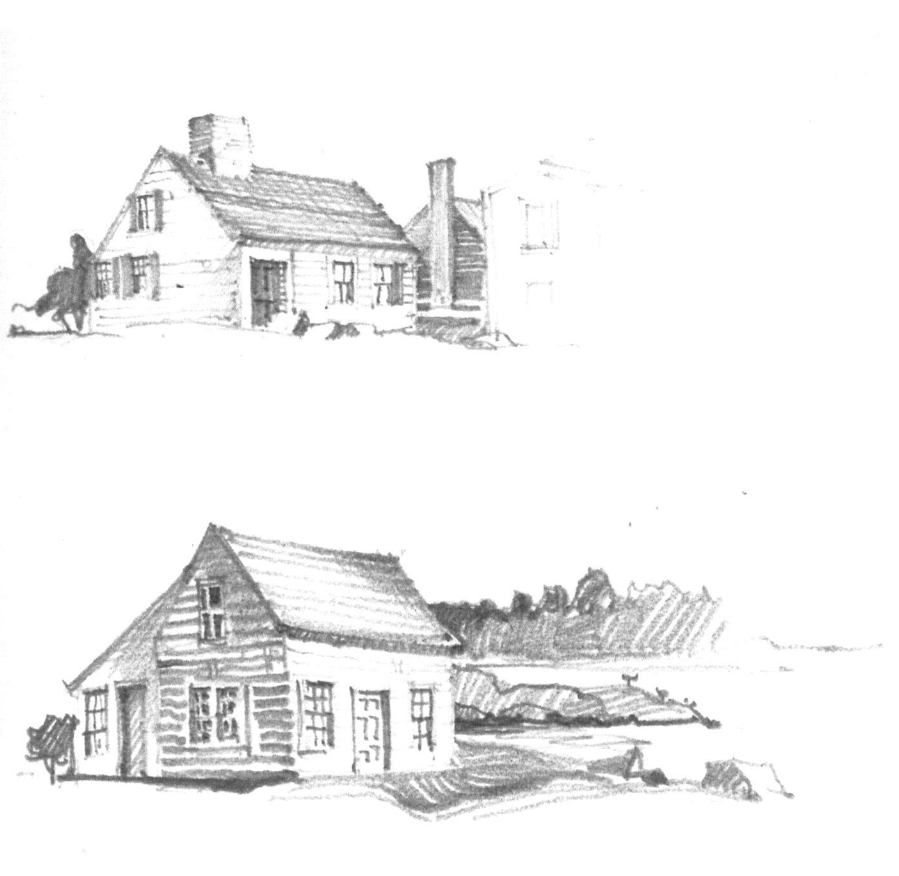

60. "Rockport, Mass. 29 Sept. 59." Soft pencil on sketchbook page.

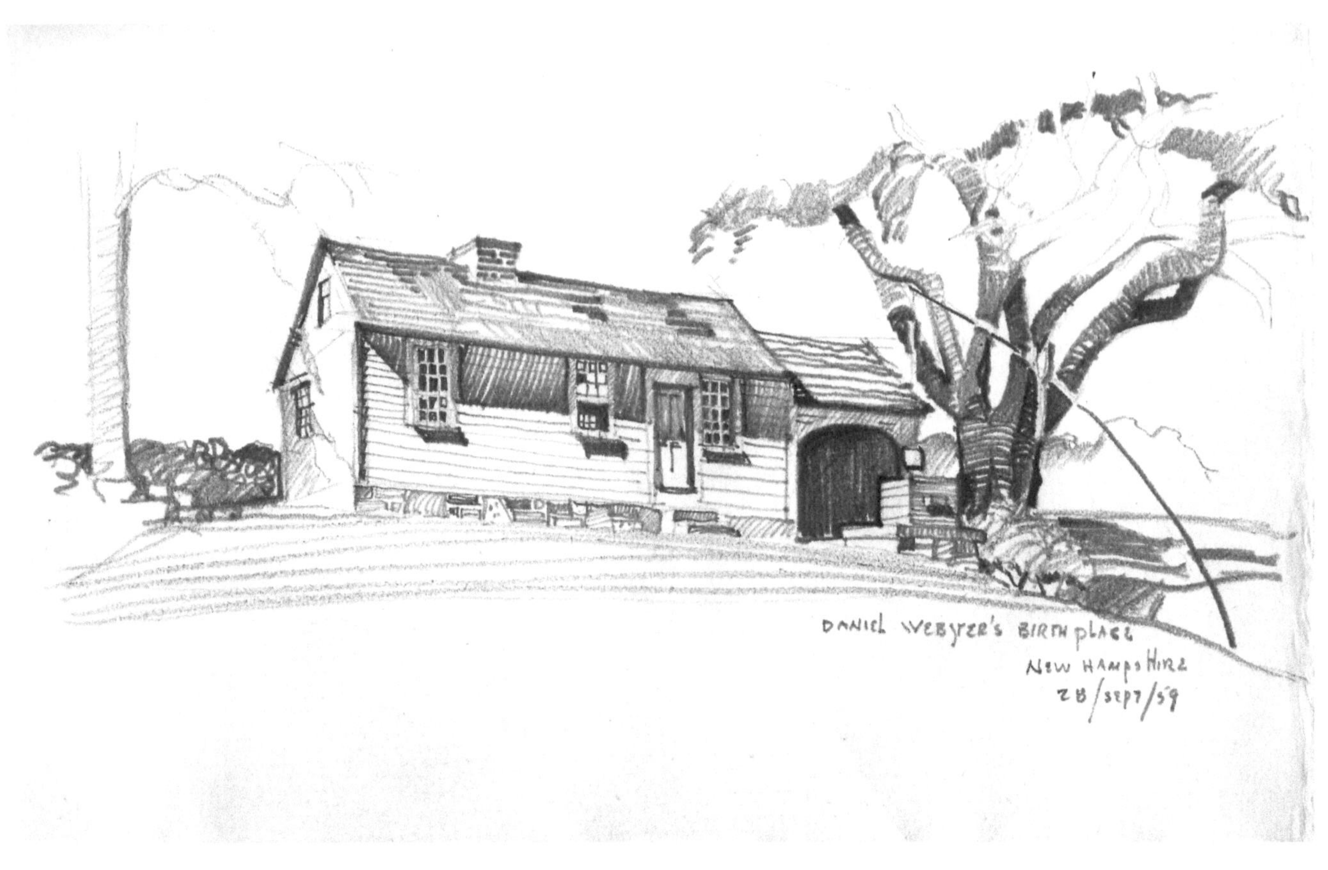

61. “Daniel Webster’s Birthplace, New Hampshire. 28 Sept. 59.” Soft pencil on sketchbook page.

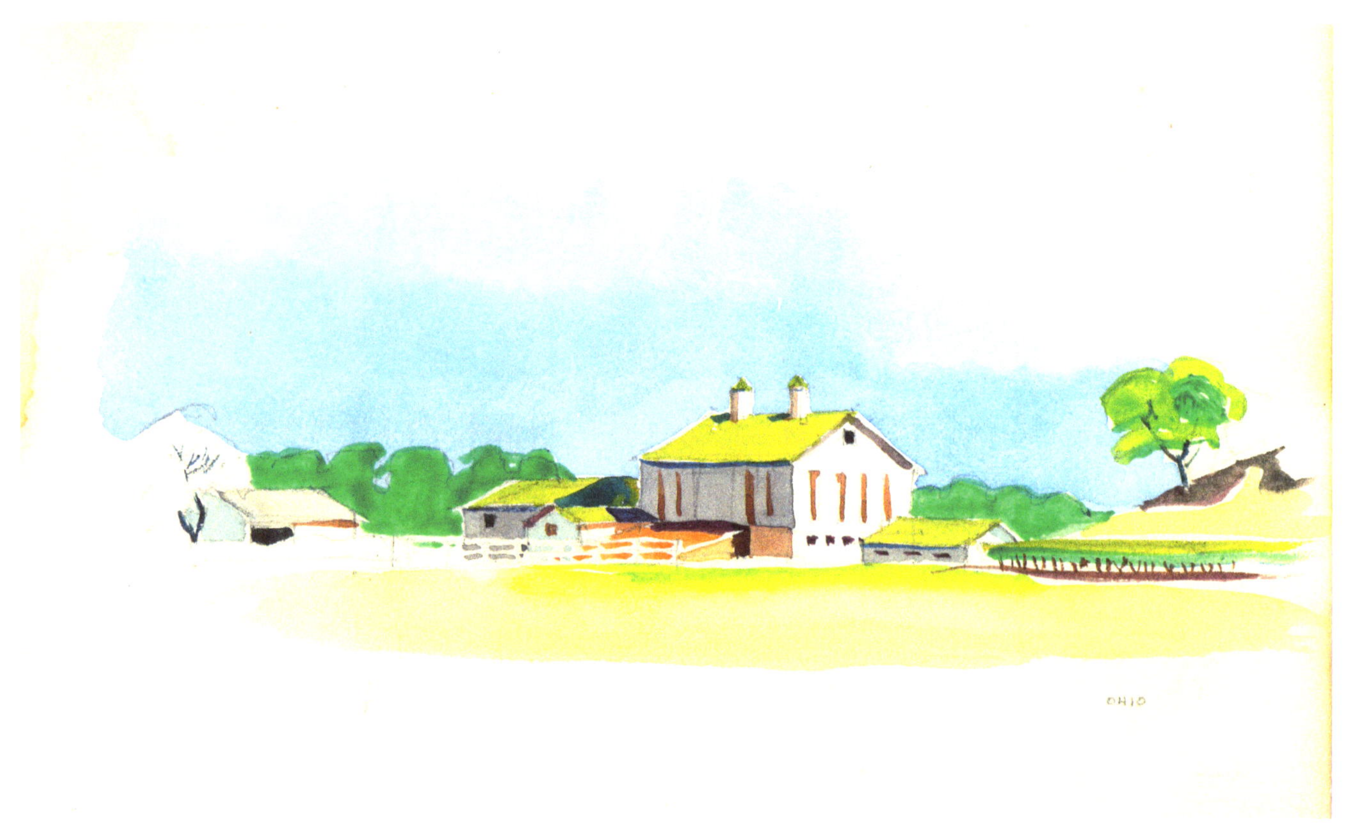

62. “Ohio.” Watercolor on sketchbook page.

Overcast, foggy, a raining most of the way up the coast.

Pleasant visit with the Kuads. Inland to Monterey, then down to the Owings place at Big Sur. House out of fable. Warm, friendly reception made it a snug harbour in the storm.

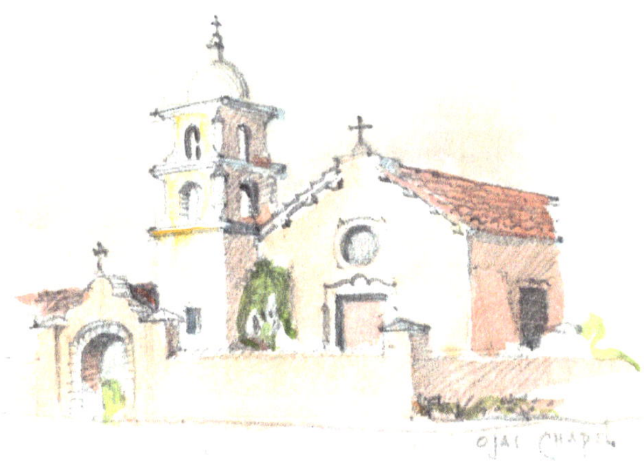

63. "Ojai Chapel." Monterey Mission church. Watercolor on sketchbook page with black ink inscription.

Travels Abroad

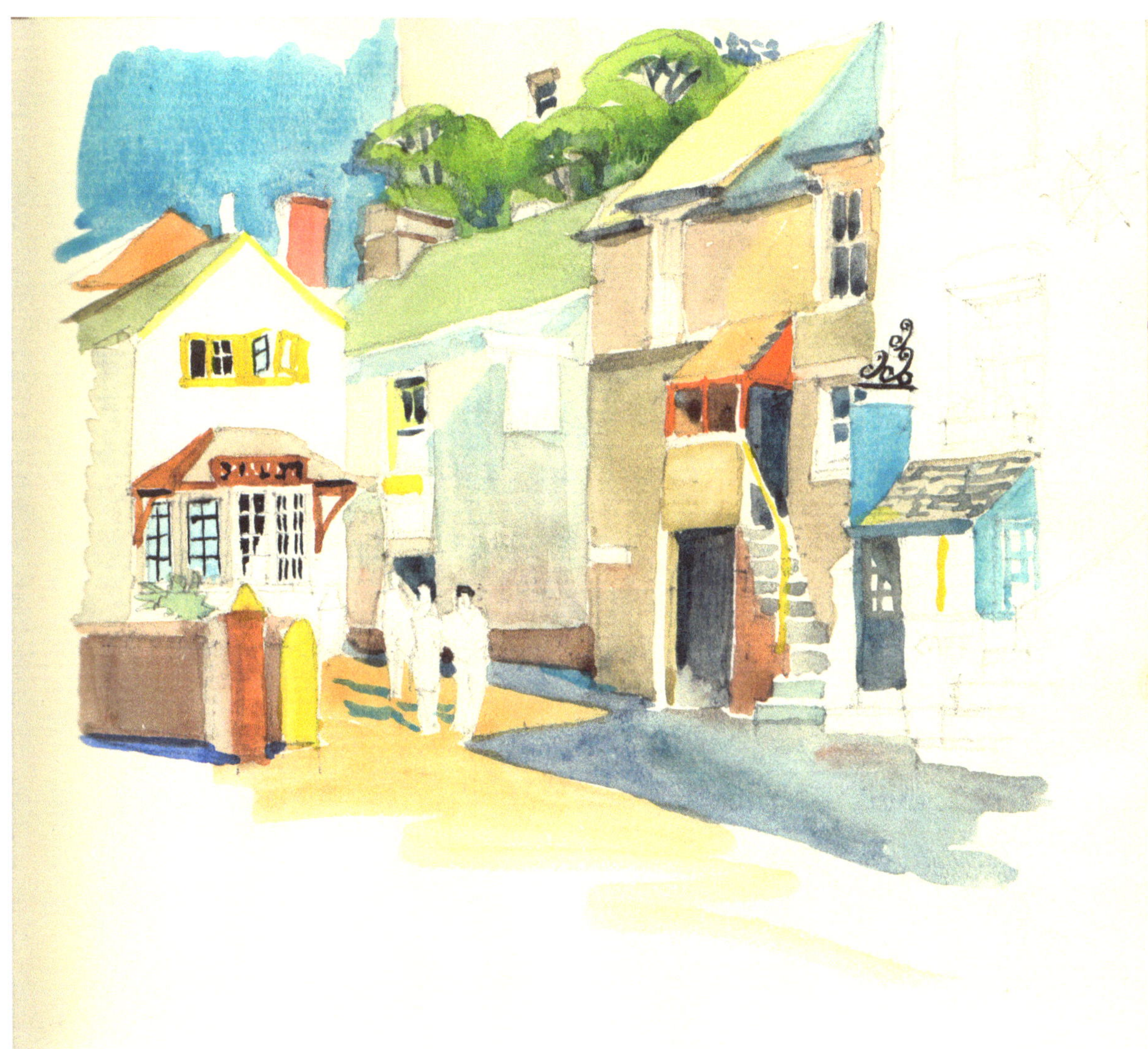

64. Scene of an English seaside town. Watercolor on sketchbook page with background watercolor wash.

Sketches from New Mexico, across the U.S., and from abroad may be seen to represent somewhat different objectives. The New Mexico sketches manifest McHugh's intentional and systematic exploration of a particular region—his new home—while sketches from travels across the U.S. for instance, as mentioned earlier, are more or less serendipitous encounters with interesting subjects. Each approach has its advantage. While the New Mexico sketches for the most part draw together moods, places, and details for the purpose of discovering what tends to unify this singularly large and varied place, the US travel sketches by comparison are largely of things and places encountered en route that happened to catch the eye. The European sketches on the other hand tend to represent a third objective. They may be seen as explorations of special things and places that characterize Europe's special qualities, especially those particular qualities that differ from the American experience. For instance, the European sketches more often depict urban ensembles rather than individual buildings. They aim to capture harmonious urban scenes where buildings flow together as ensembles in contrast to the more individually distinguishable buildings as comprise most American towns. In addition, the European sketches, when they do single out individual buildings, tend to select certain uniquely European building types that fascinated John McHugh, for instance, English half-timbered medieval buildings.

Sketches 64 through 74 are European street scenes and towns and villages, those ensembles of buildings and the public spaces they frame that characterize European traditional urbanism. Sketches 75 through 104, on the other hand, do select out individual buildings and other objects, sometimes including their natural setting, such as sketches 75 and 83, and at other times they focus on certain buildings, objects, or details or upon urban clusters that have been selected out of a larger urban ensemble for special consideration, such as the bridge in sketch 94, the tower in sketch 97, the tight cluster of forms in sketch 100 and boats in sketches 100, 101 and 104.

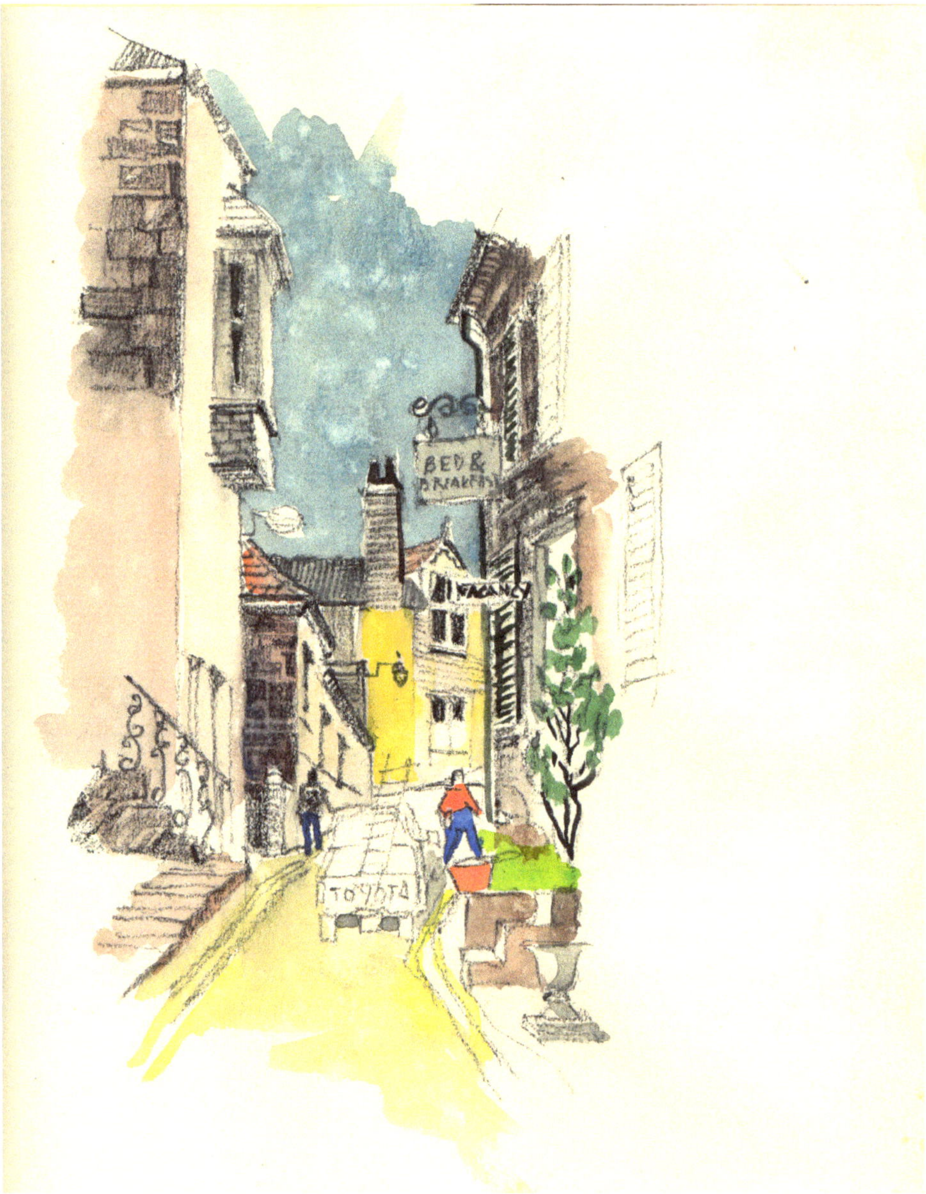

65. European street scene. Watercolor and graphite pencil on sketchbook page.

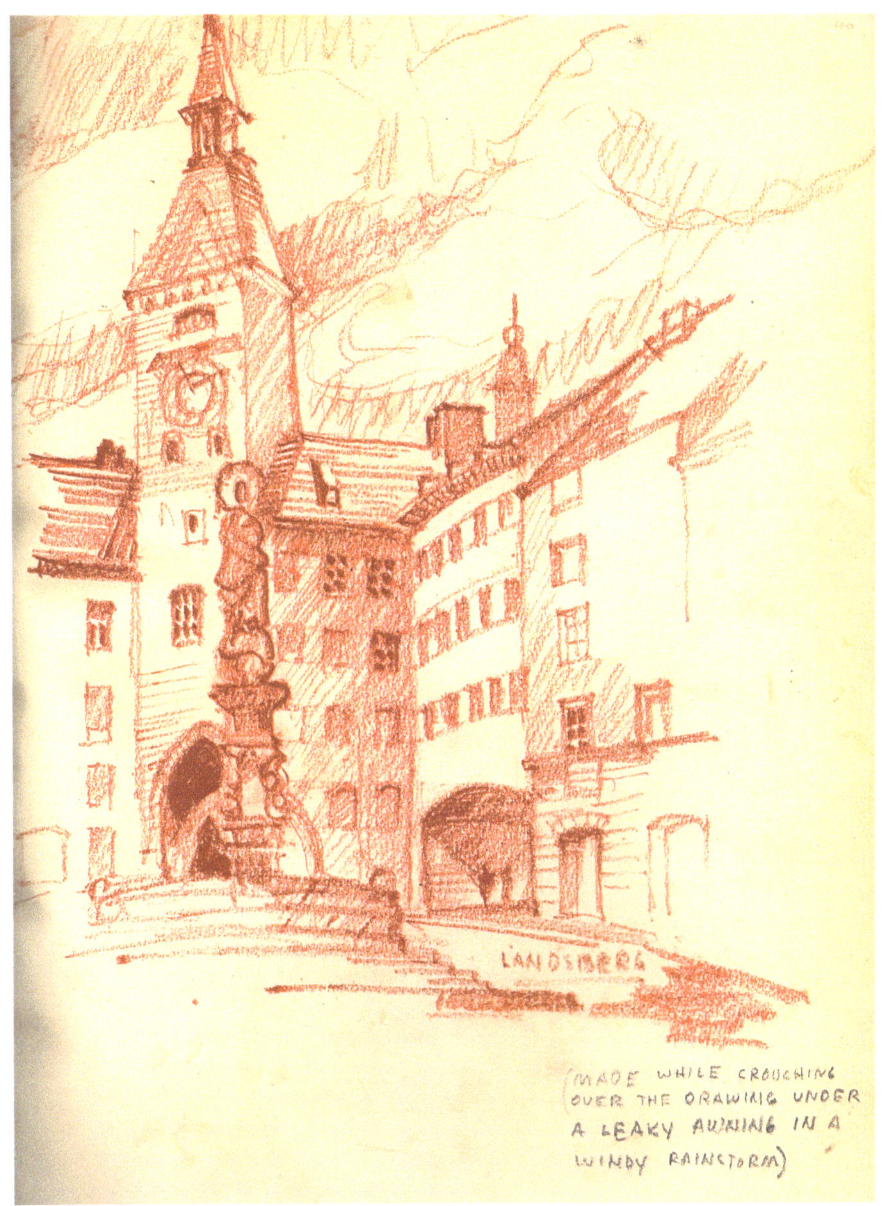

66. "Landsberg." European street scene, Conté crayon on sketchbook page.

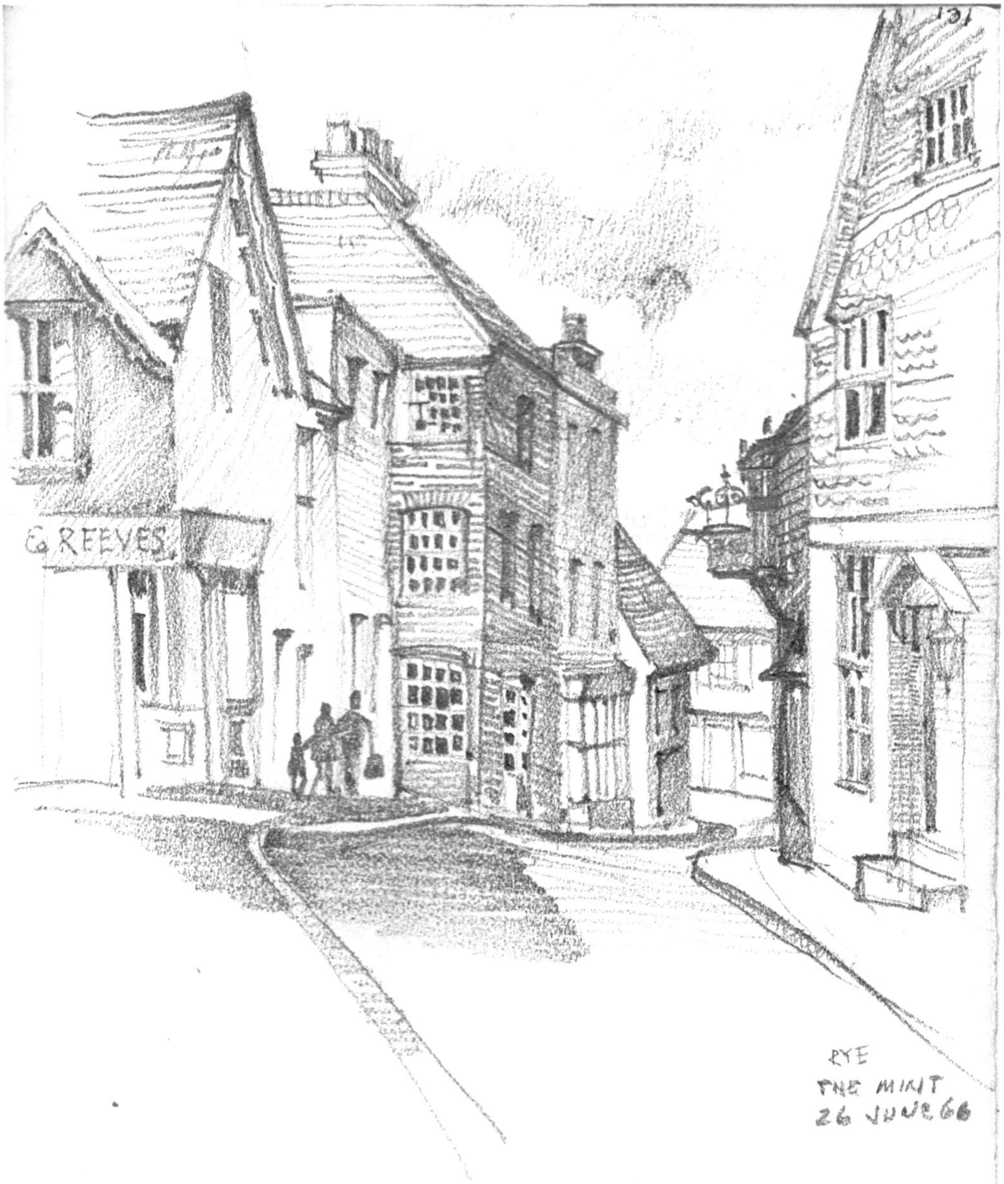

67. “Rye, The Mint. 26 June 66.” Soft pencil on sketchbook page.

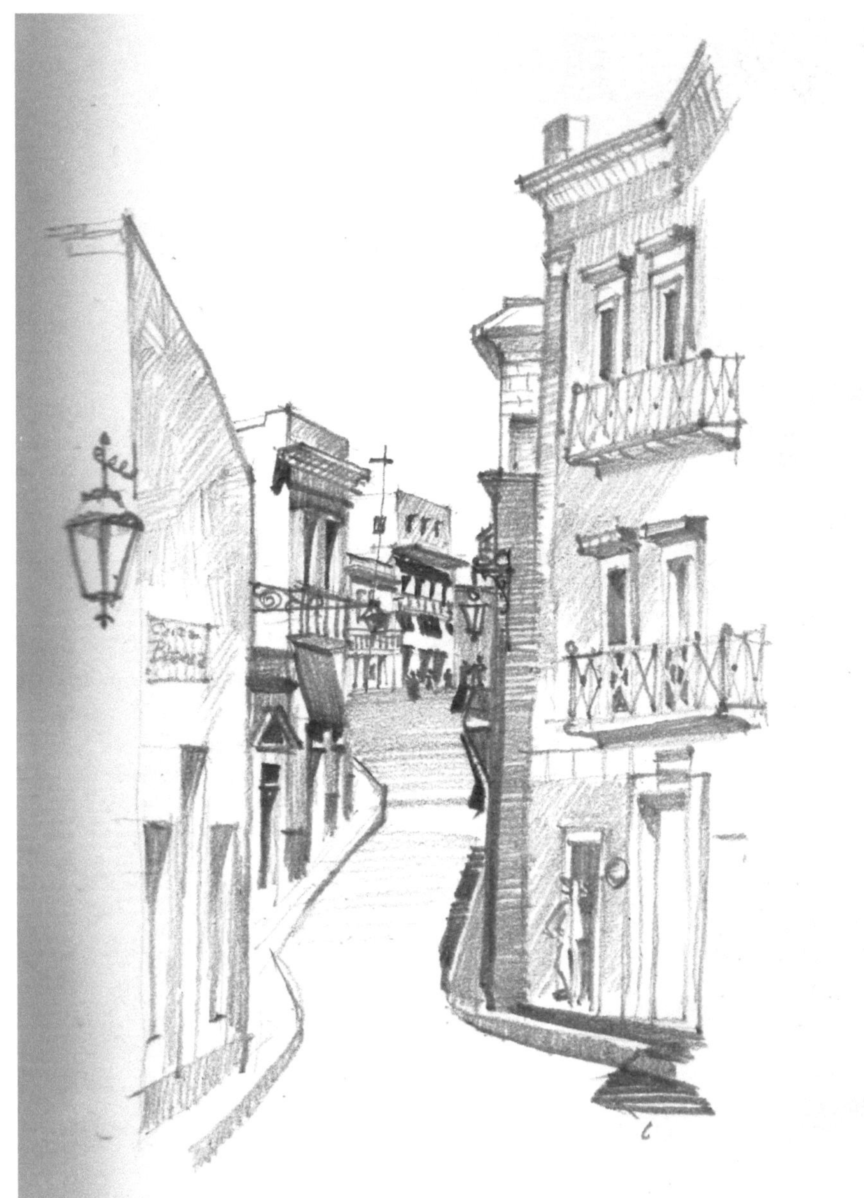

68. European street scene. Soft pencil on sketchbook page.

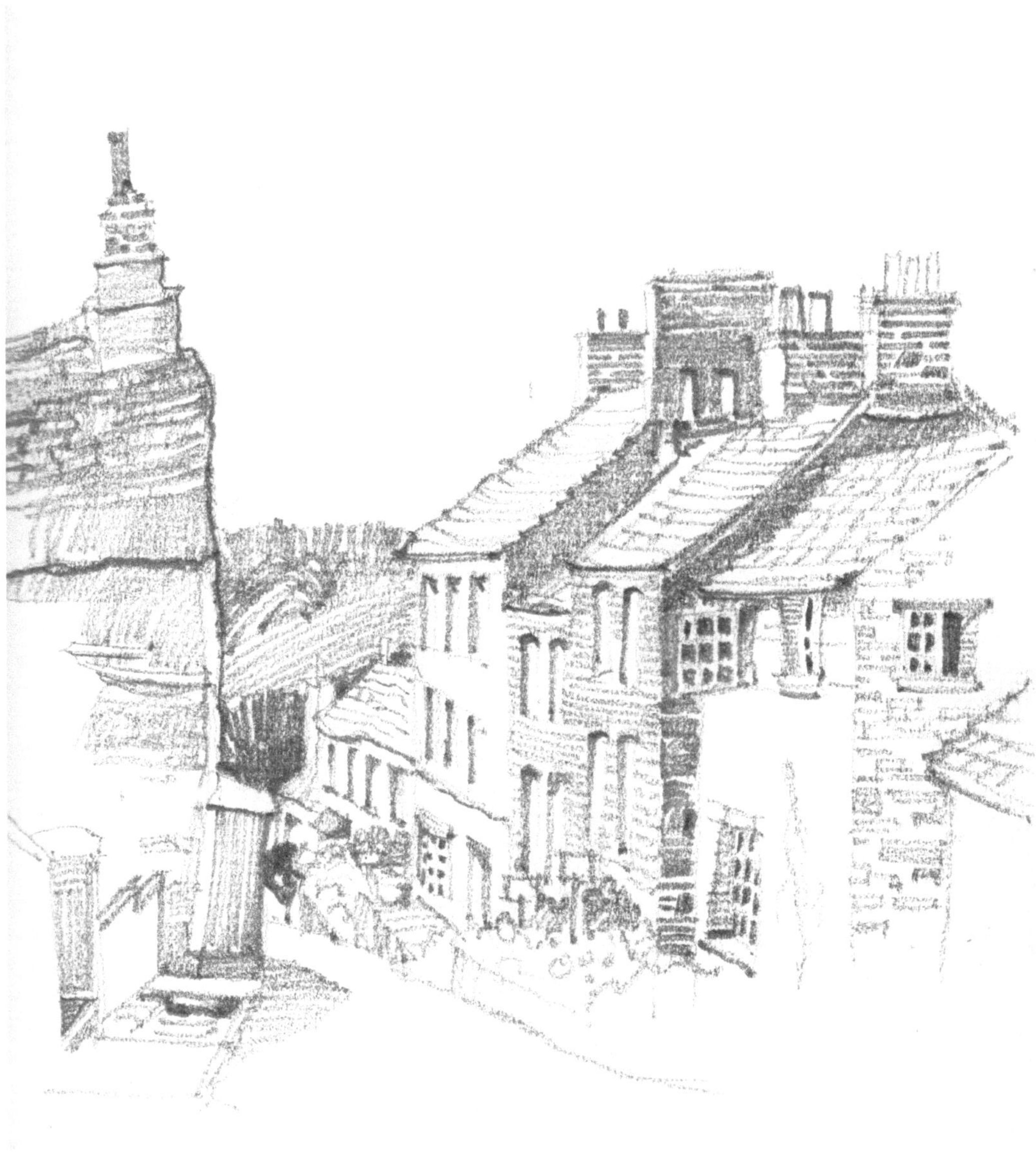

69. European street scene. Soft pencil on sketchbook page.

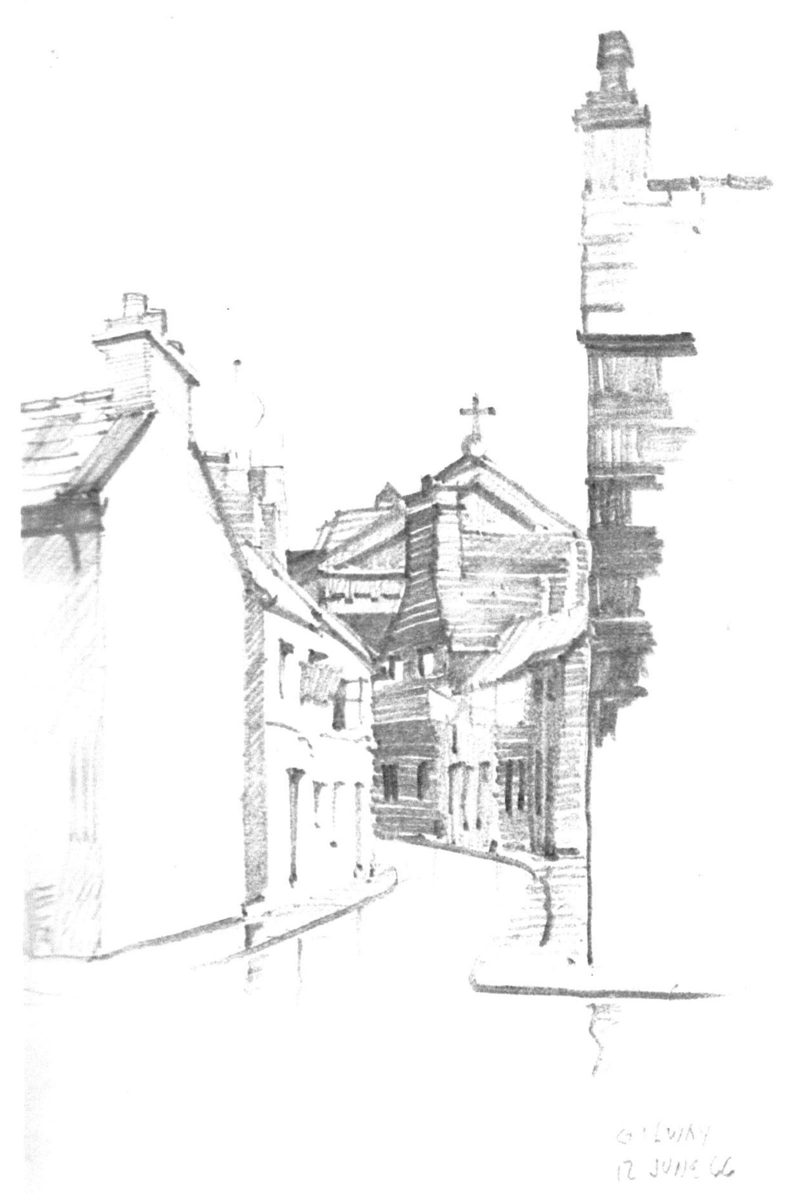

70. “Galway. 12 June 66.” Soft pencil on sketchbook page.

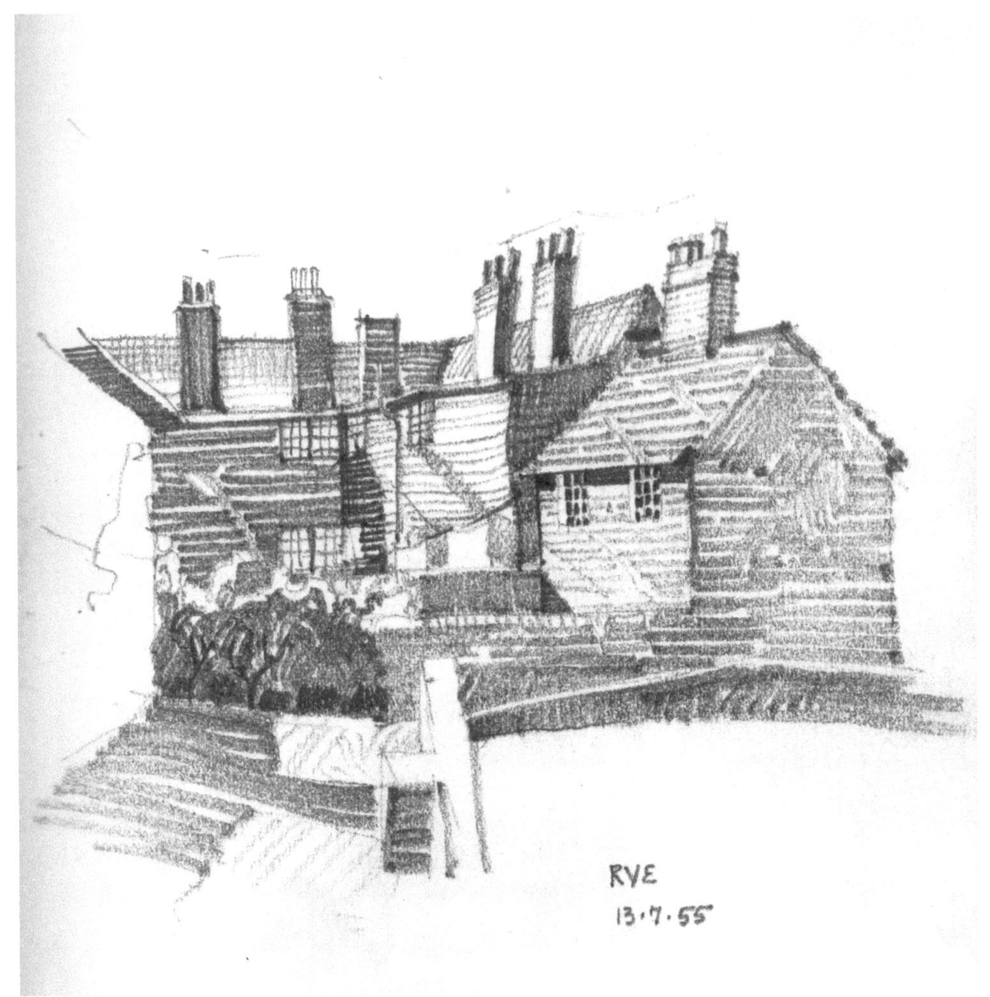

71. “Rye. 13-7-55.” Soft pencil on sketchbook page.

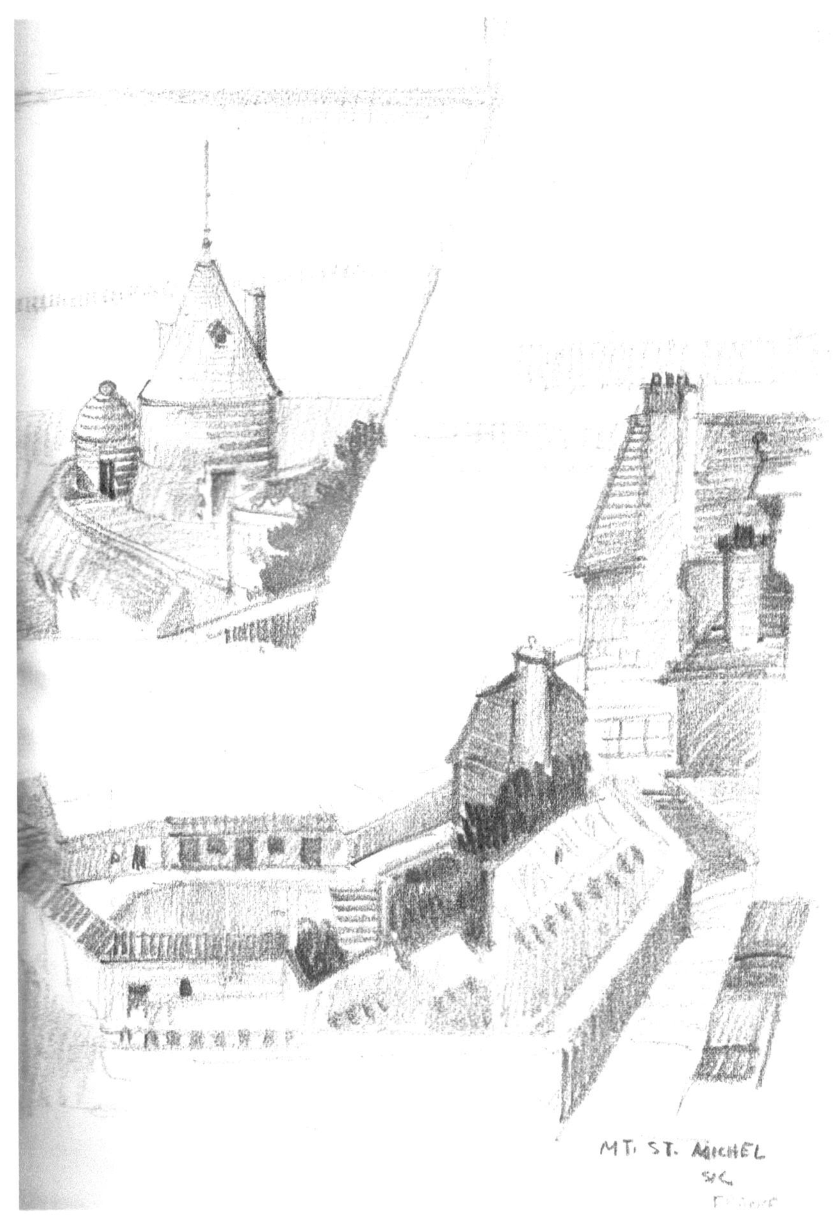

72. "Mt. St. Michael." Soft pencil on sketchbook page.

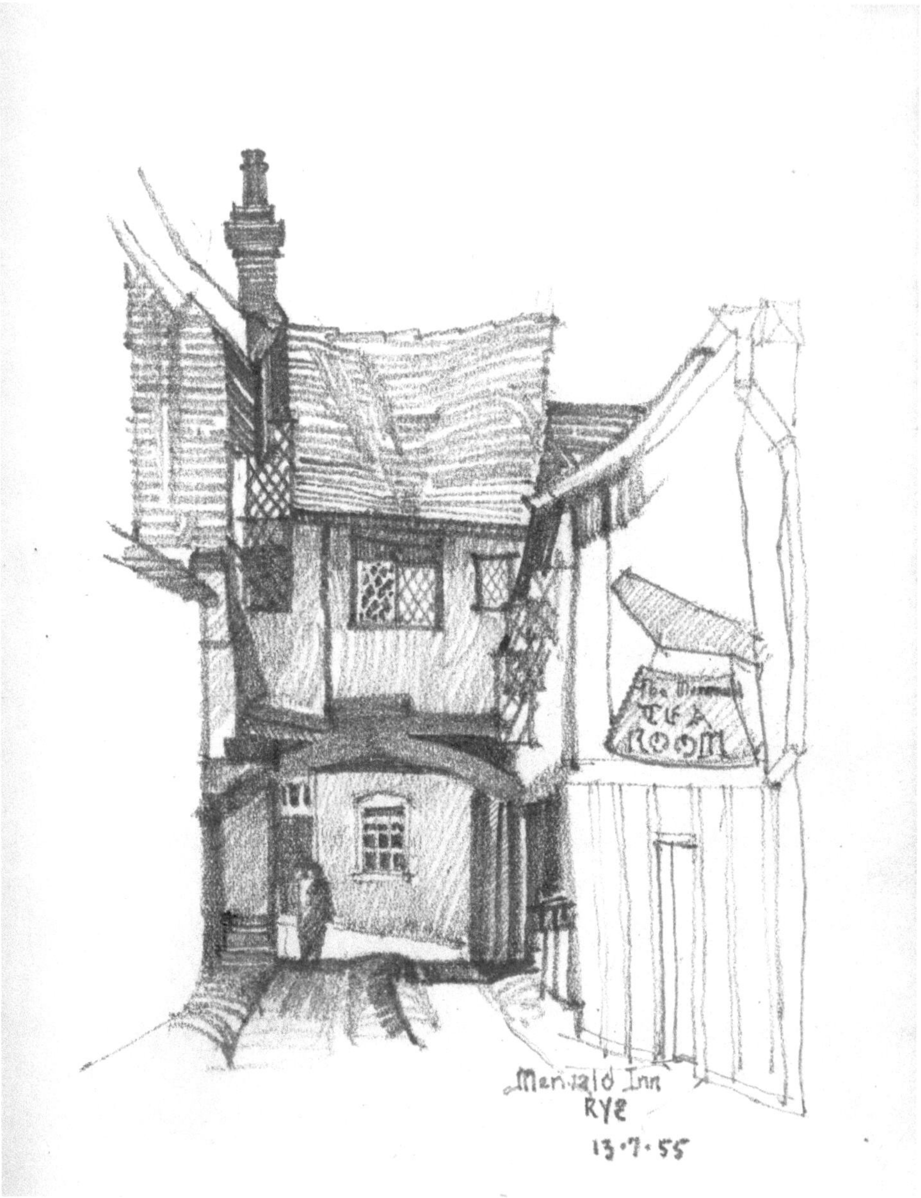

73. “Menald Inn, Rye. 13-7-55.” Soft pencil on sketchbook page.

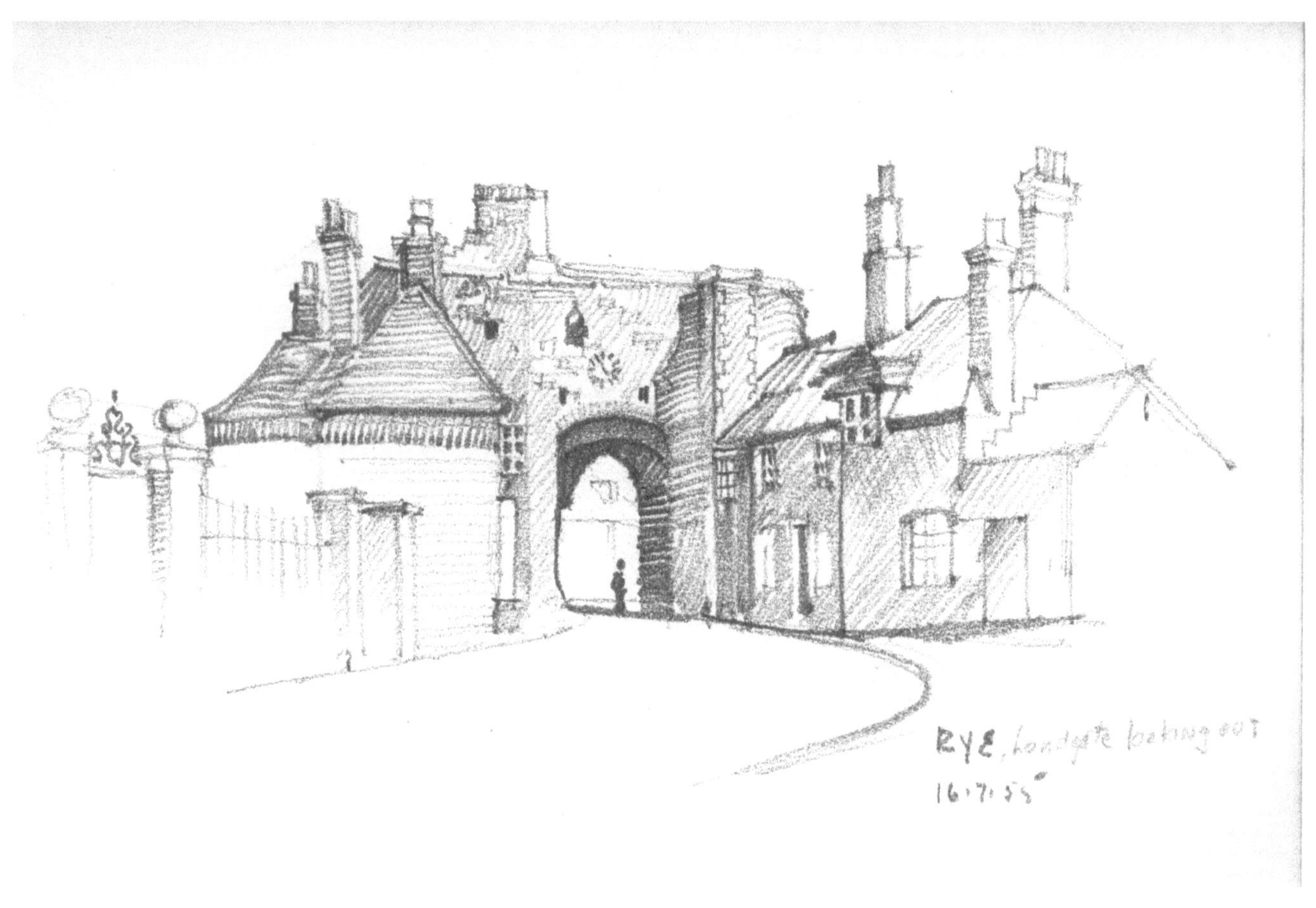

74. "Rye, Landgate Looking Out. 16-7-55." Soft pencil on sketchbook page.

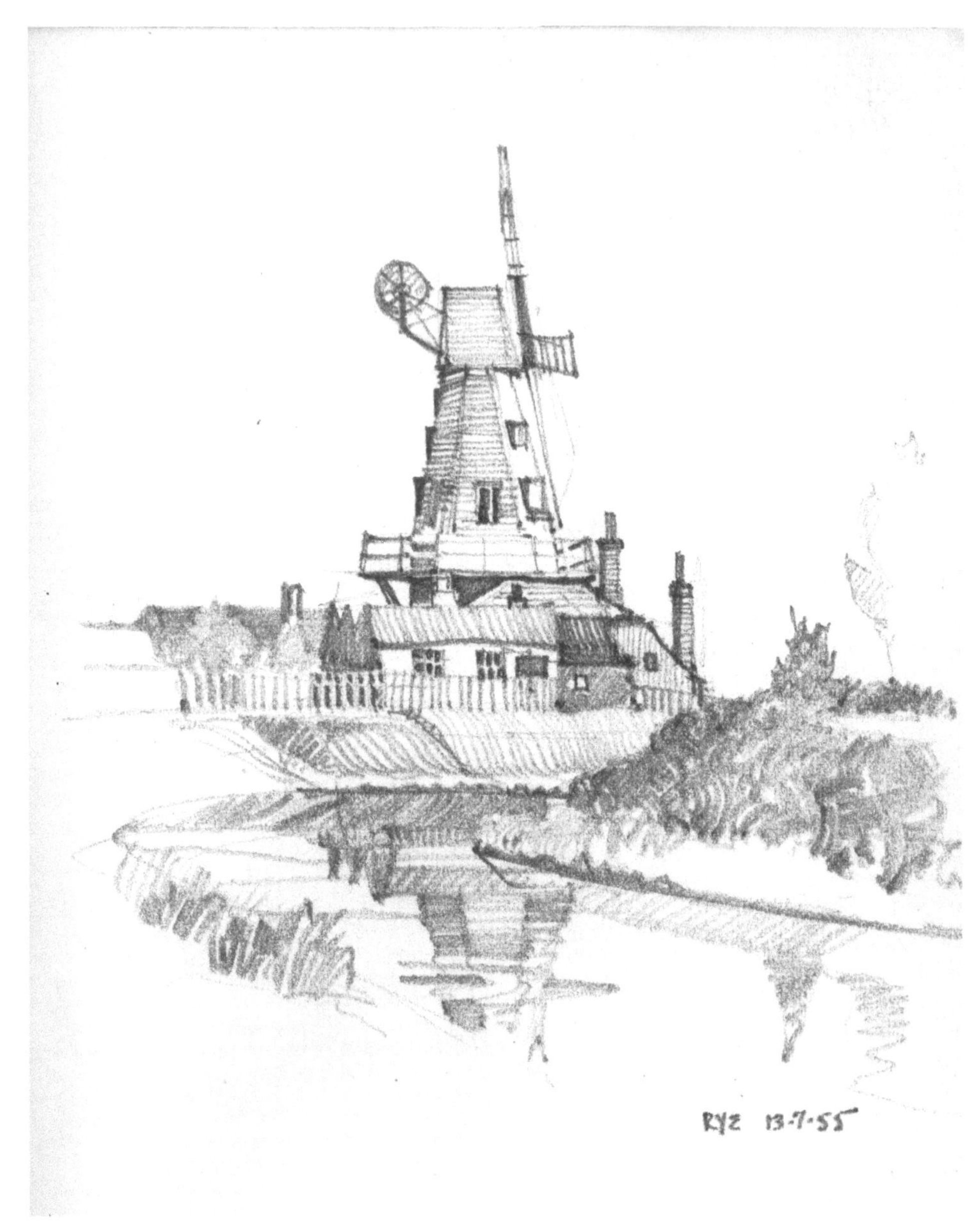

75. “Rye. 13-7-55” Soft pencil on sketchbook page.

Finished at
Mountsfield House
Rye Sussex
28 June 1966

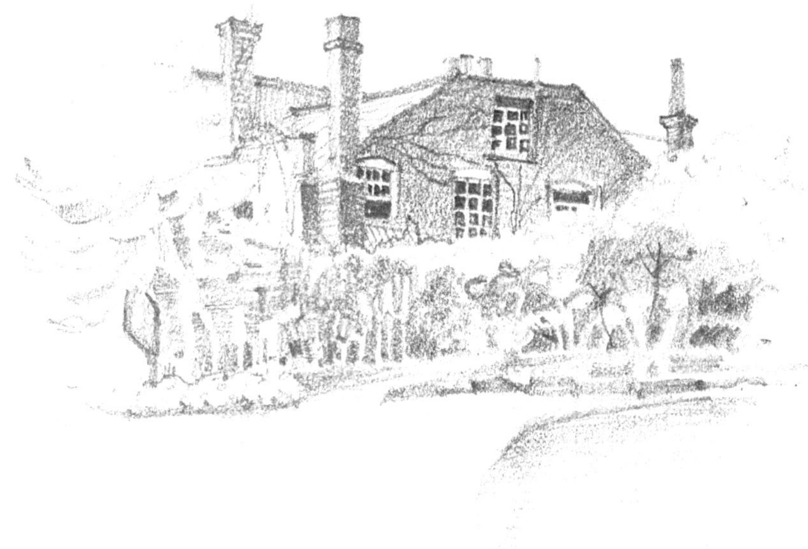

76. "Mountsfield House, Rye, Sussex. 28 June 1966." Soft pencil on sketchbook page.

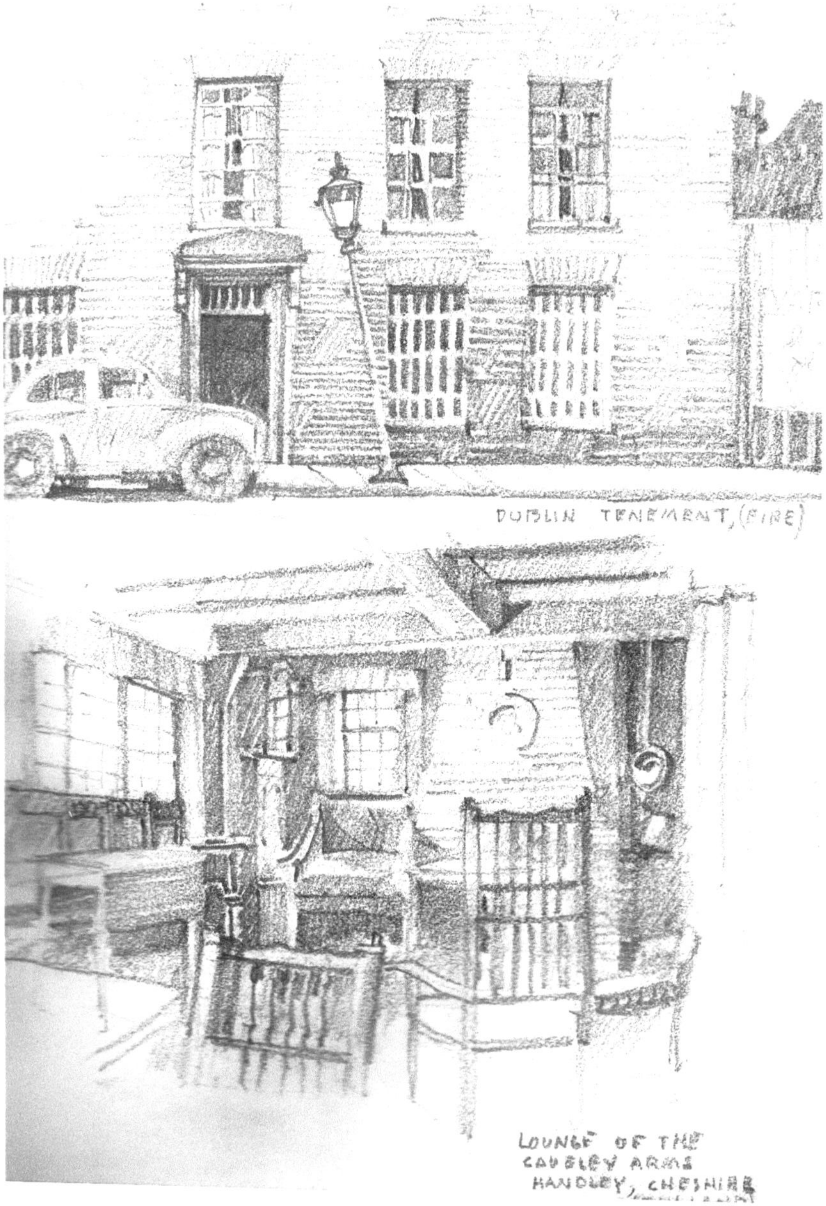

77. "Dublin Tenement" and "Lounge of the Carely Arms, Handley, Cheshire." Soft pencil on sketchbook page.

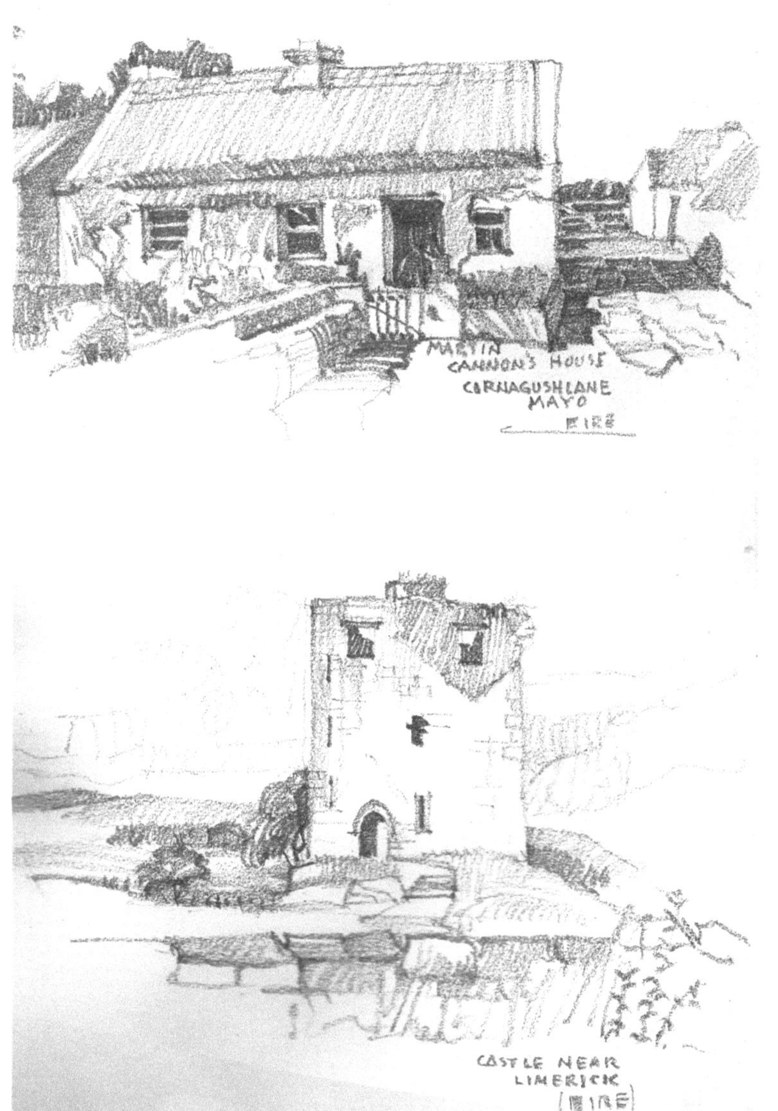

78. "Martin Cannon's House" and "Castle Near Limerick." Soft pencil on sketchbook page.

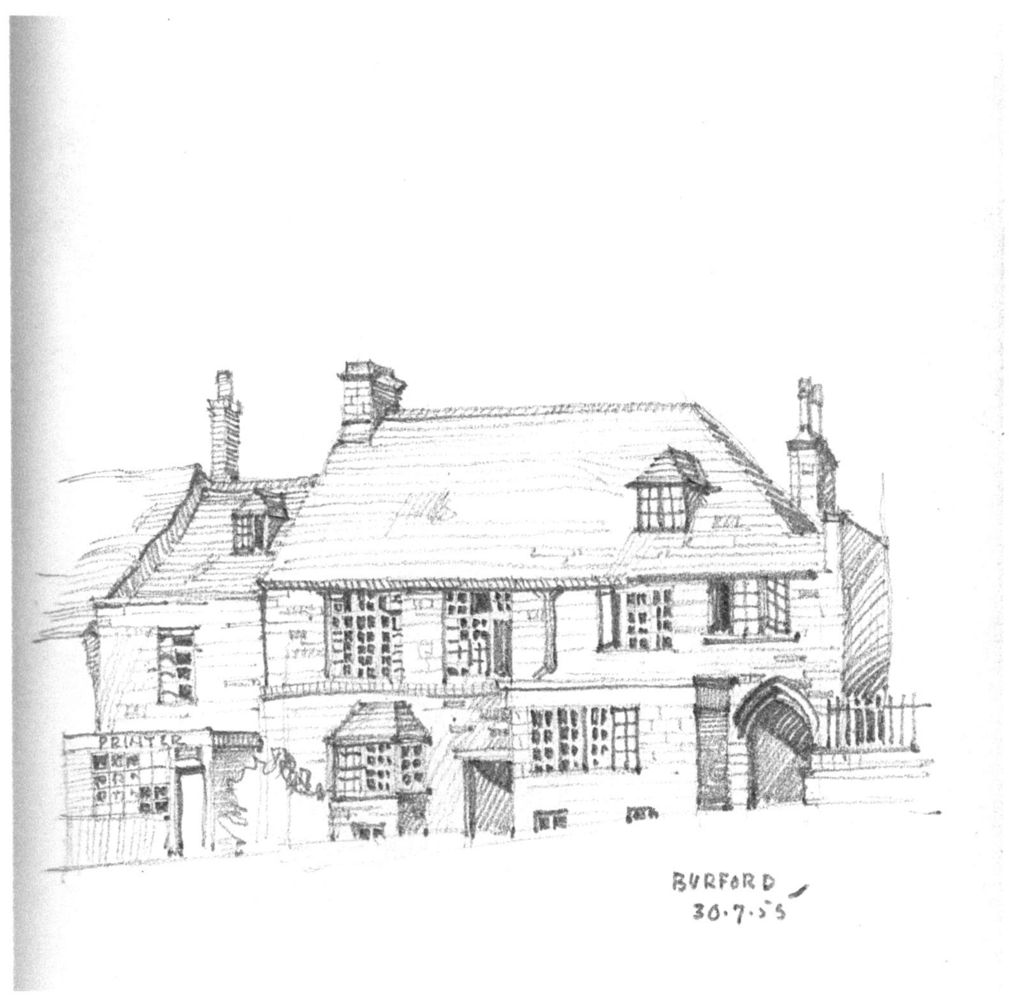

79. "Buford. 30-7-55." Soft pencil on sketchbook page.

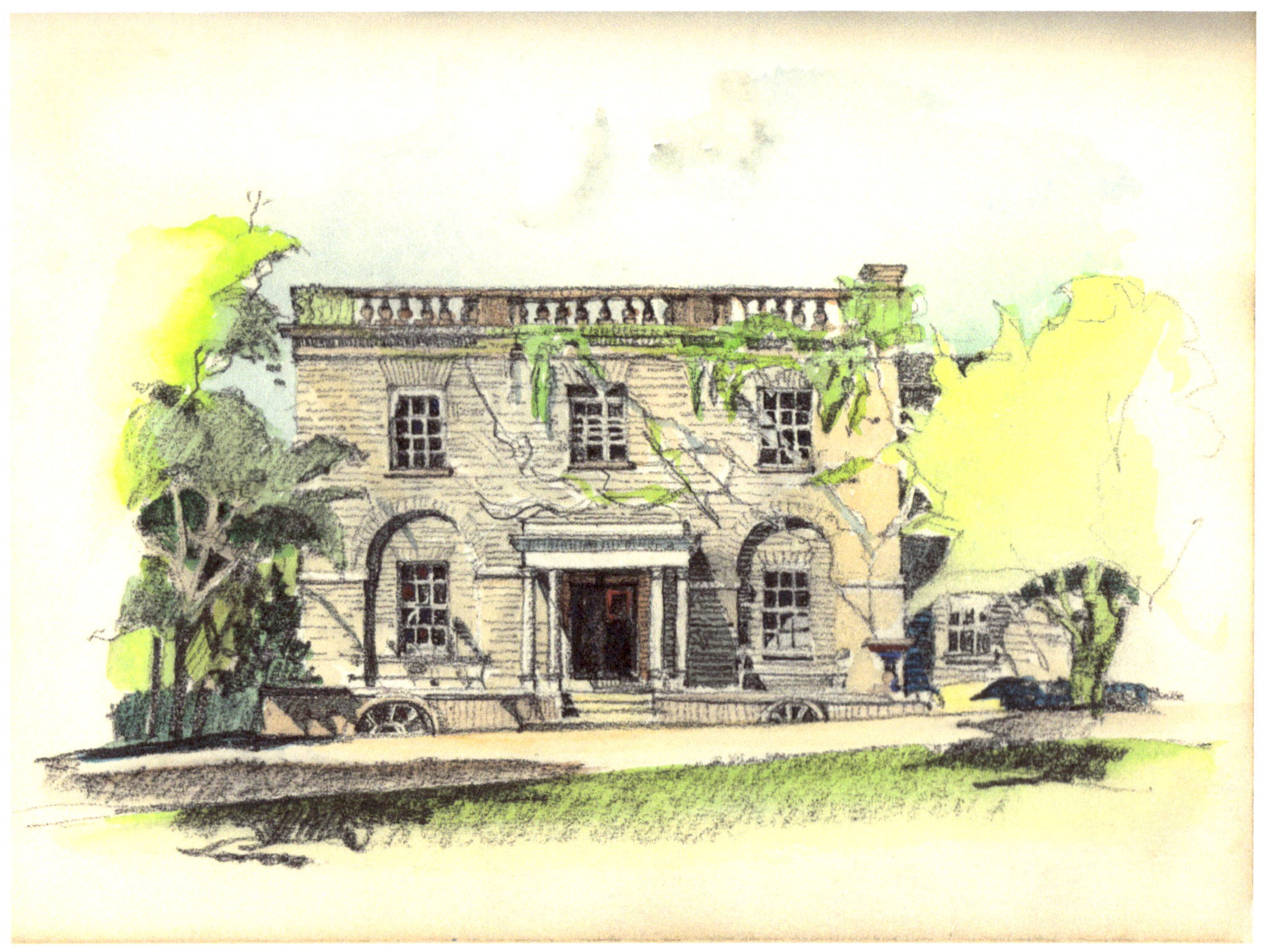

80. Country Residence. Graphite pencil and watercolor on sketchbook page.

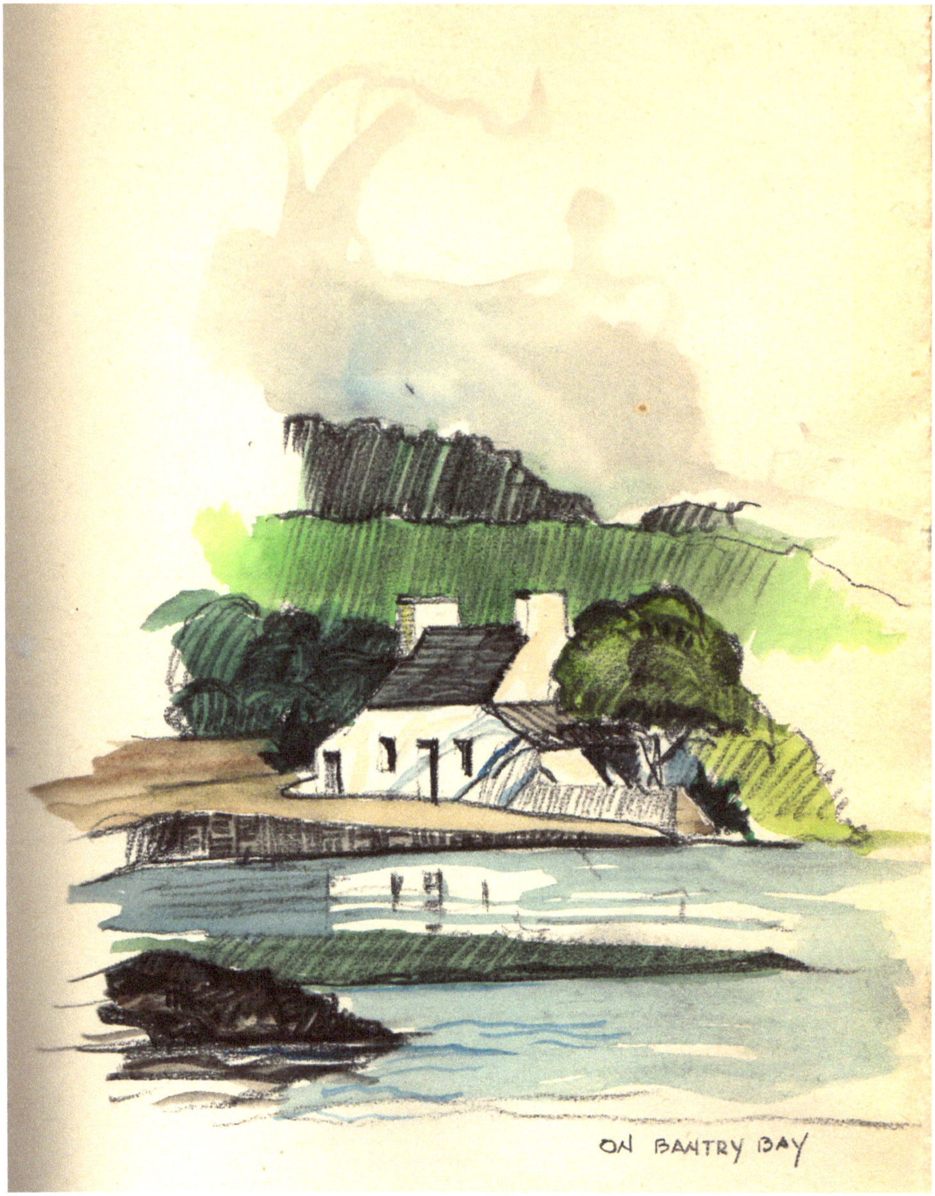

81. "On Bantry Bay." Watercolor and graphite pencil on sketchbook page.

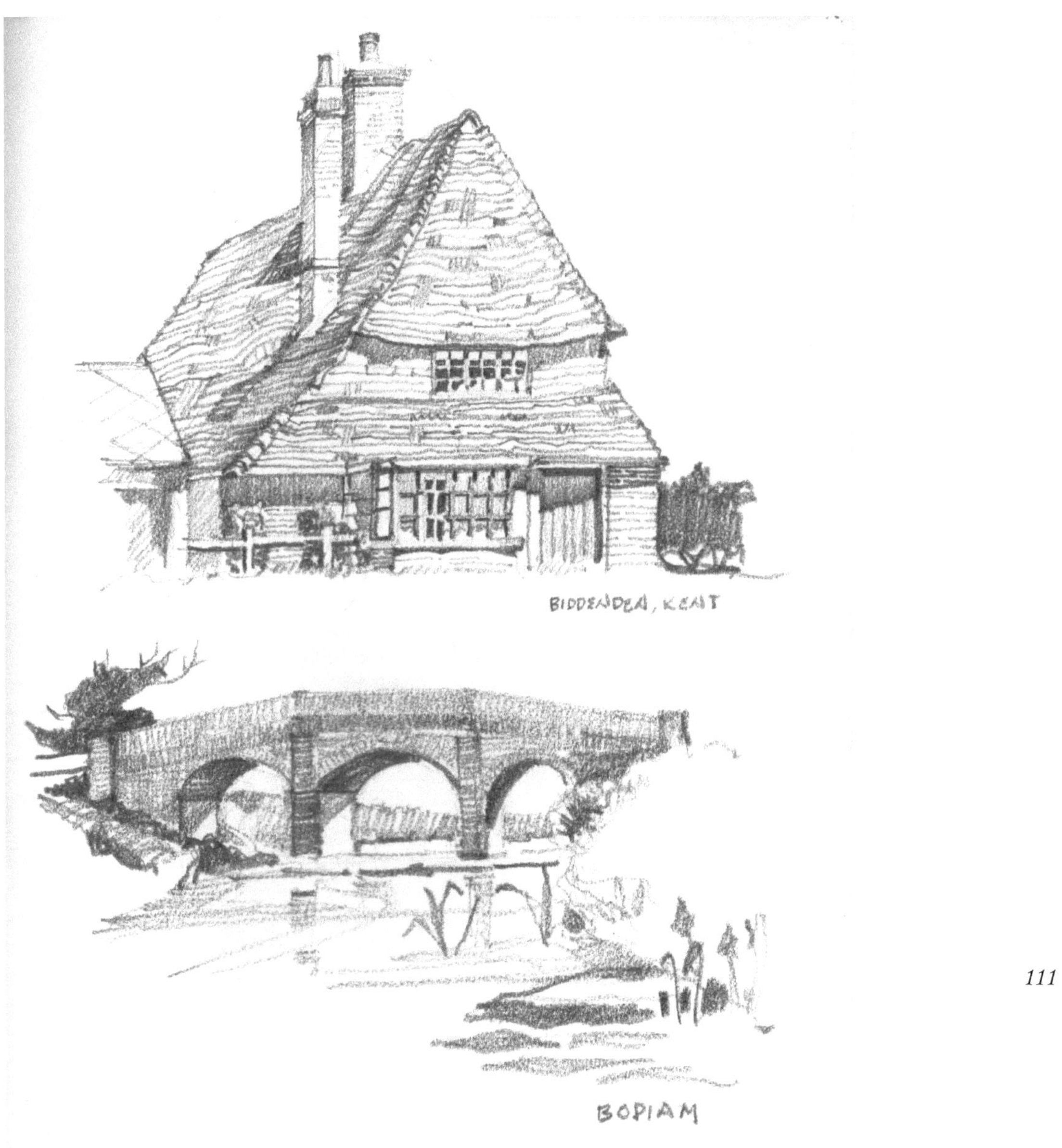

82. “Biddendea, Kent” and “Bodiam.” Soft pencil on sketchbook page.

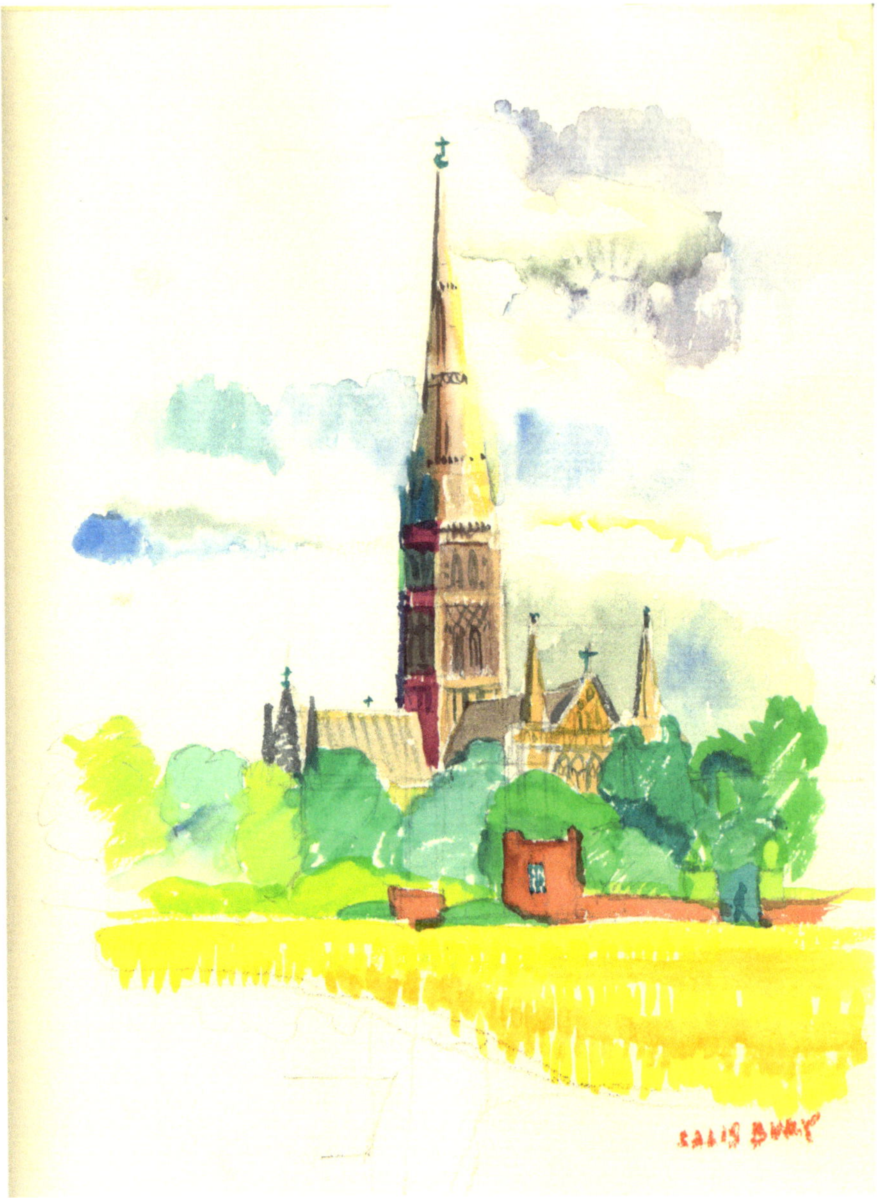

83. "Salisbury." Watercolor on sketchbook page.

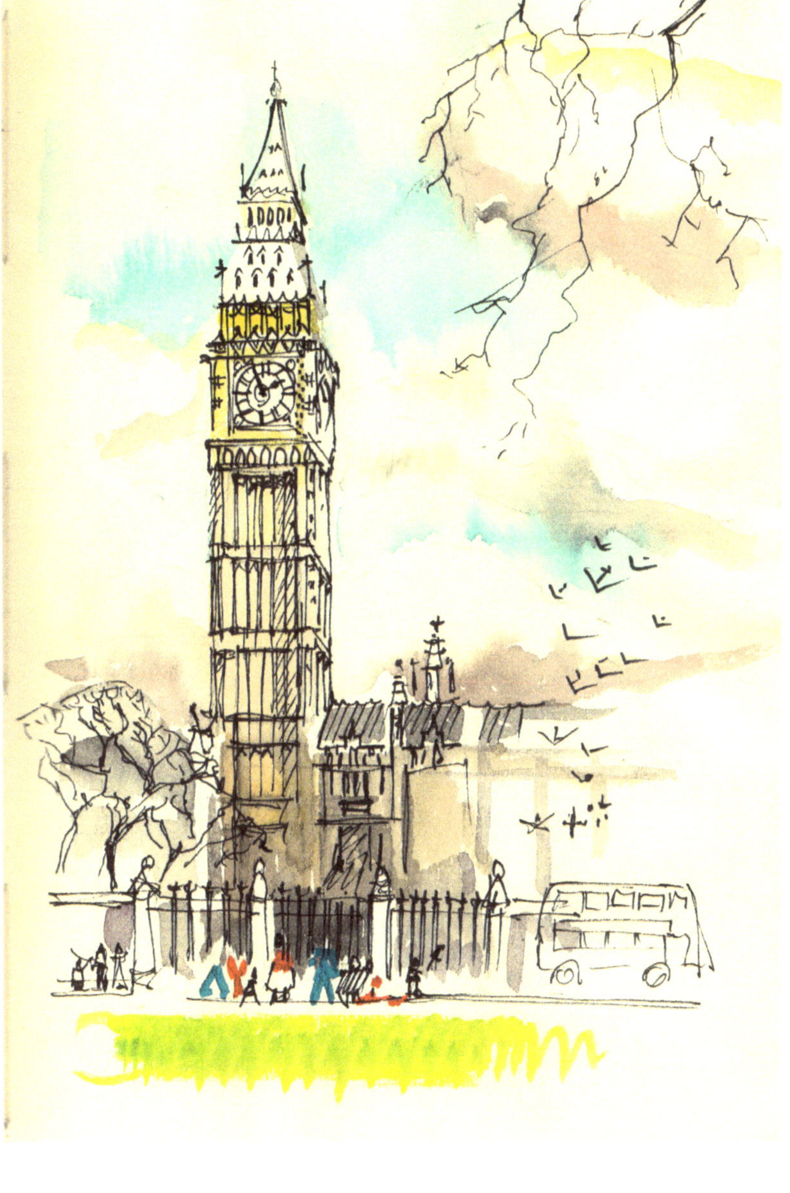

84. Big Ben, London. Watercolor and black ink applied with fine-line pen on sketchbook page.

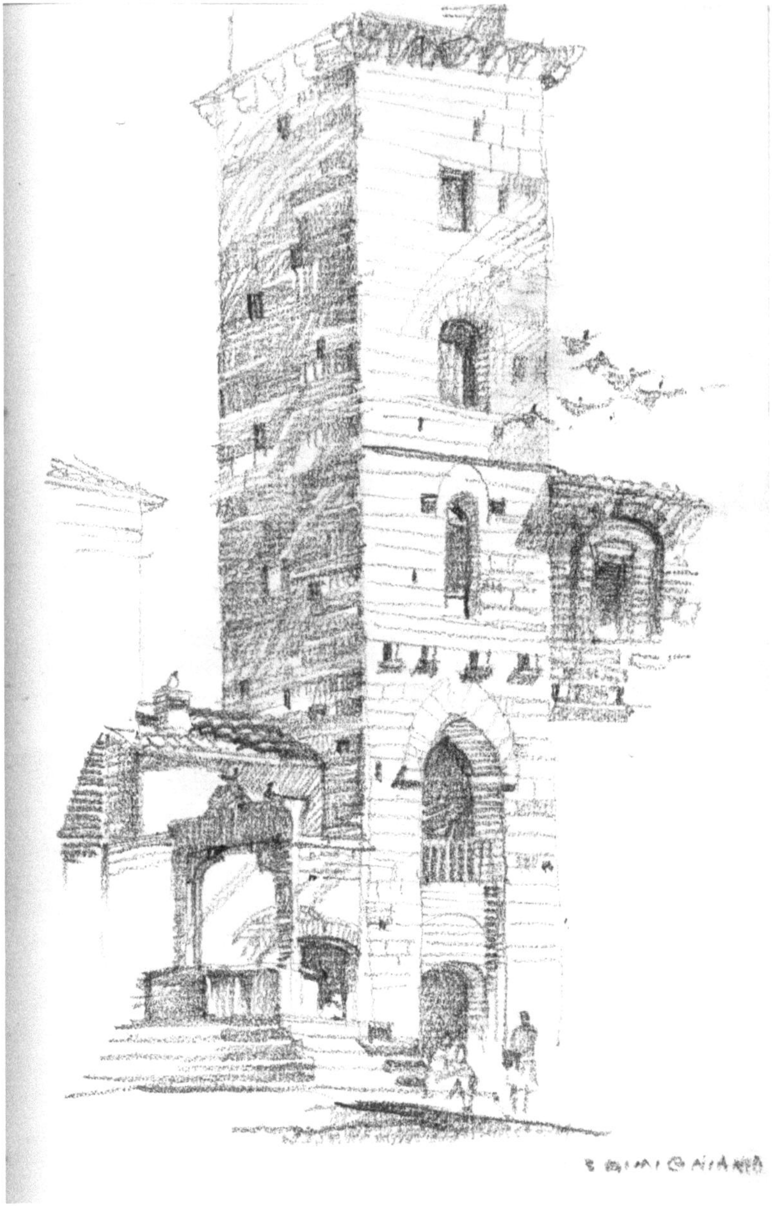

85. Tower, European city. Soft pencil on sketchbook page.

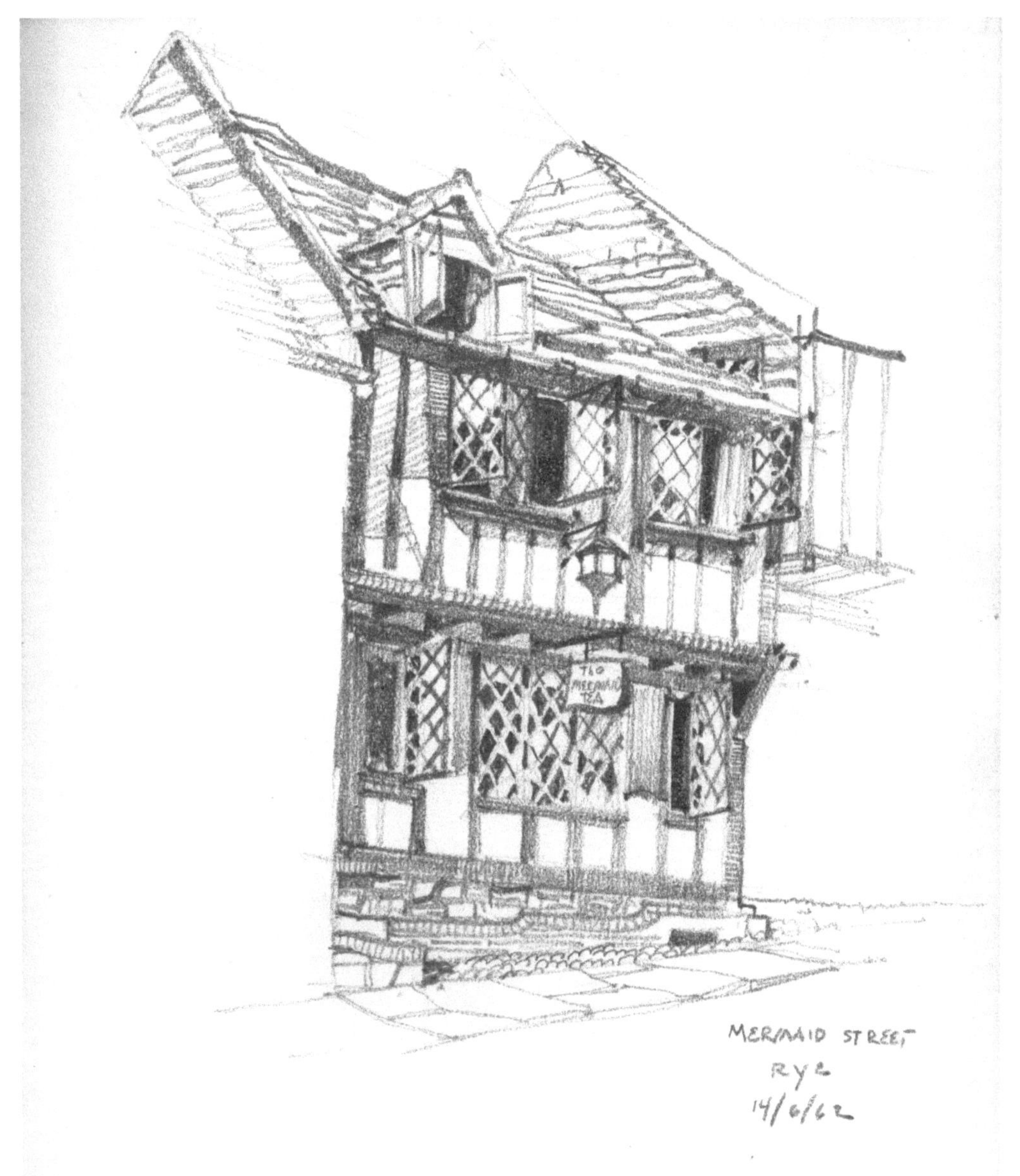

86. “Mermaid Street, Rye. 14-6-62.” Soft pencil on sketchbook page.

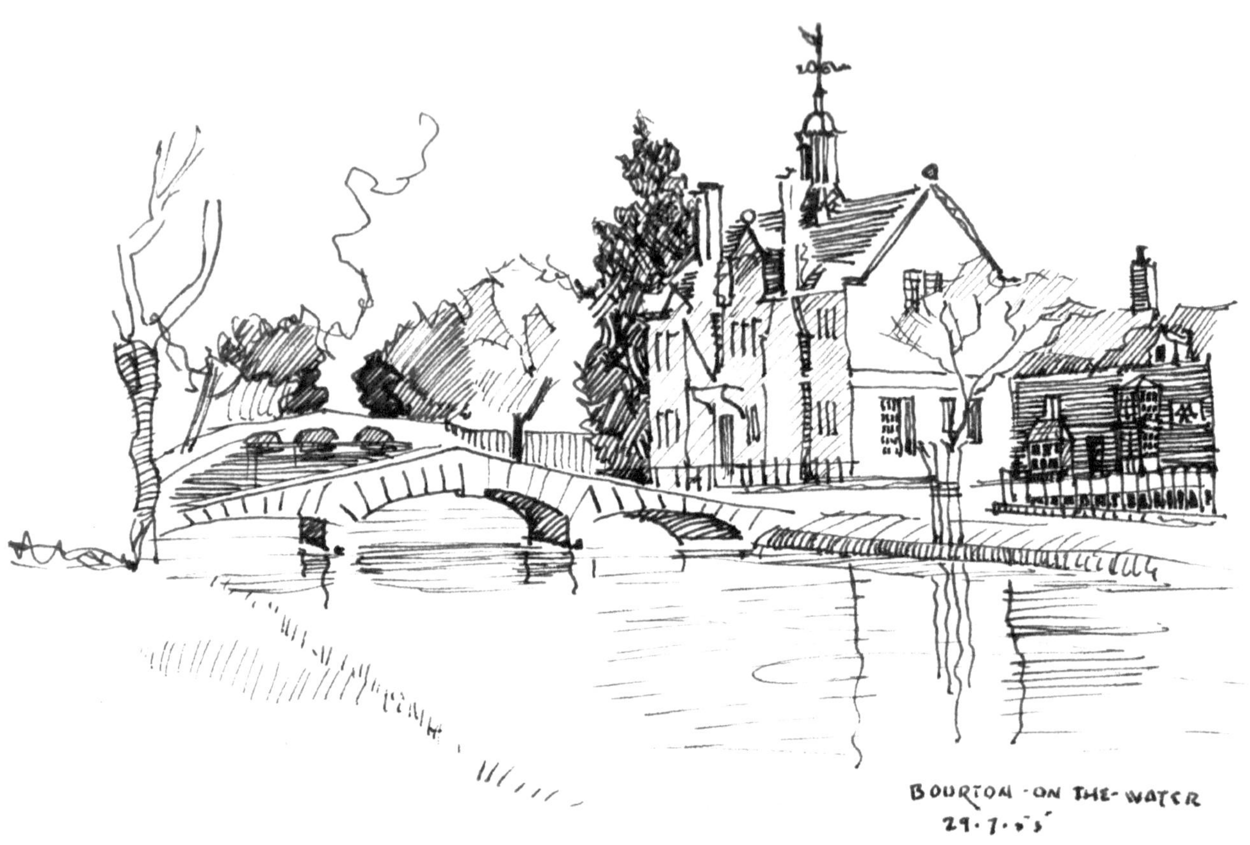

87. "Bourton-On The-Water. 29-7-55." Black ink applied with felt tip or fiber tip pen on sketchbook page.

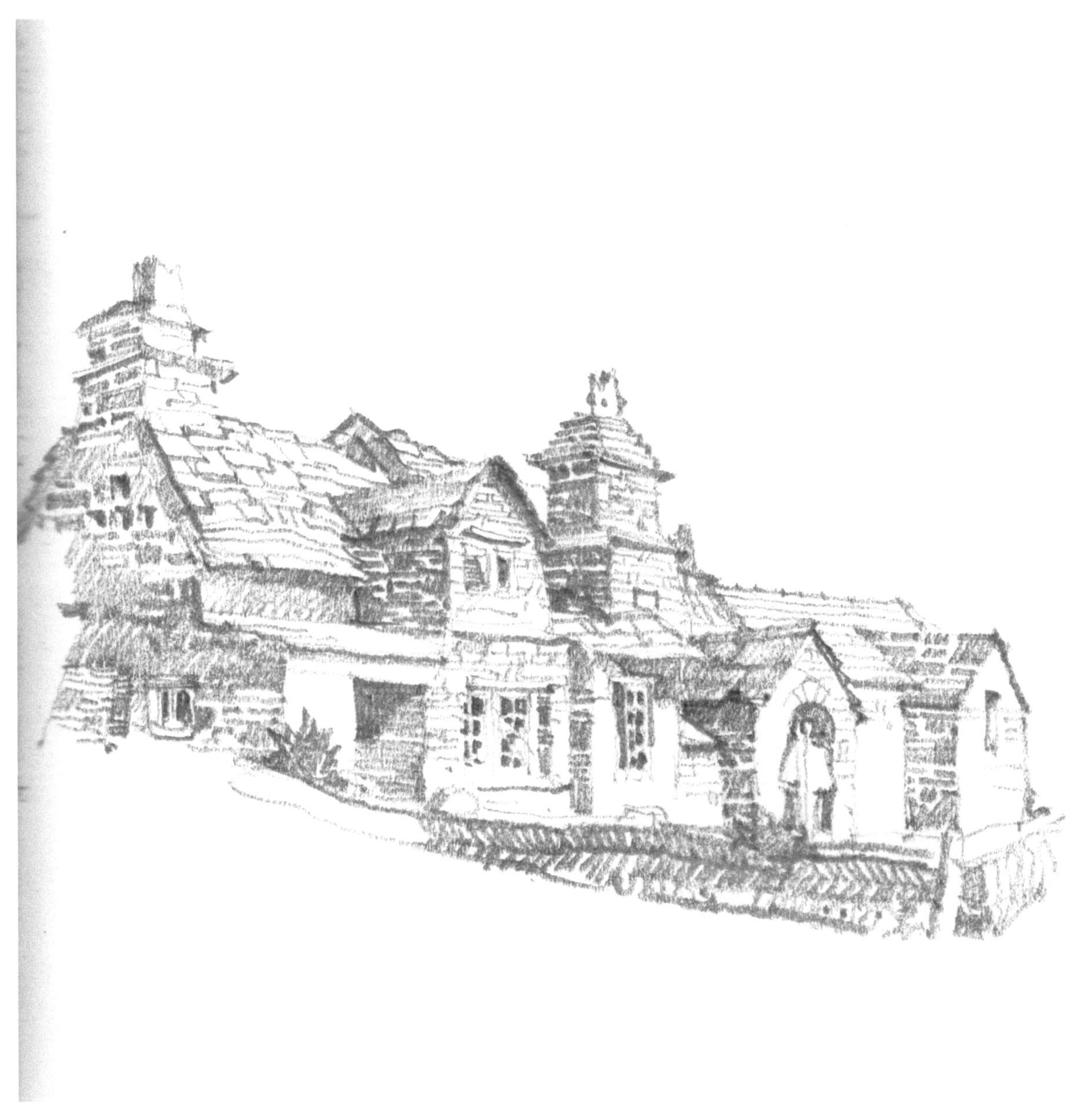

88. Ensemble of buildings, U.K. Soft pencil on sketchbook page.

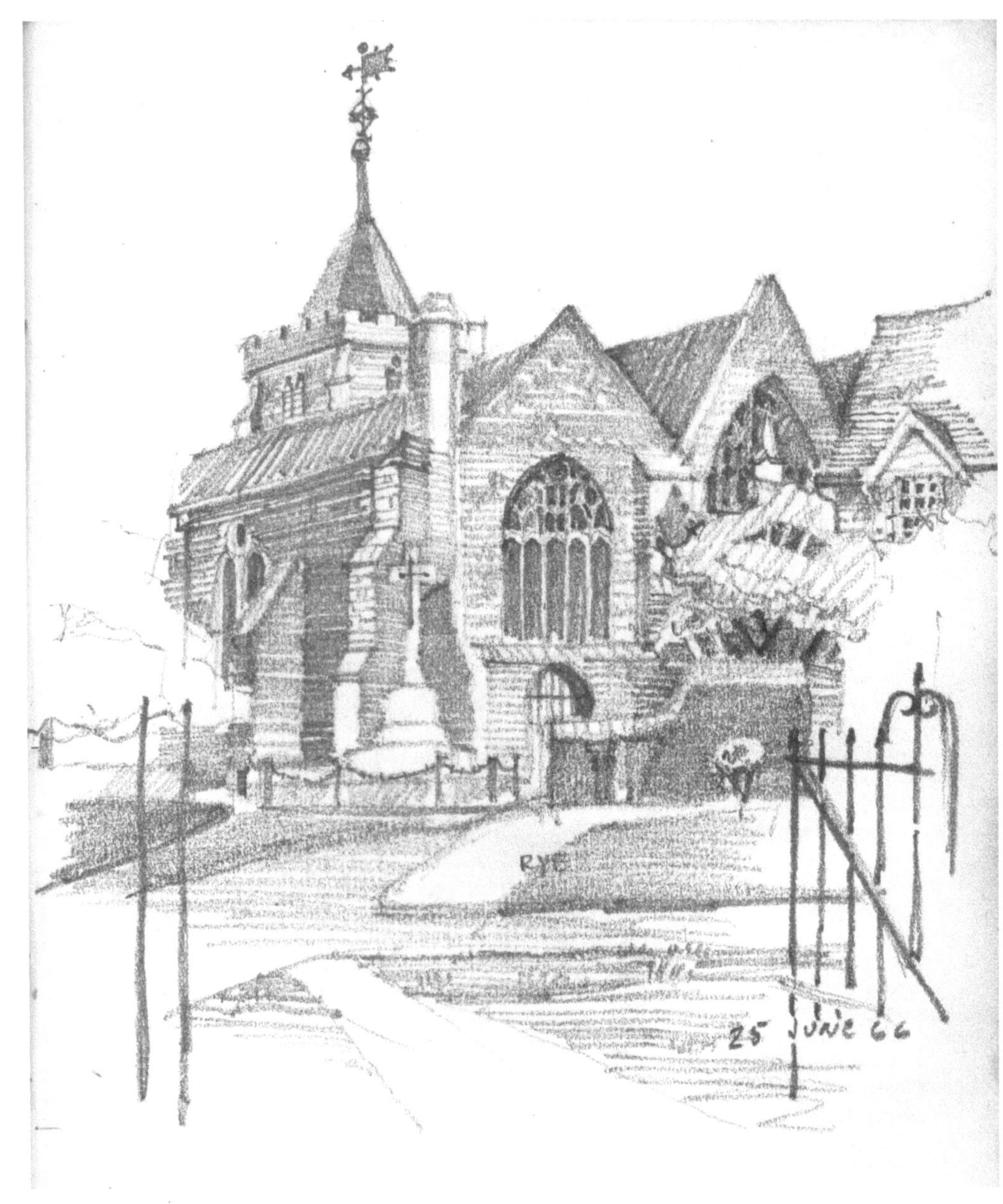

89. "Rye. 25 June 66." Soft pencil on sketchbook page.

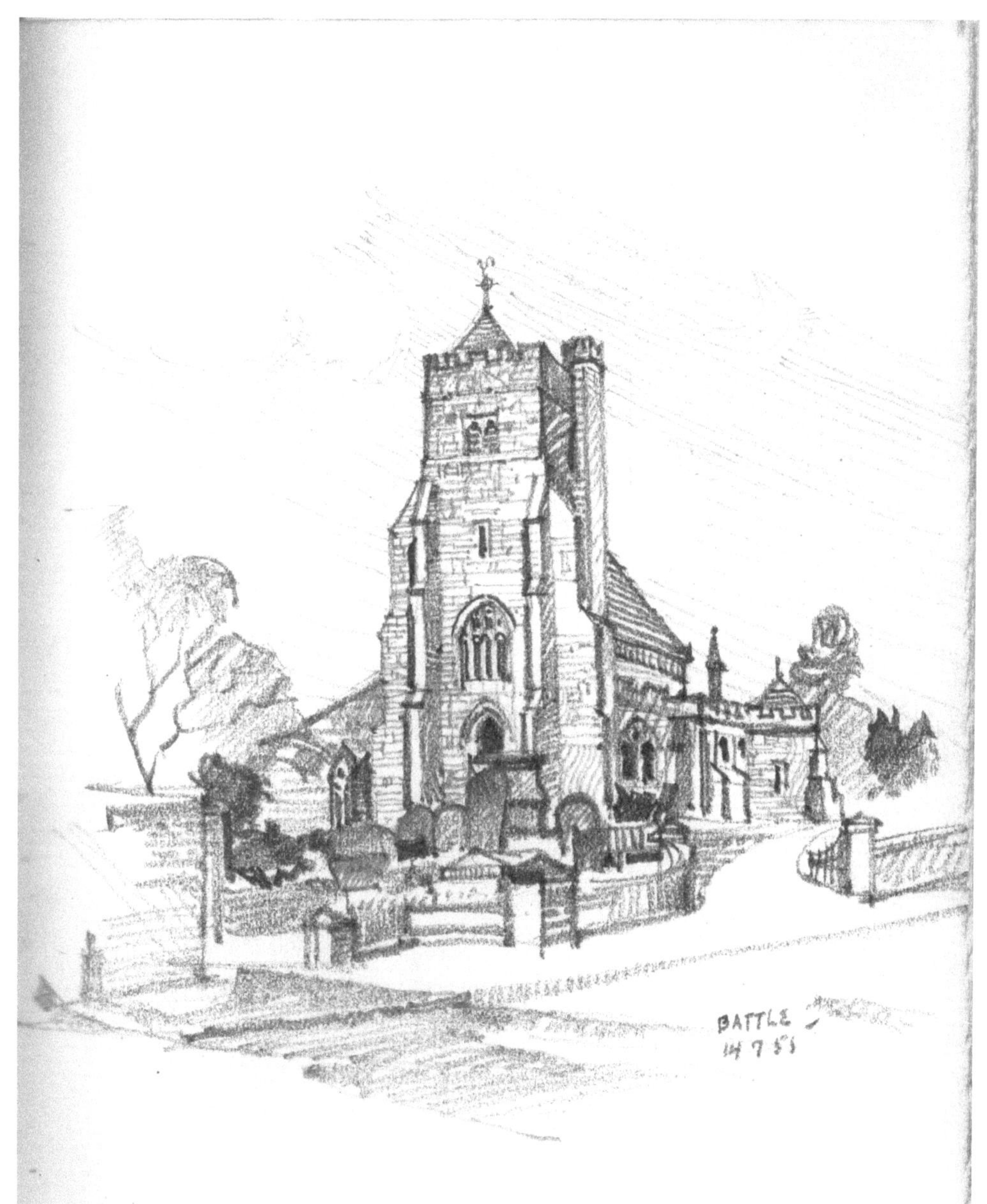

90. "Battle. 14-7-51." Soft pencil on sketchbook page.

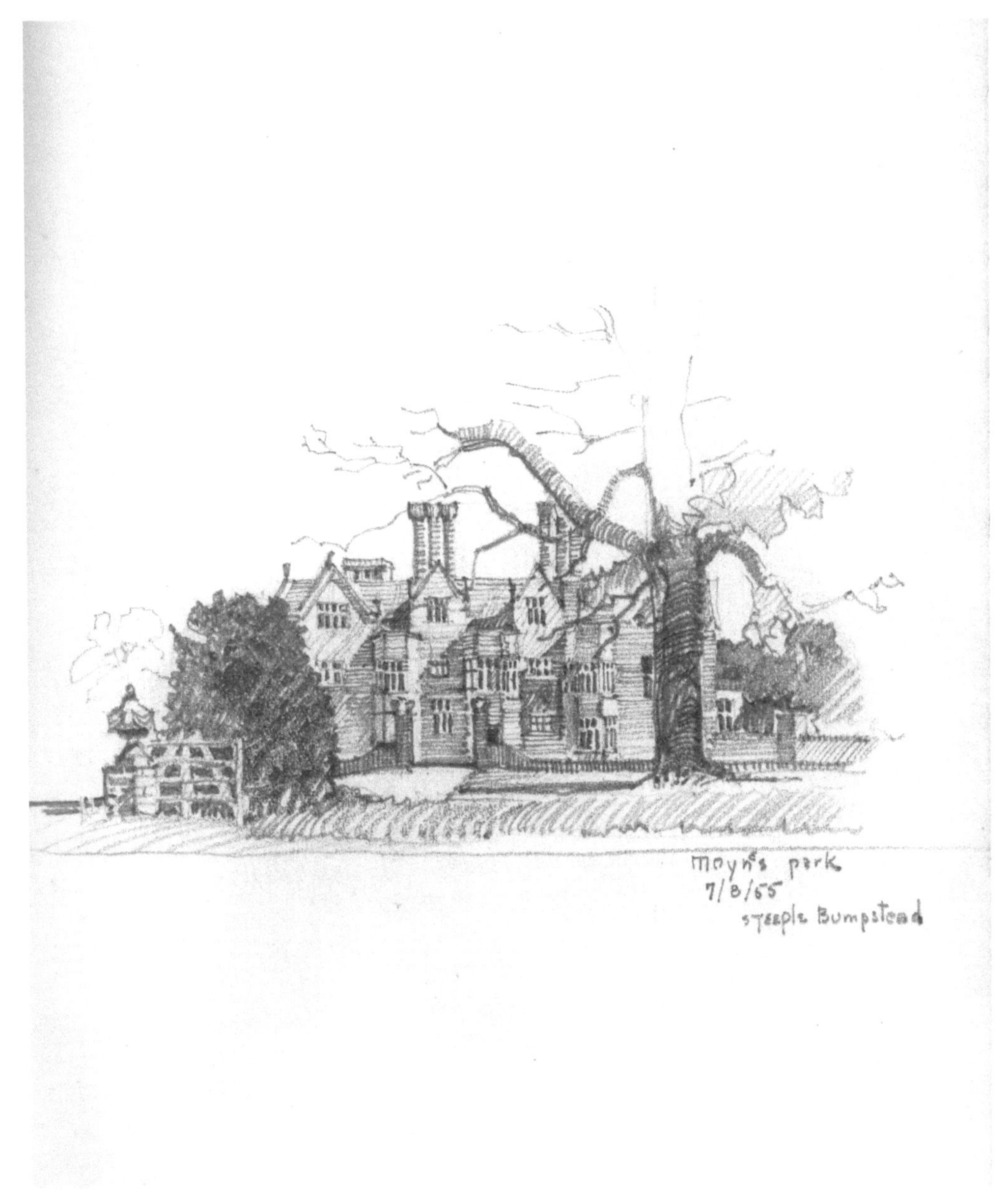

91. "Moyn's Park. 7-8-55." Soft pencil on sketchbook page.

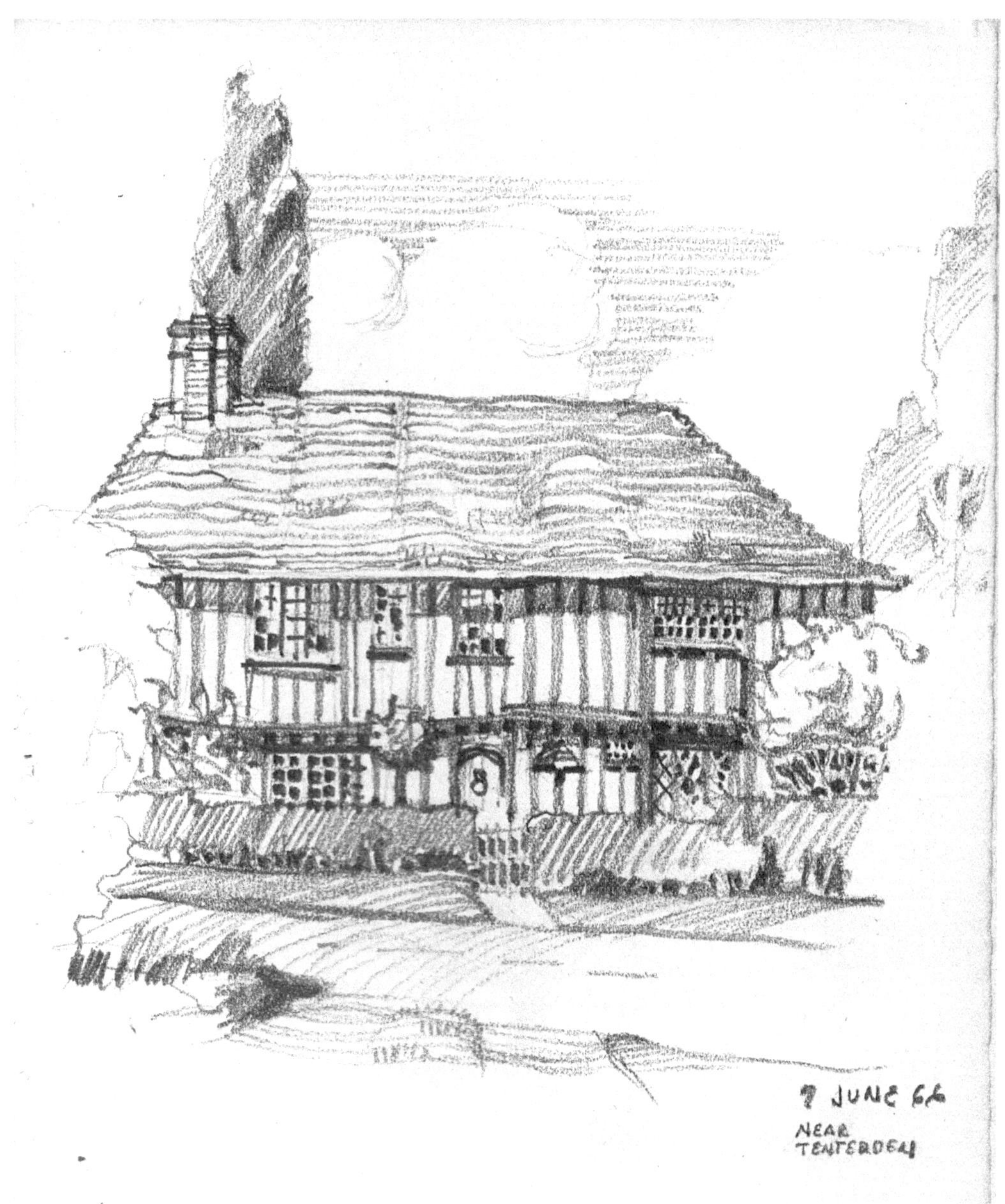

121

92. "Near Tenterdan. 7 June 66." Soft pencil on sketchbook page.

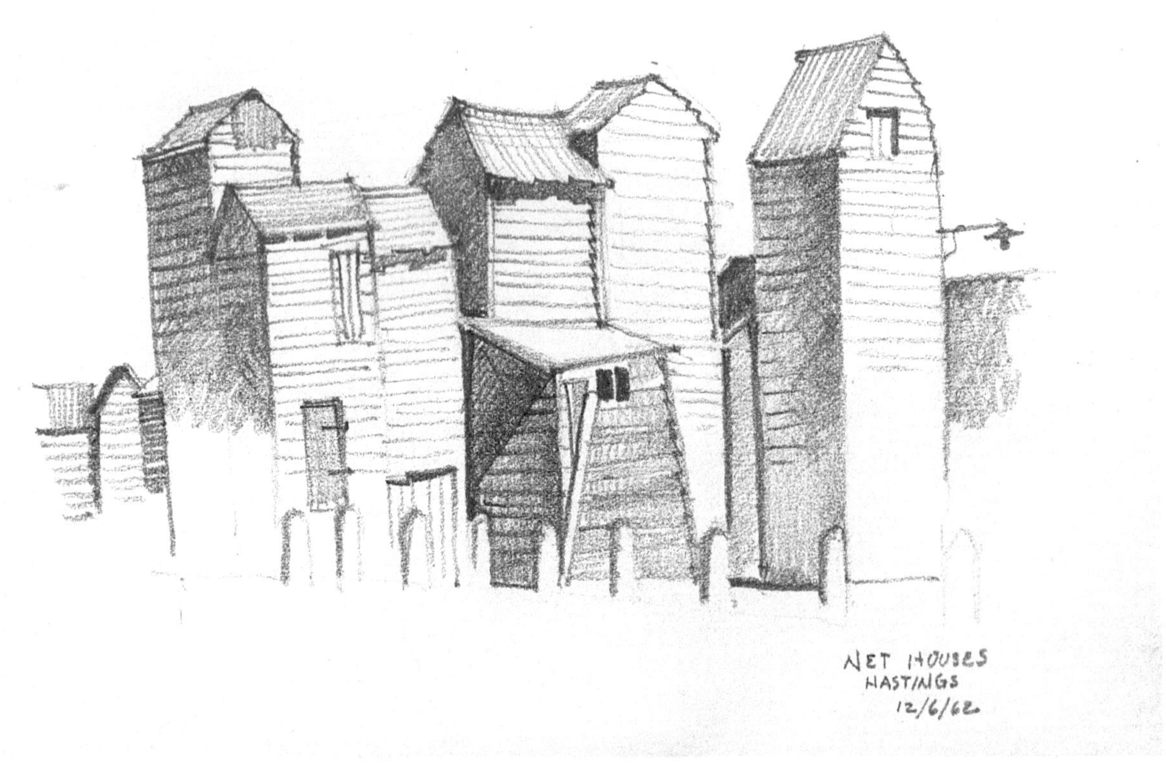

93. "Net Houses, Hastings. 12/6/62." Soft pencil on sketchbook page.

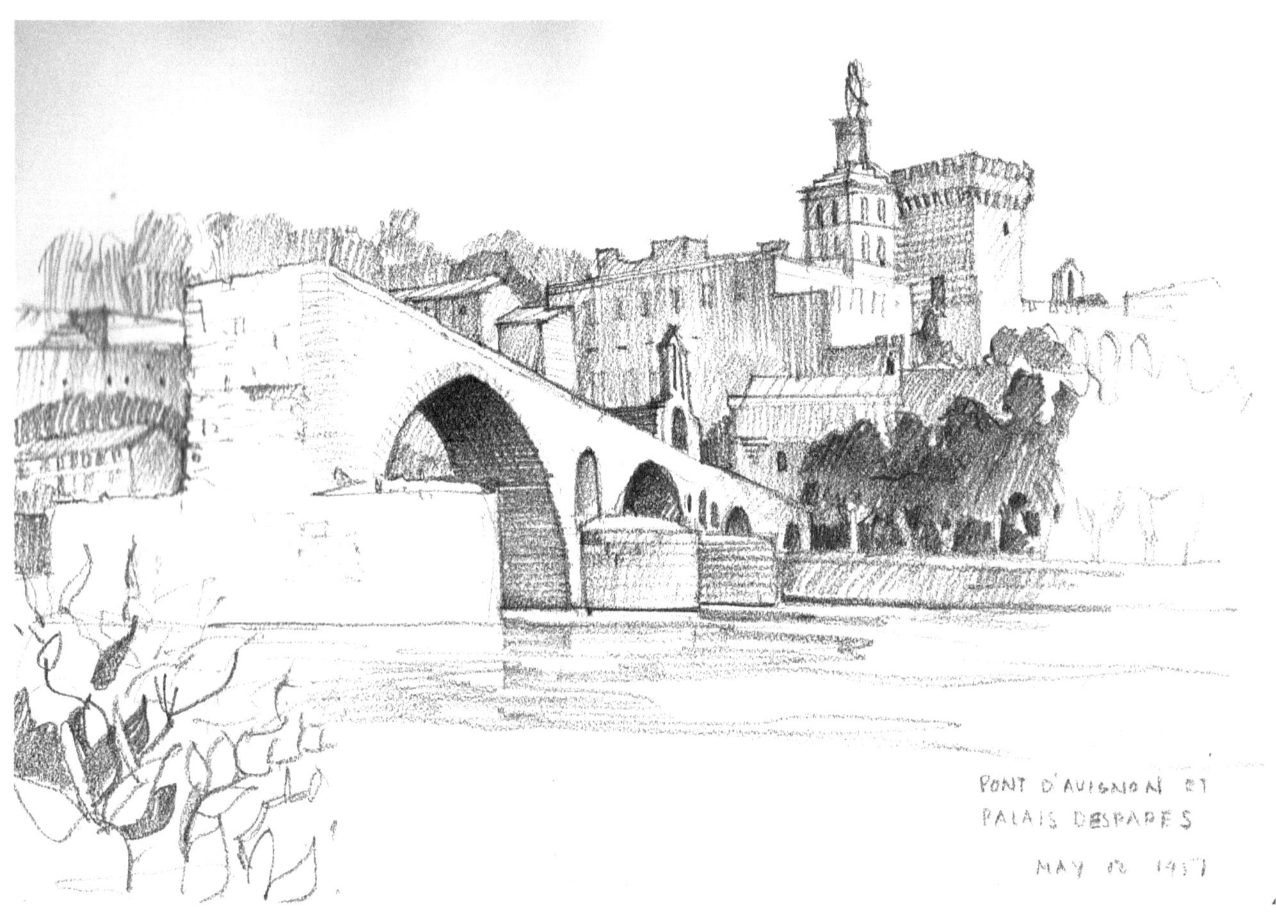

94. "Pont D'Avignon et Palais Despares. May 12, 1957." Soft pencil on sketchbook page.

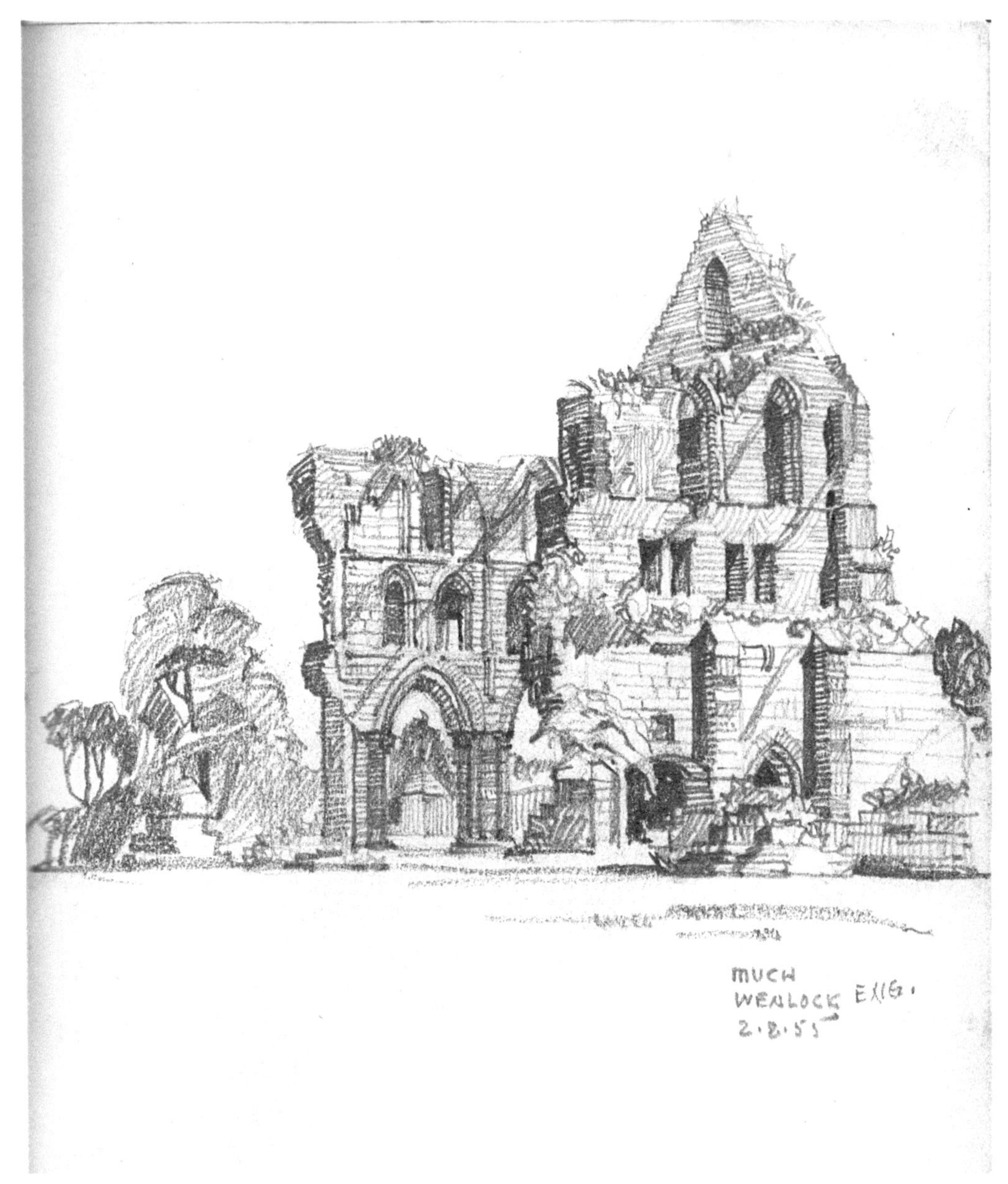

95. "Much, Wenlock, Eng. 2-8-55." Soft pencil on sketchbook page.

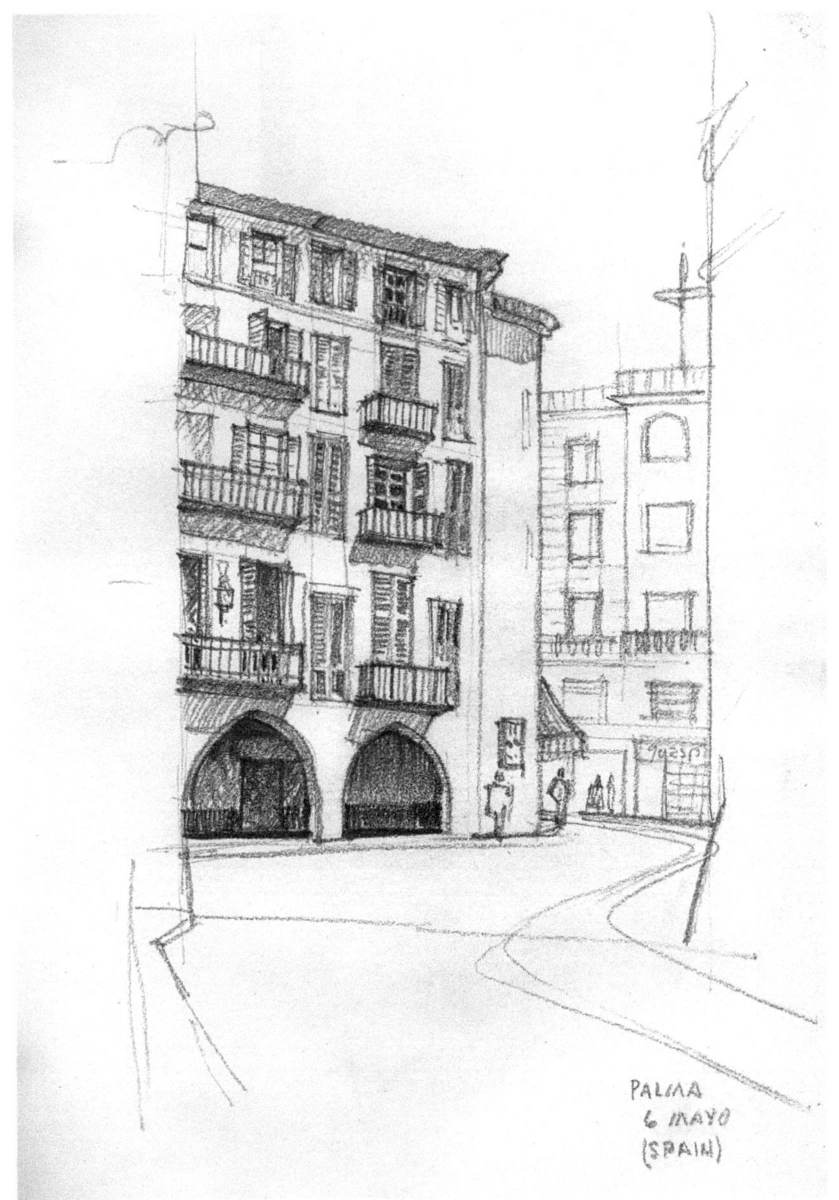

96. "Palma. 6 May." Soft pencil on sketchbook page.

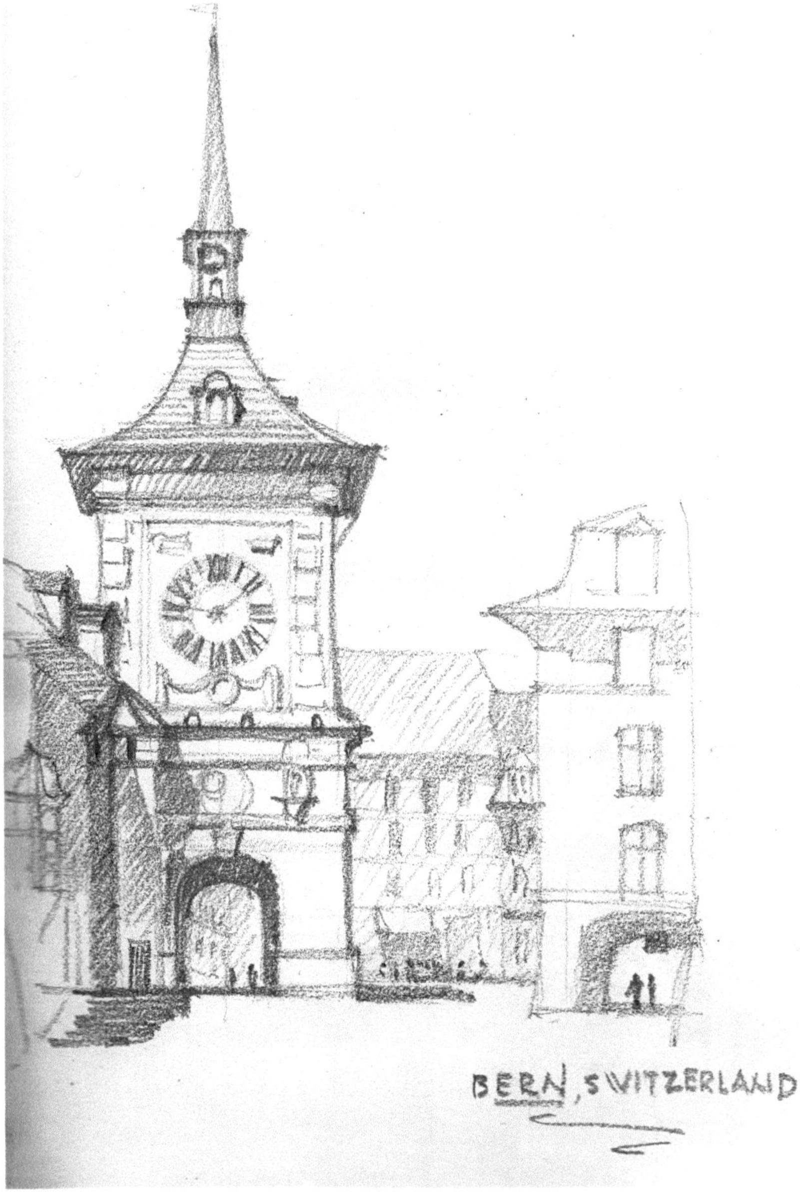

97. “Bern, Switzerland.” Soft pencil on sketchbook page.

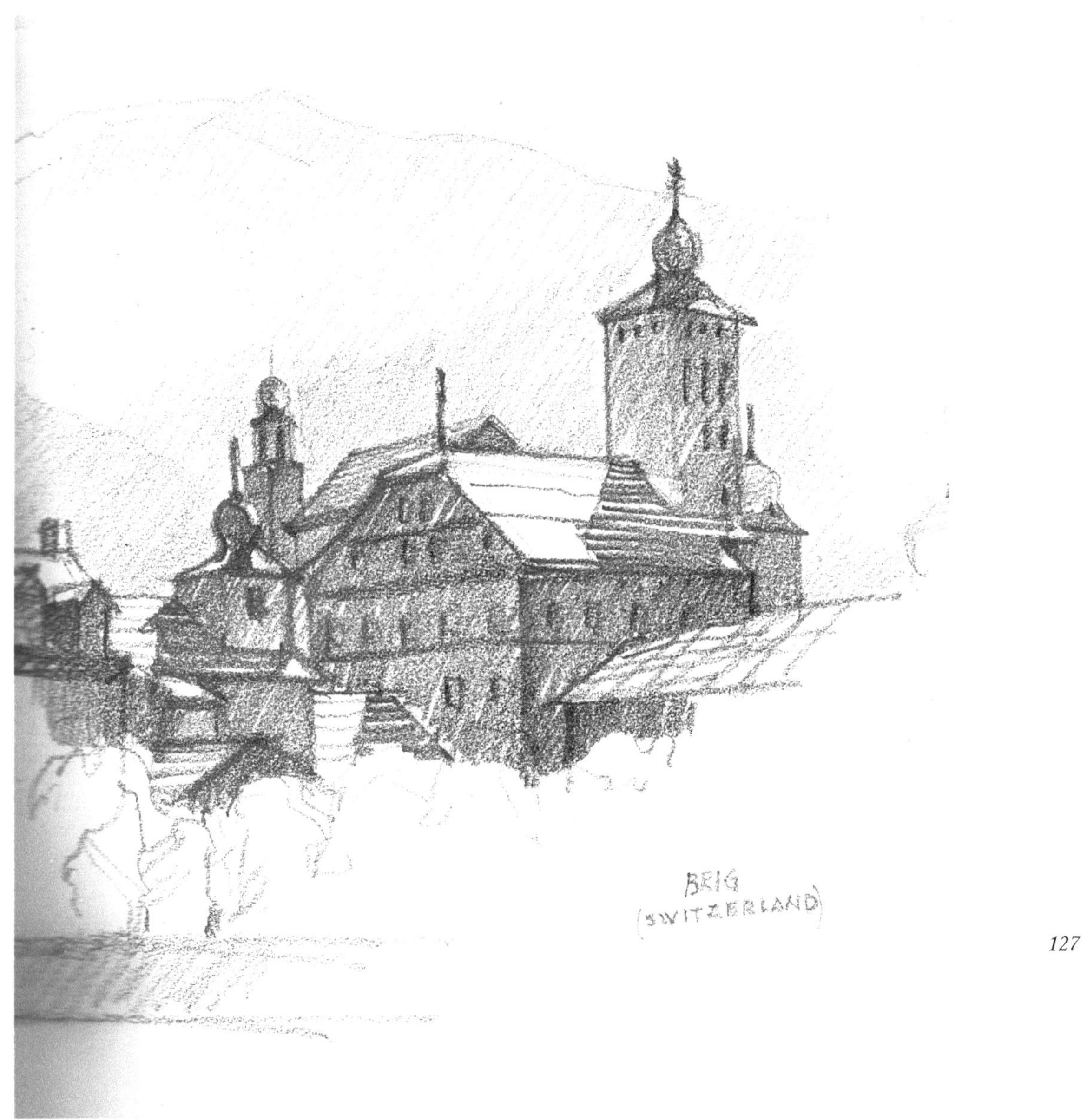

98. “Brig, Switzerland.” Soft pencil on sketchbook page.

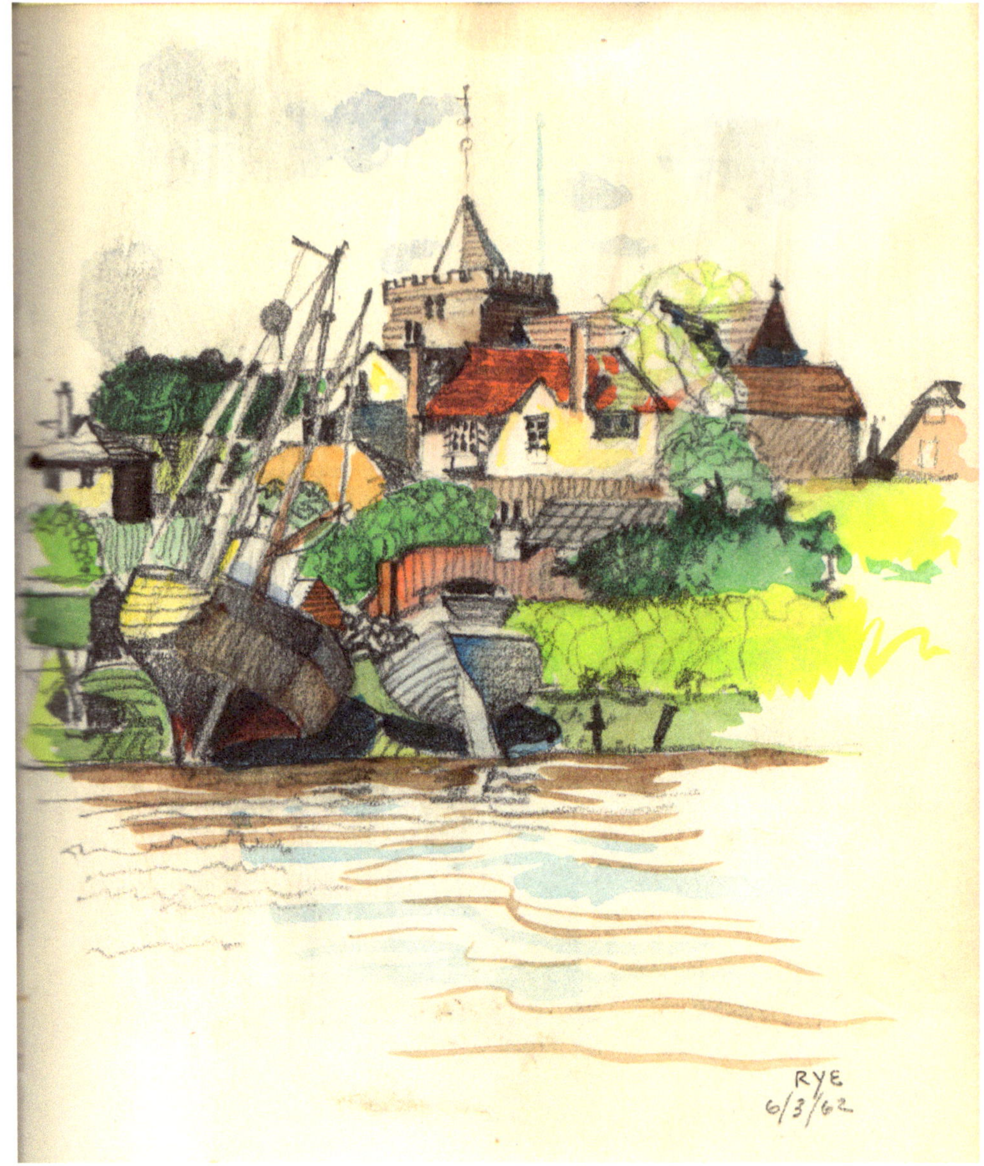

99. "Rye. 6/3/62." Watercolor and soft pencil on sketchbook page.

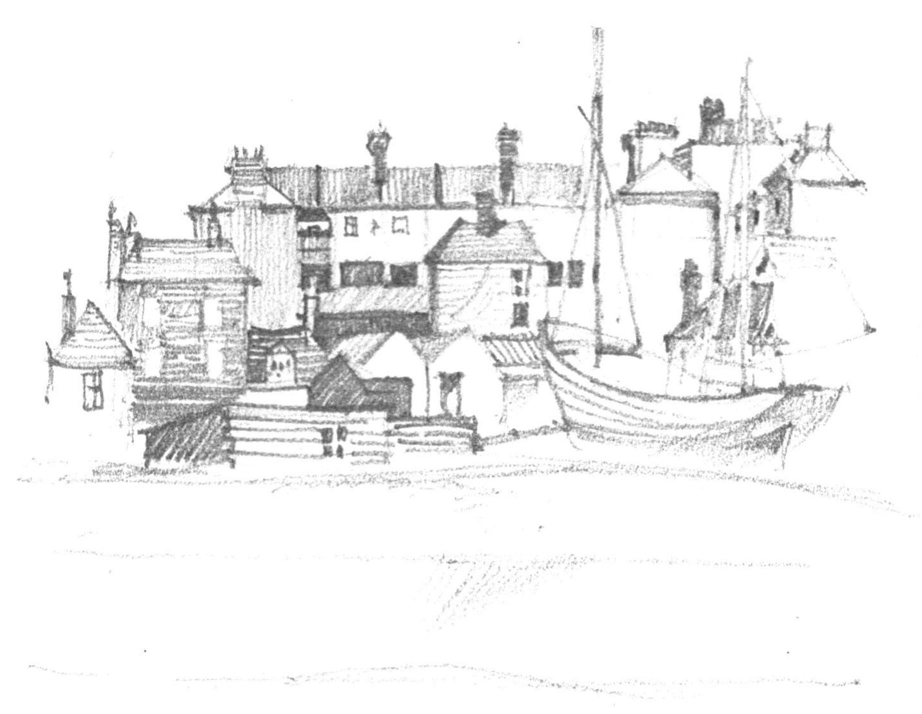

100. "Hastings. 7 May '66." Graphite pencil on sketchbook page.

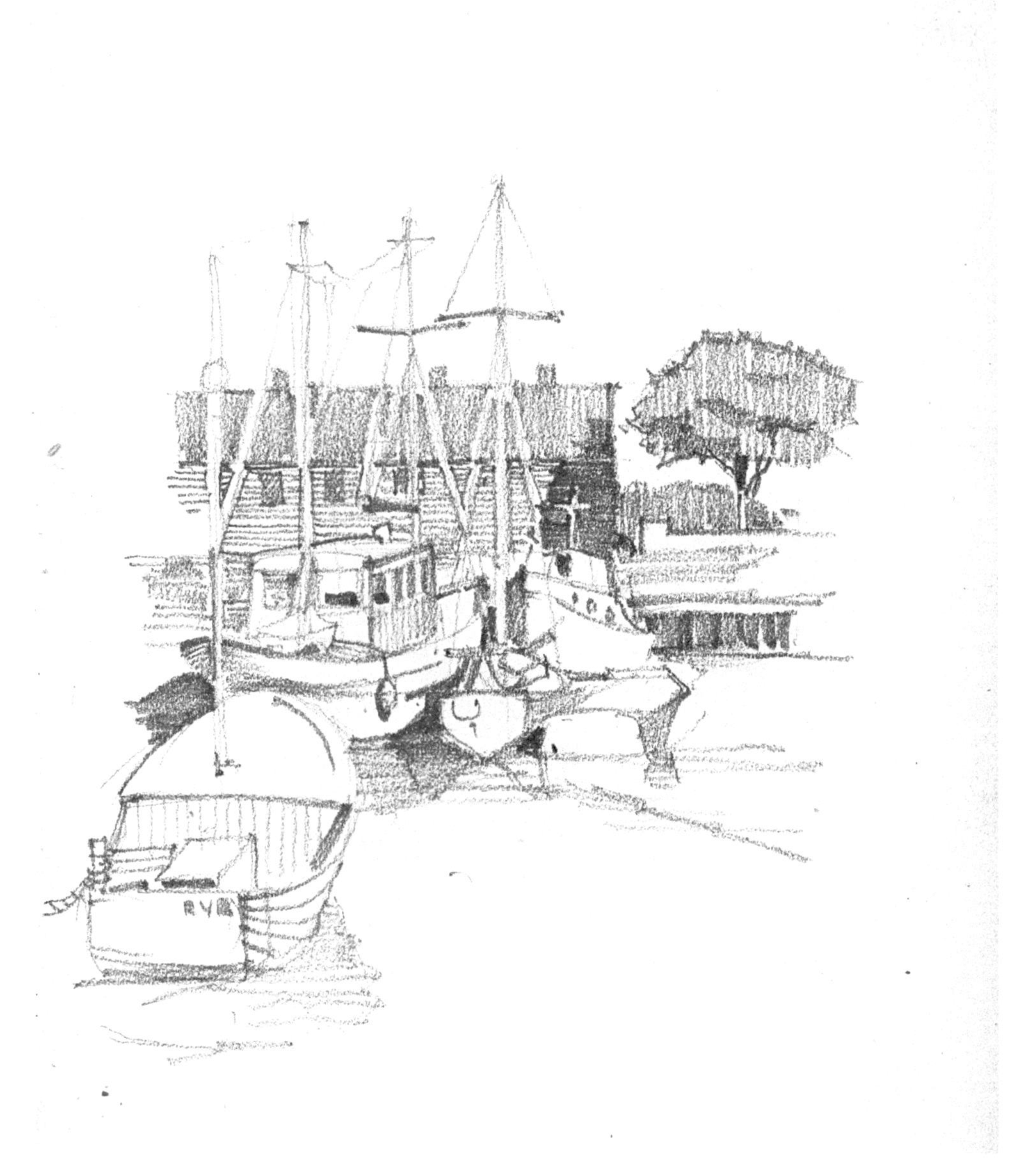

101. Rye, U.K. Soft pencil on sketchbook page.

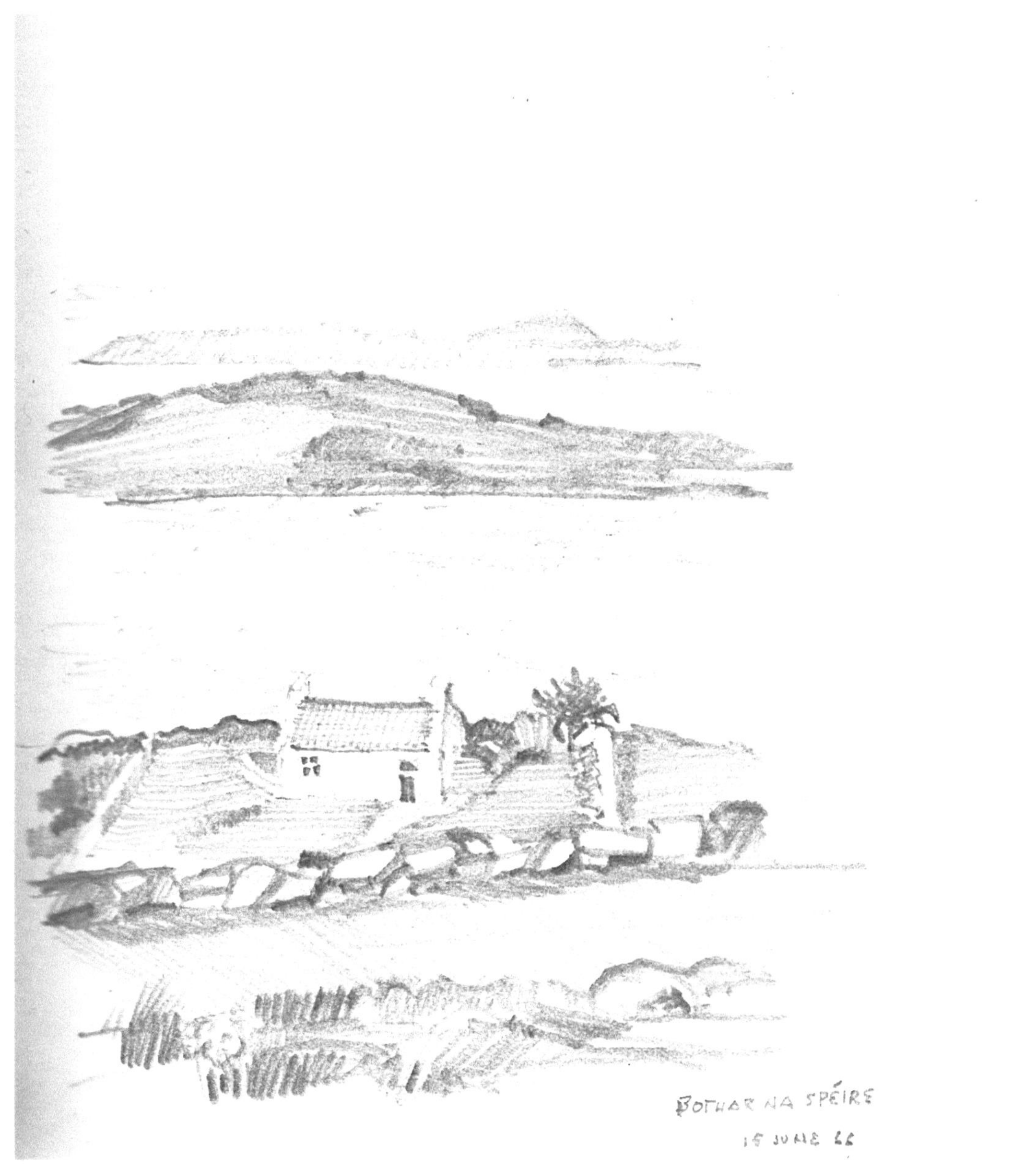

102. "Bothan Na Spéirs. 15 June '66" Soft pencil on sketchbook page.

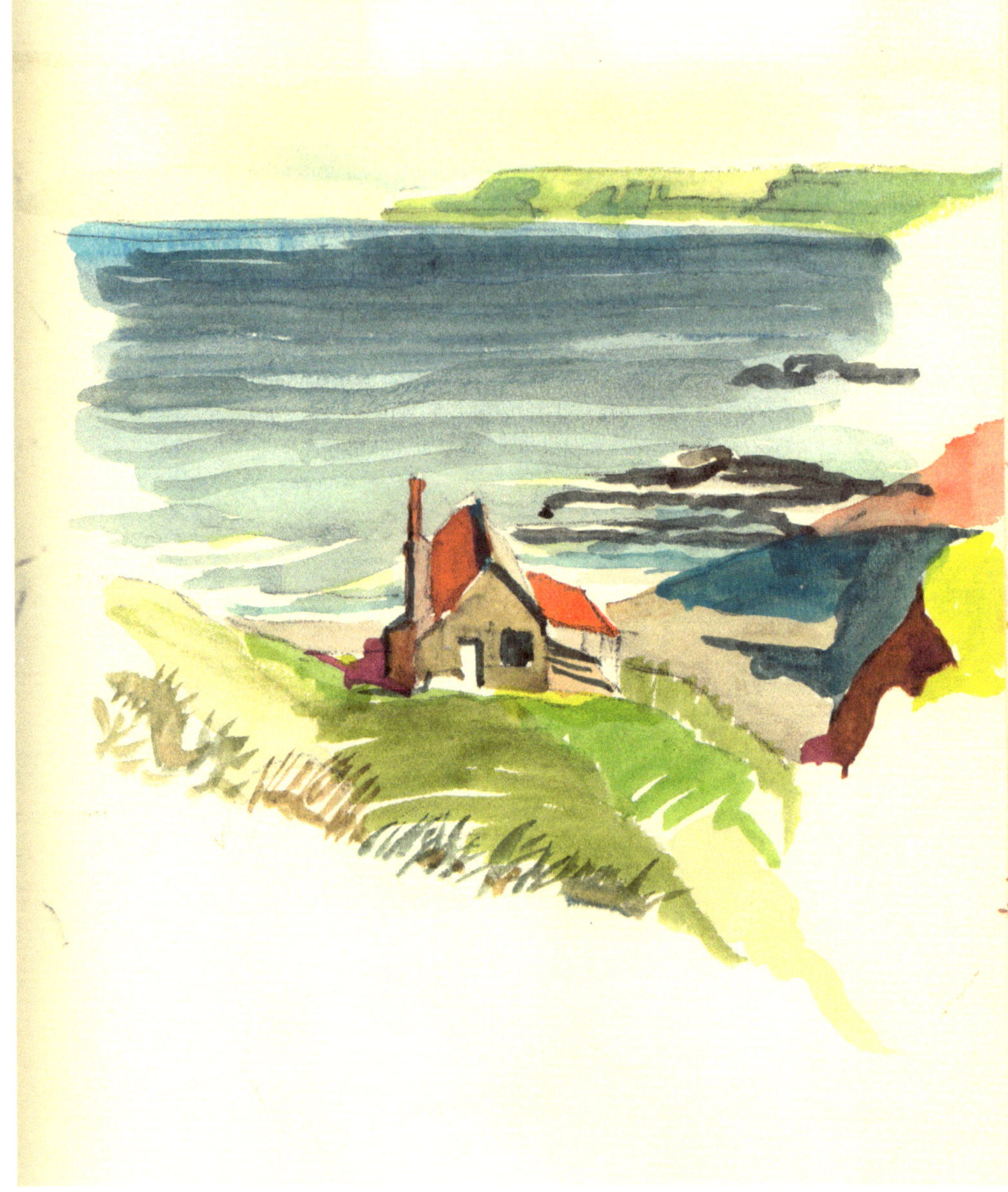

103. House near beach. Watercolor on sketchbook page.

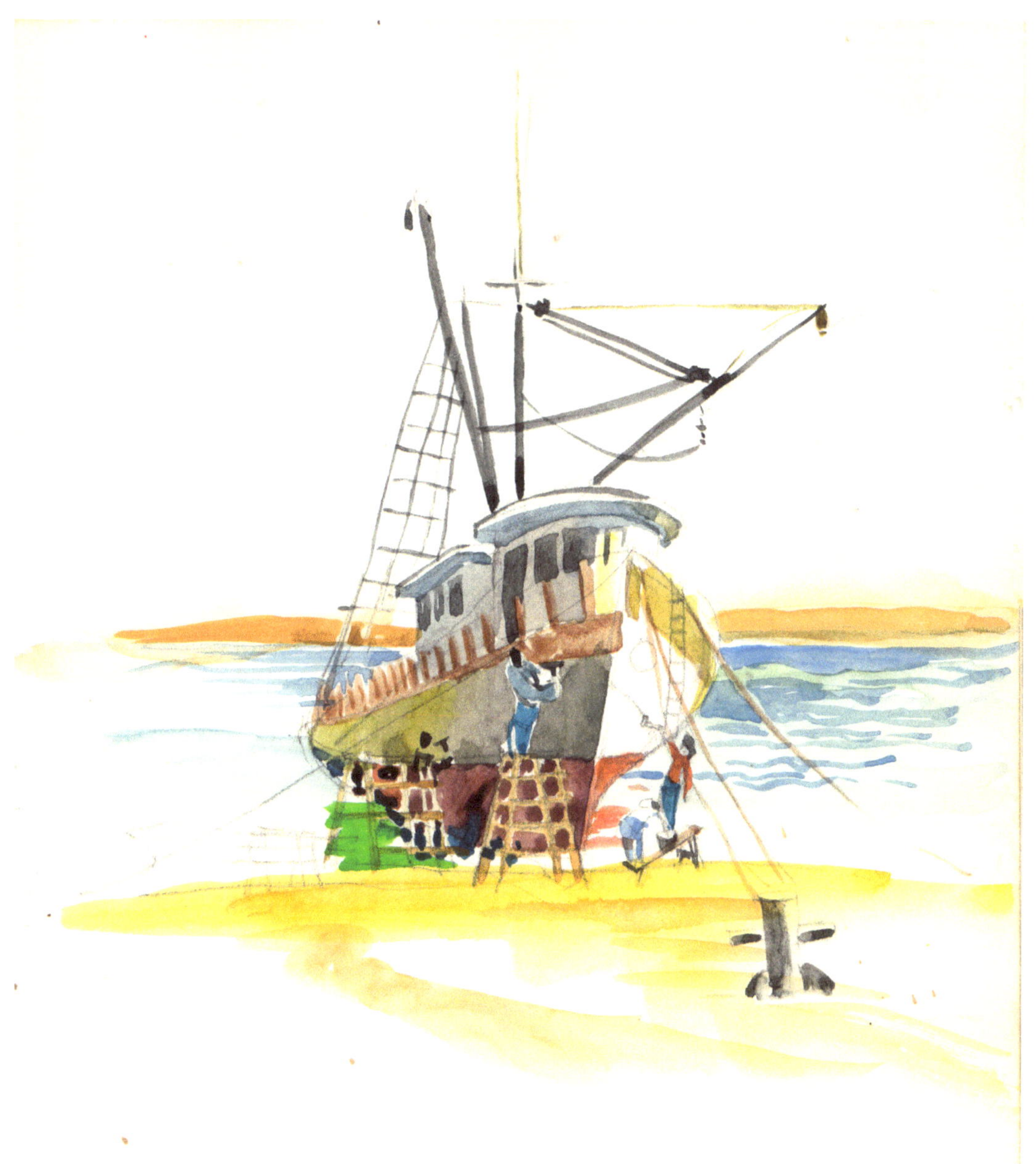

104. "Shrimp boat ..." Watercolor on sketchbook page.

Nature

The drive south was so beautiful I almost couldn't stand it. Crystalline air, enamel blue skies, all shades of brilliant green in the grass and trees, and golden sands.

Uncrowded highways allowed me to drive slowly or to stop for photos and sketches.

Wandered down to a secluded beach and spent an hour or so in a proper hippie beach colony.

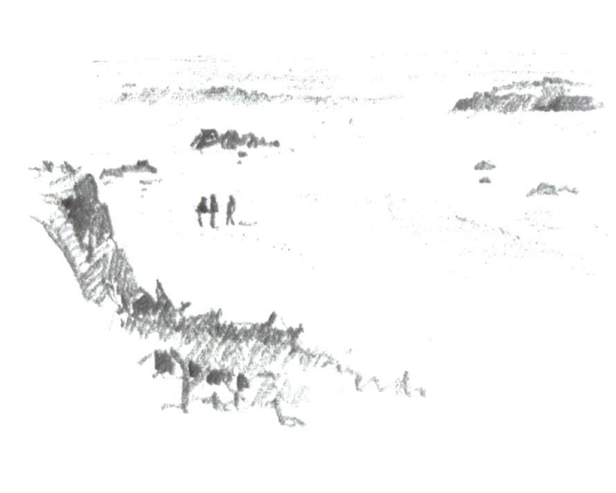

105. "The Drive South ..." Fiber tip pen for the inscription and soft pencil for the beach scene.

For the most part, John McHugh preferred to focus on architecture and urbanism in his sketches, but here and there, throughout his travels, he captured scenes of natural landscape without man-made intervention (sketches106 through 108 for instance). Then there are scenes of landscape in which architecture is so integrated with its natural setting that it appears as part of nature itself. This latter type may be seen especially in illus. 103 of the previous section and to an extent in sketches 83 and 87. Sketches of typical English small towns seen from a distance and frequently found to be nestled in the natural landscape of the agricultural valleys where they reside may be considered as "nature sketches" as well.

The first sketch in this series, (105) is a quick sketch in soft pencil that captures the essence of a beach scene and includes a note in which McHugh refers humorously to the beach scene as "a proper hippie beach colony." The figures on the beach provide a sense of scale, contrasted against the horizontal flatness and quiet of the ocean. Following that sketch are others that appear to be experiments in media. The first of these (106) evokes the softness of a typically misty day in British Columbia, Canada. Colored pencil over a background wash of watercolor are combined to capture the mood of blue-grey stillness. A similar quality is achieved in sketch. 107 with an especially wet watercolor technique. Further experimentation involves the use of opaque colored media for sketch 108, and the familiar soft pencil for sketch109. The next two, sketch 110 and 111, continue the experimentation with media and technique, a subject to be discussed in the next chapter. The last sketch of this short series, (112) places an English village into nature with soft pencil, recognizing the unique character of so many English villages that seem an integral part of the natural landscape.

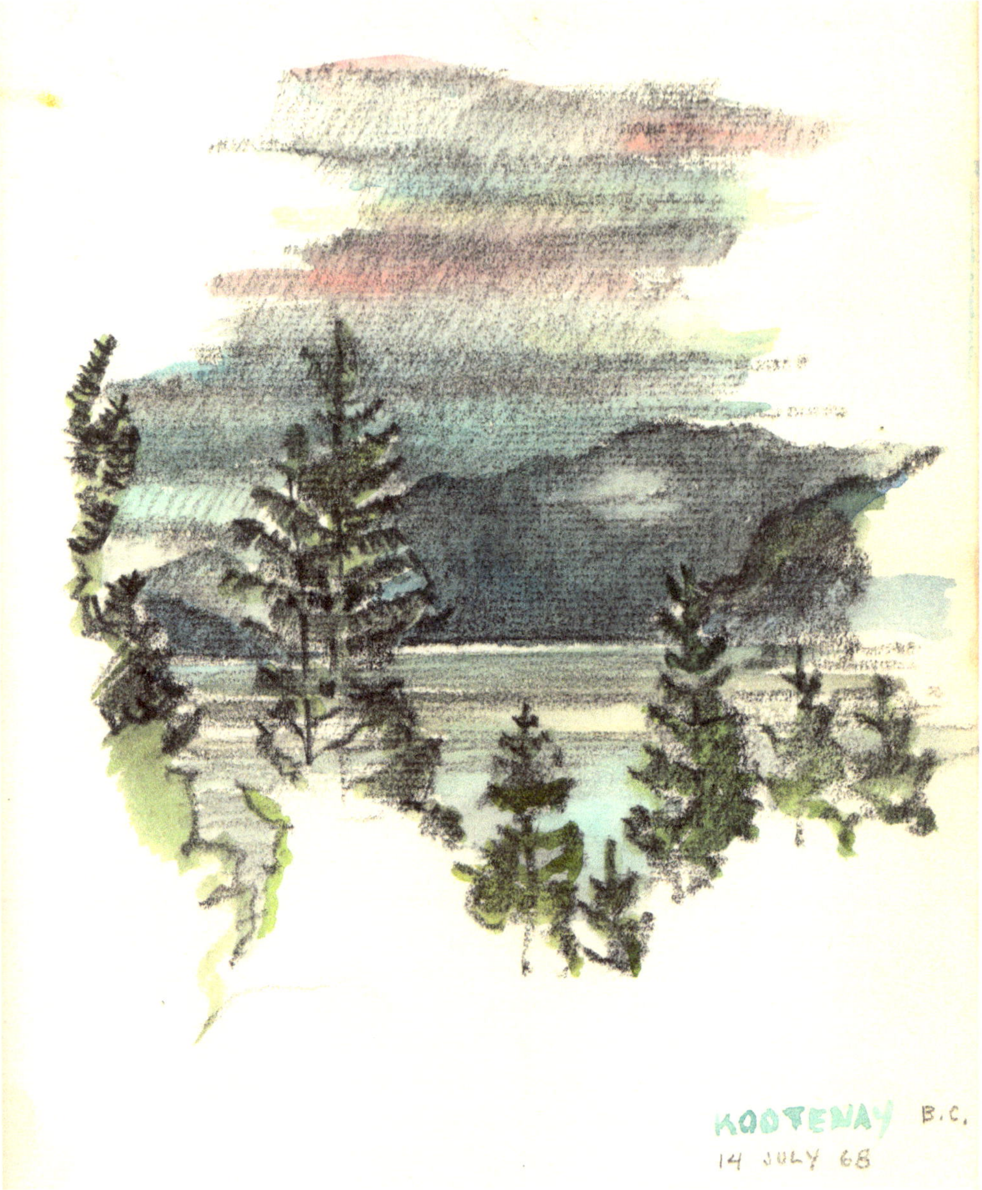

106. “Kootenaly B.C. 14 July 68” Watercolor and colored pencil on textured sketchbook paper.

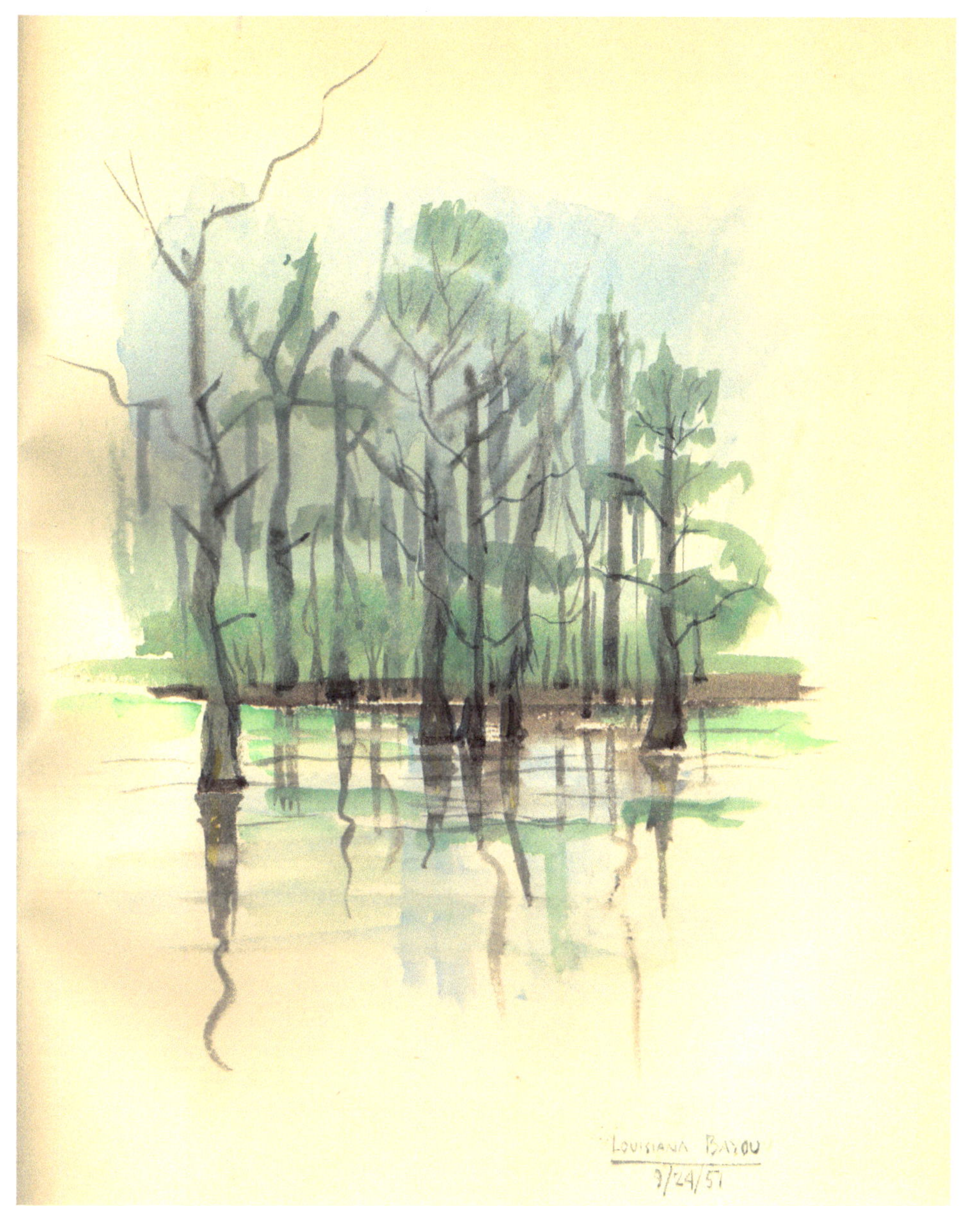

107. "Louisiana Bayou. 9/24/57." Watercolor on sketchbook page.

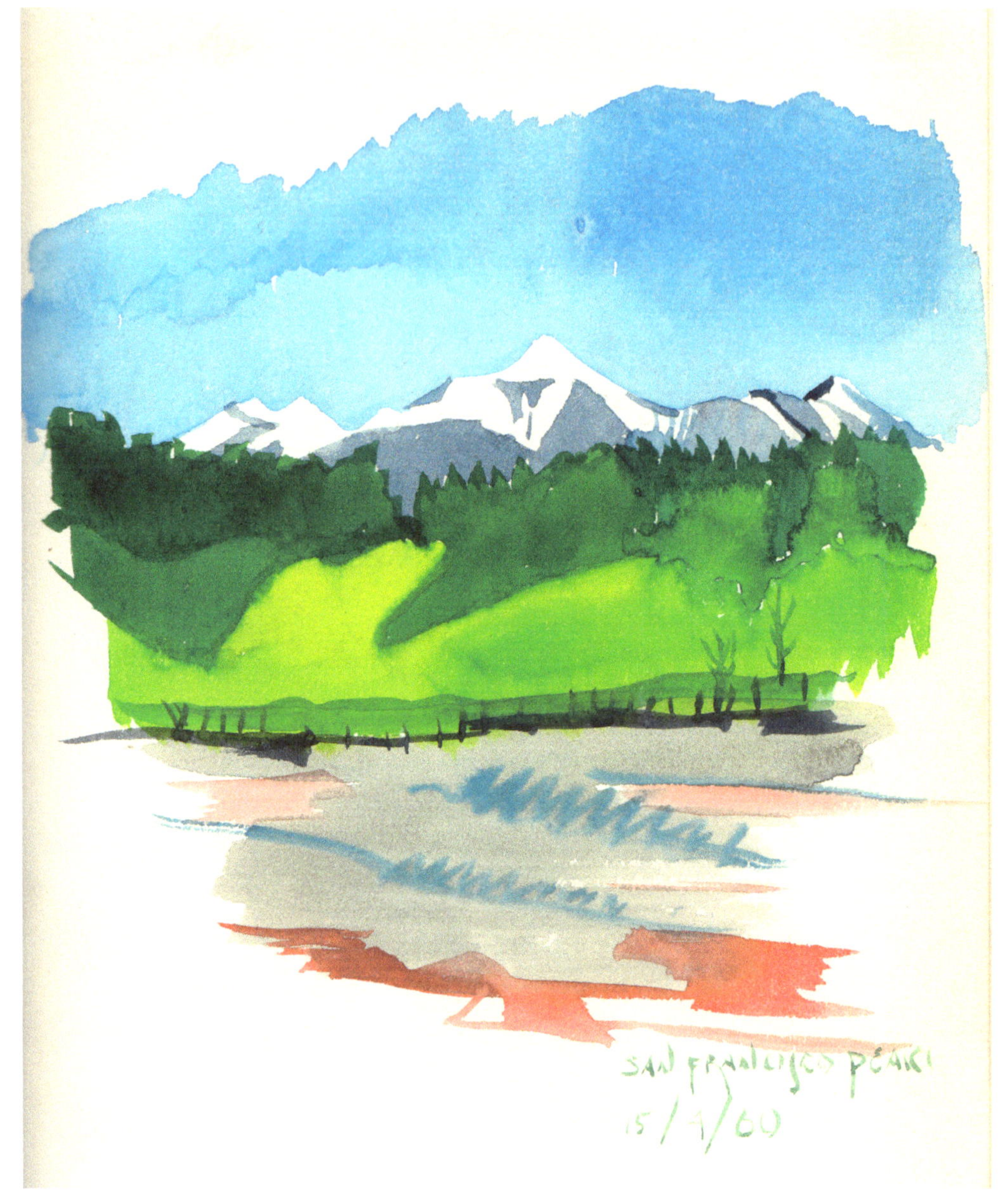

108. "San Francisco Peaks. 15/4/60." Watercolor on sketchbook page.

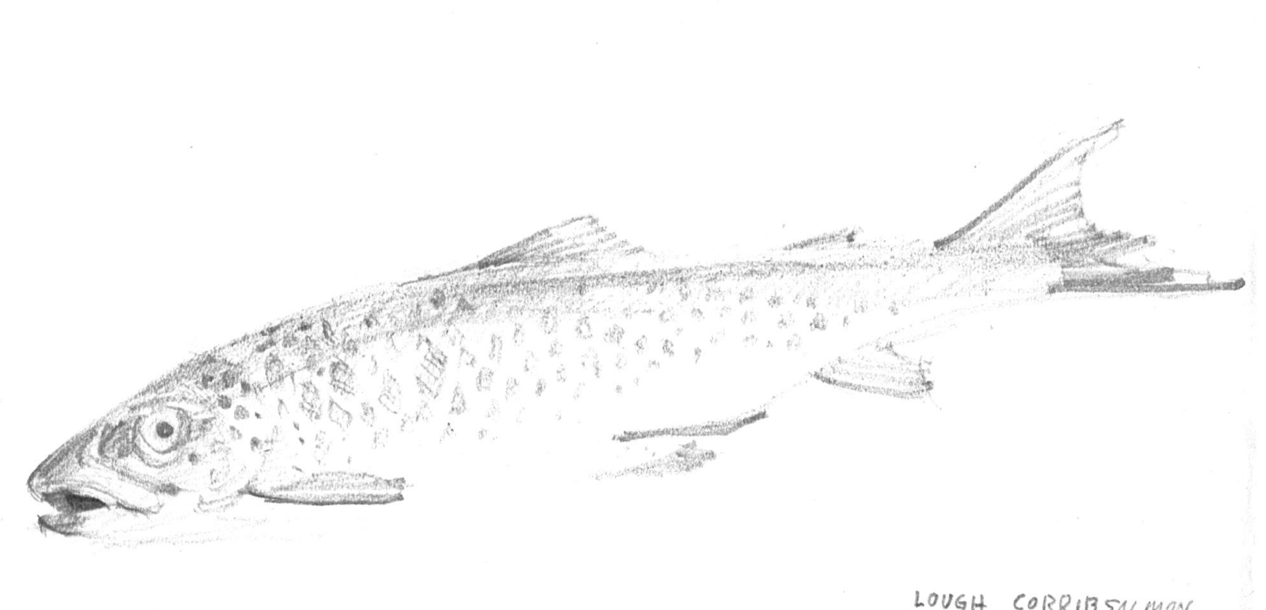

109. “Lough Corribsalmon. 8 June 66.” Soft pencil on sketchbook page.

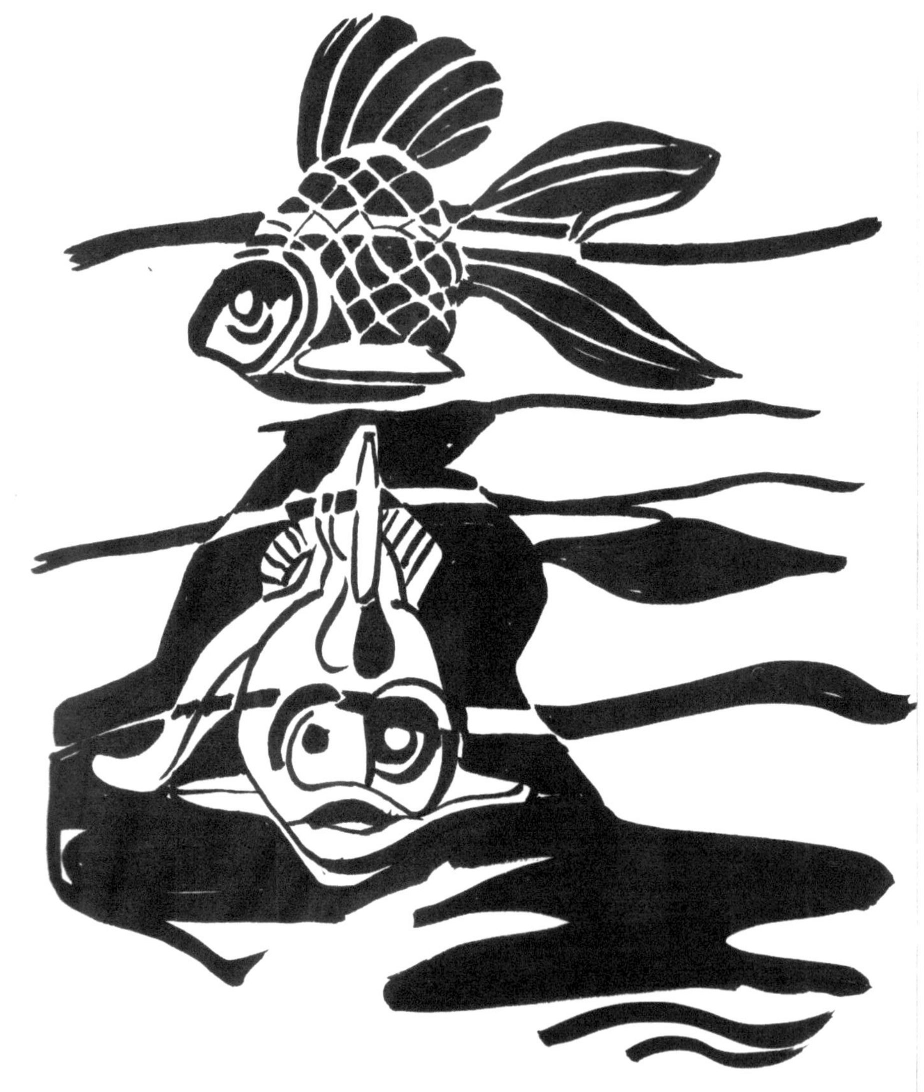

110. Fish. India ink on sketchbook page.

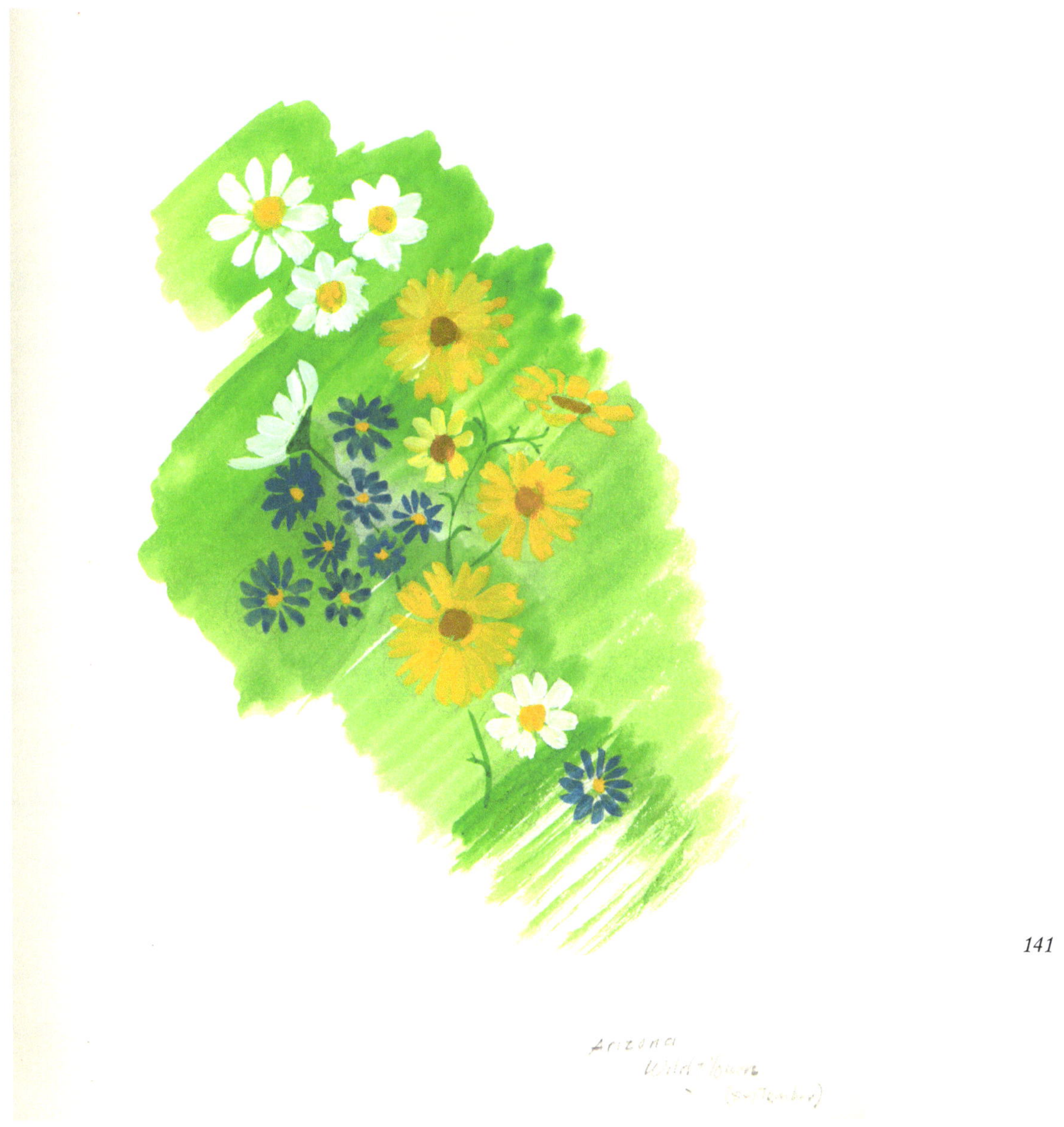

111. "Arizona Wildflowers. September." Watercolor and opaque color media on sketchbook page.

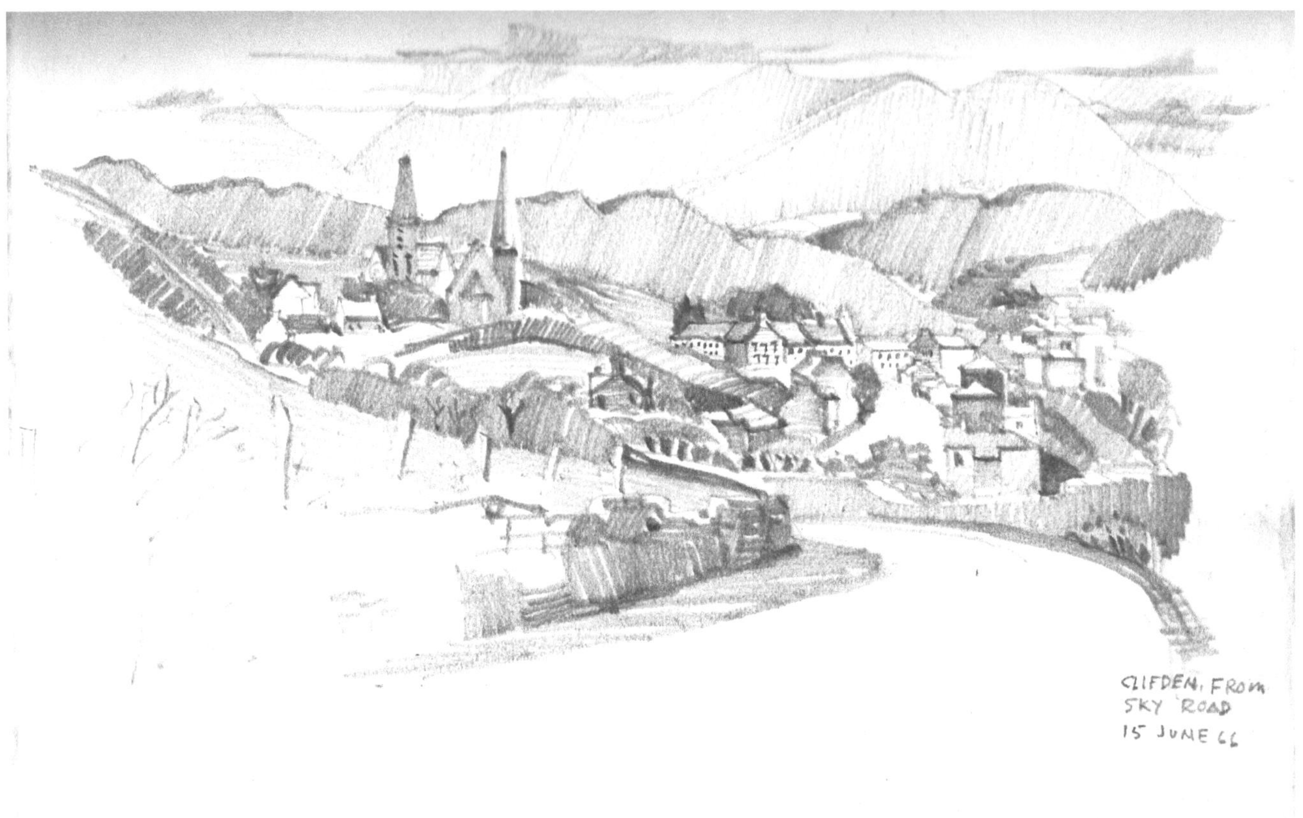

112. "Clifden from Sky Road. 15 June 66." Soft pencil on sketchbook page.

Techniques and Media 3

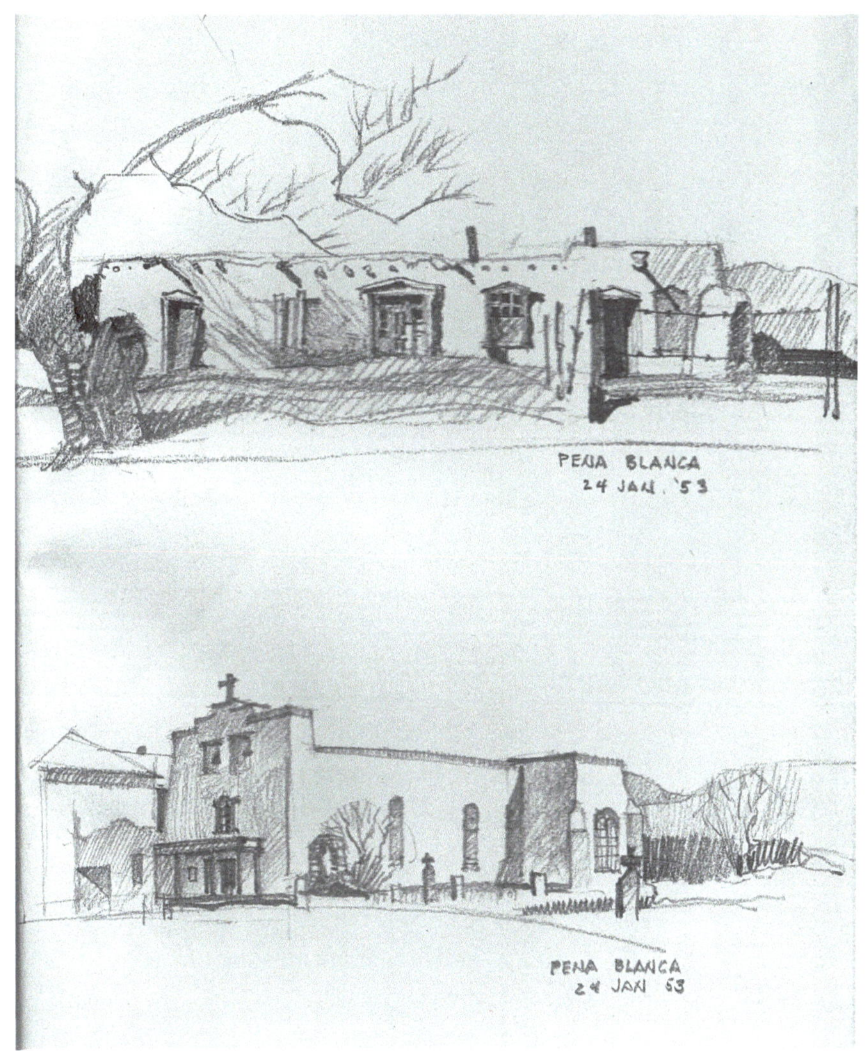

113. "Pena Blanca 24 Jan. 53." Soft pencil on sketchbook page.

Learning to sketch involves looking at examples then trying it on your own. Each time your own sketch doesn't look right, a closer look at the example you are trying to emulate is in order. The following sketches from John McHugh's travels represent the full range of techniques and media that he used over the years. While soft pencil on sketchbook pages was his preferred approach, he, nonetheless, experimented with other media and techniques from time to time, providing us with plenty of varied examples from which to learn.

Sketch 113 is an example of the most frequently used media and technique in McHugh's sketchbooks. In this drawing, however, the paper is quite smooth. This technique produces a soft, modeled form on the page, especially when the paper is textured. The procedure usually involves sharpening the pencil to the desired edge, then lightly tracing the scene as though it were a line. Once this linear drawing is complete, the same pencil may be used to produce soft texture and shading, providing a modeled surface effect by replicating how surfaces reflect light. Most in-the-field sketchers keep a small piece of sandpaper at the ready, to sharpen their pencils to the desired shapes. The result can be a 'soft' drawing with obvious pencil strokes in background material (trees and sky for instance) and not so obvious in the foreground subject. The effect differs when the pencil, sharpened to a chisel point, makes lines with the edge versus when it renders areas of texture and smooth surface with the flat of the chisel. Notice how the pads of the prickly pear cactus in sketch 114 are rendered differently from one another as they are slanted toward or away from the sun. A variation of the soft pencil technique may be used to give forms hard edges using the side of the chisel point or a pointed pencil as in sketch 115, giving the object a stronger presence, especially when floated on the page as is this drawing of an agave. The use of graphite pencil may be varied as well depending on the texture of the paper. Smooth paper produces what we see in the latter sketches, while sketch 39 in a previous section is a good close up example of the effect of soft pencil on a highly textured surface.

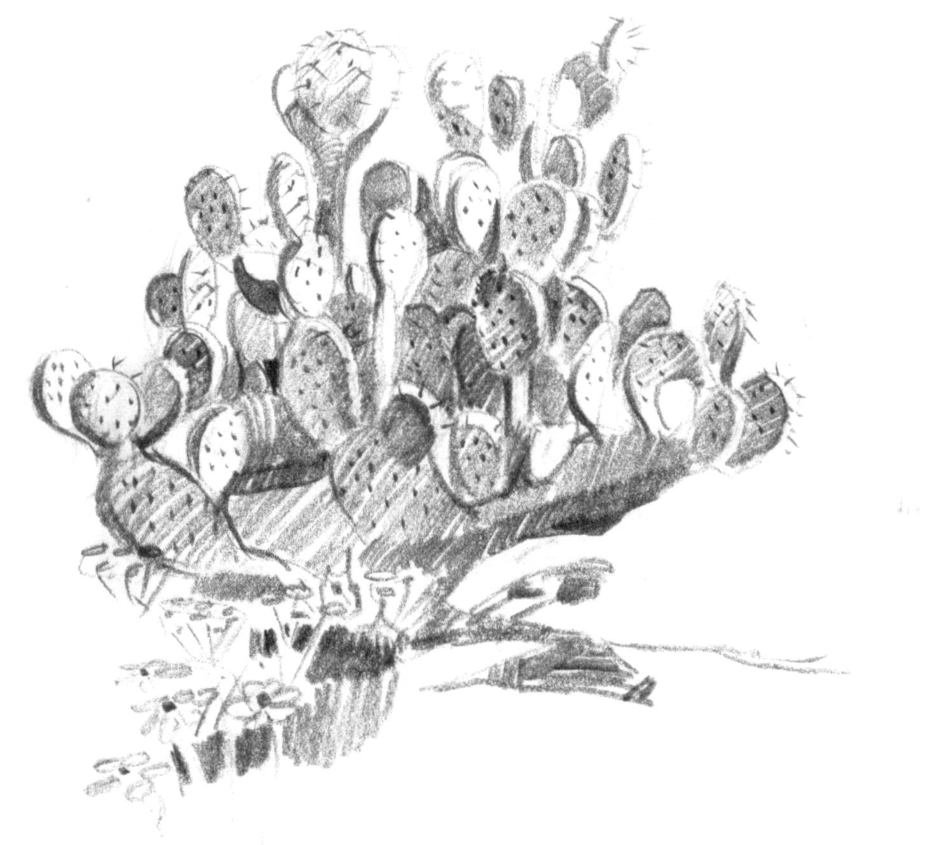

114. "In Tonto Forest north of Phoenix." Soft pencil on sketchbook page.

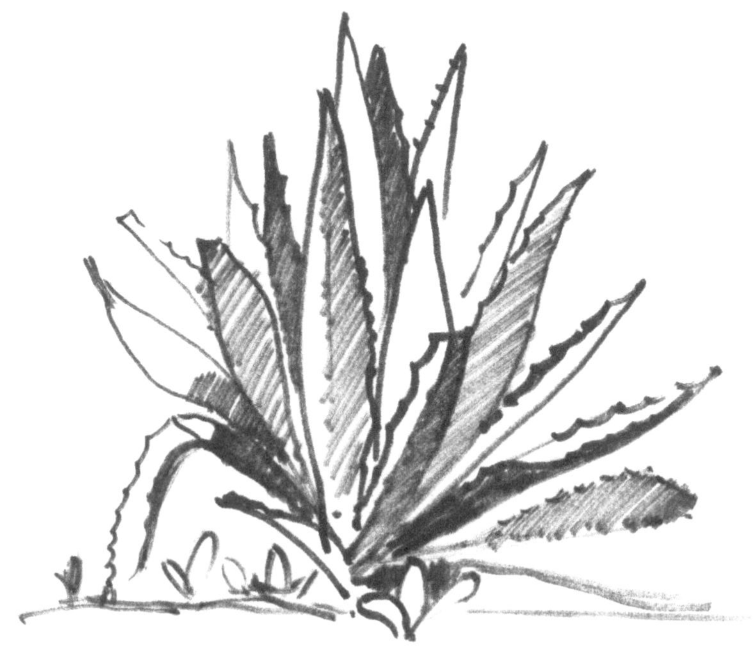

115. “Puerto Peñasco, Sonora.” Soft pencil on sketchbook page.

Sketches 116 and 117 are ink on sketchbook pages, likely done with a felt tip pen. They are executed in a free and casual sketch style. This technique may be accomplished quickly compared to the previous examples, while still conveying the most important characteristics of a subject that give it form and recognition. At the same time, it forces the sketcher to ascertain what are indeed the important characteristics of a subject necessary for understanding its basic formal structure.

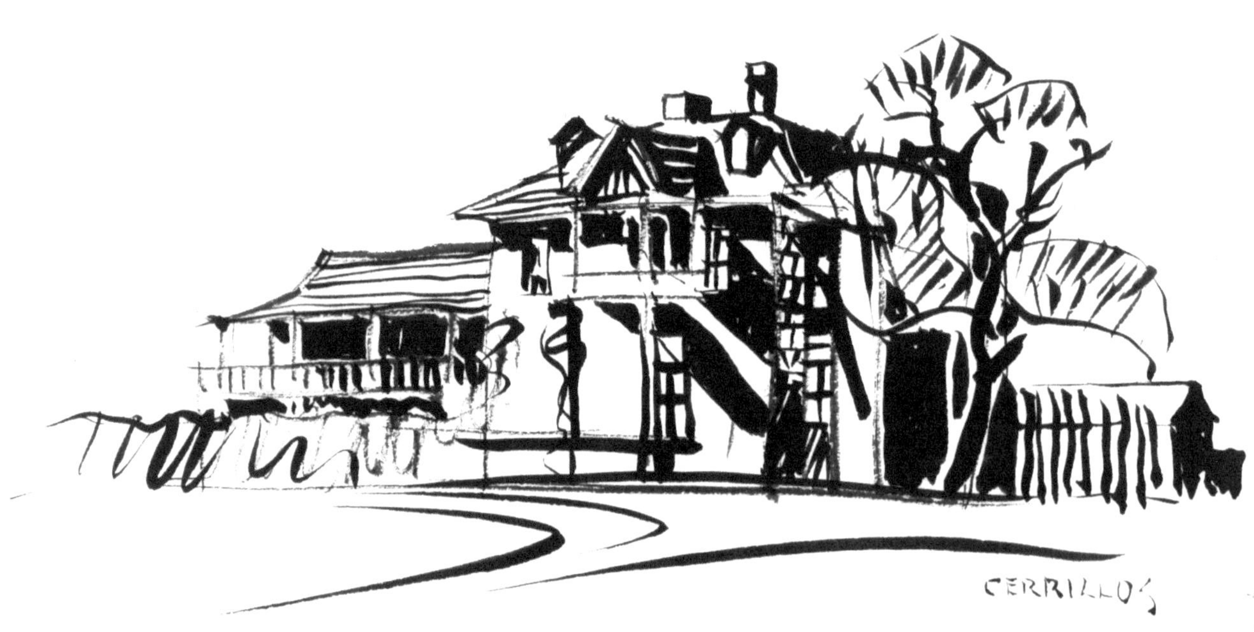

116. "Cerrillos." Felt tip pen, black ink on sketchbook page.

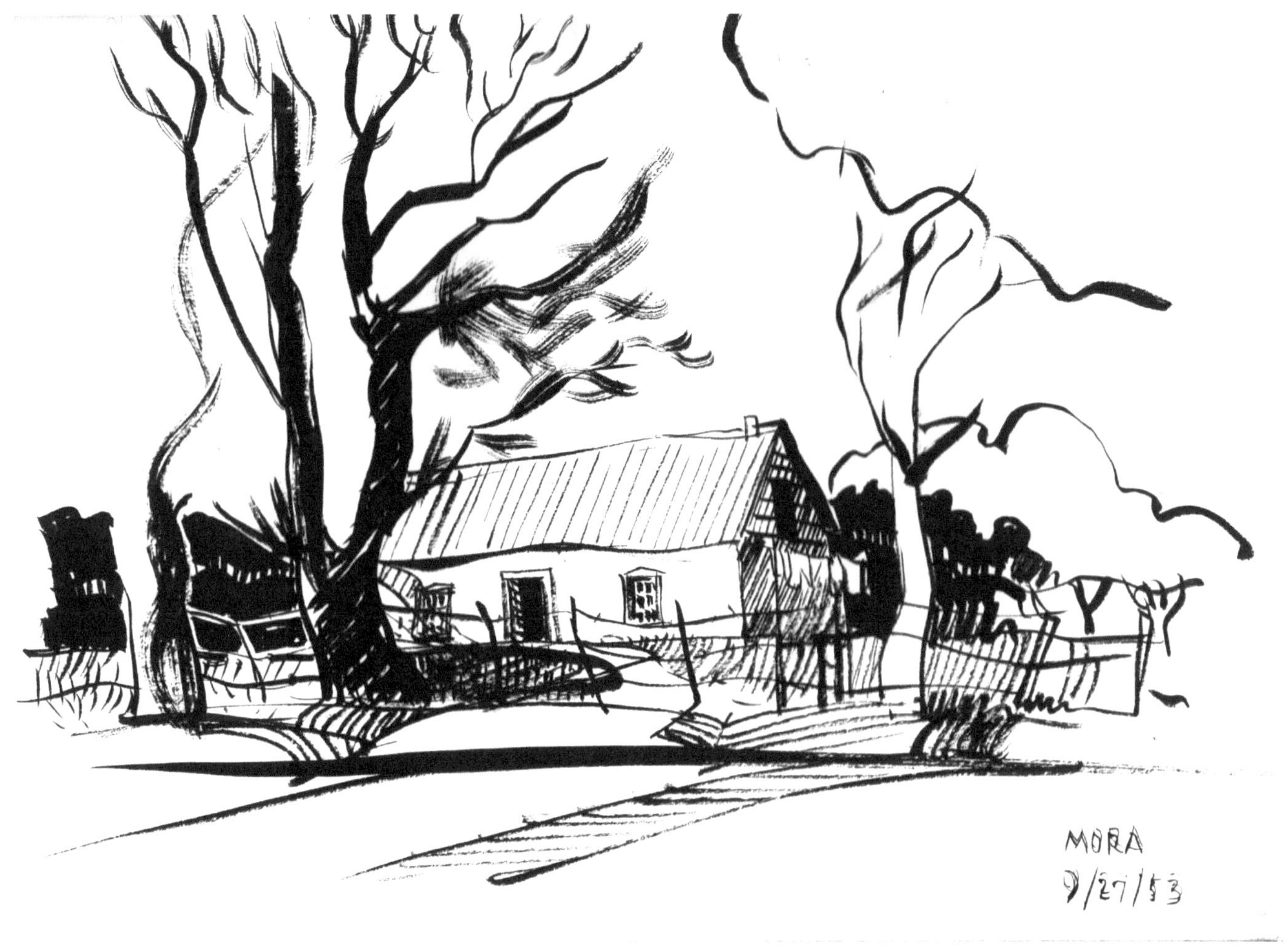

117. "Mora. 9/27/53." Felt tip pen, black ink on sketchbook page.

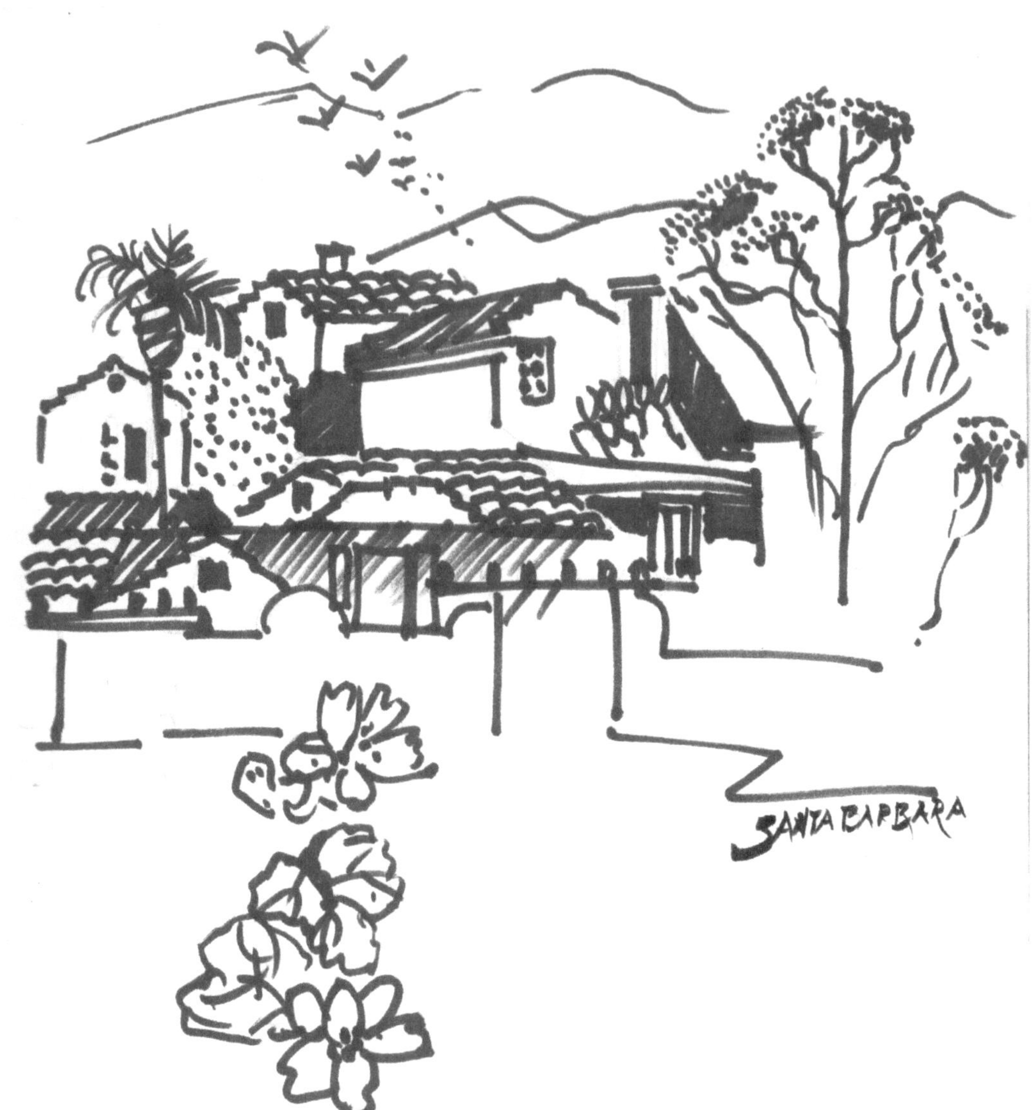

118. “Santa Barbara.” Felt tip pen on sketchbook page.

Like the last three drawings, sketch 119 is a quick sketch, but this time using a narrower felt tip pen with less opaque ink. This may be accomplished by using a felt tip or fiber tip pen that is low on ink, and so produces a dry line. In these sketches, depicting shadows in particular provides a primary means to defining form. It is perhaps surprising to discover that shadows alone can render the overall form perceptible, without depiction of accompanying details.

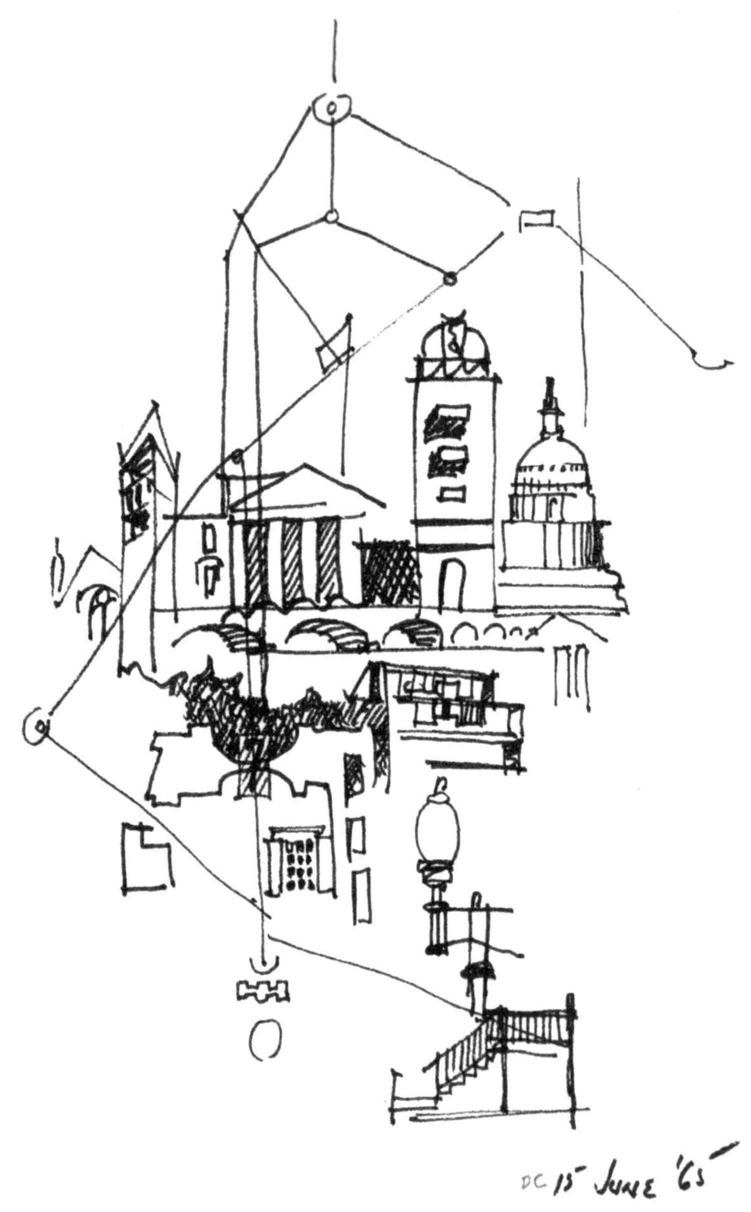

119. "D.C. 15 June '65." Felt tip or fiber tip pen on sketchbook page.

Sketch 119 is not of a particular scene, but rather it is a collage of images brought together to evoke a sense of place. Certain iconic buildings and incidental but characteristic street fixtures such as street lamps and stairs, are brought together to characterize a particular city or to generalize about a particular district of that city.

Sketches 120 through 126 introduce color. The color is watercolor applied directly on sketchbook pages. The first one uses a quick sketch technique like the black ink drawings preceding it, and the three that follow are progressively more detailed. Brightness of color suggests a lively, sunny scene in 120, while muted tones suggest a scene in low or filtered light in 122, perhaps at dawn or dusk. Sketch 123 suggests a blowing rain streaking across an otherwise bright urban scene. Note that 121 was prepared beforehand with a background wash of transparent watercolor.

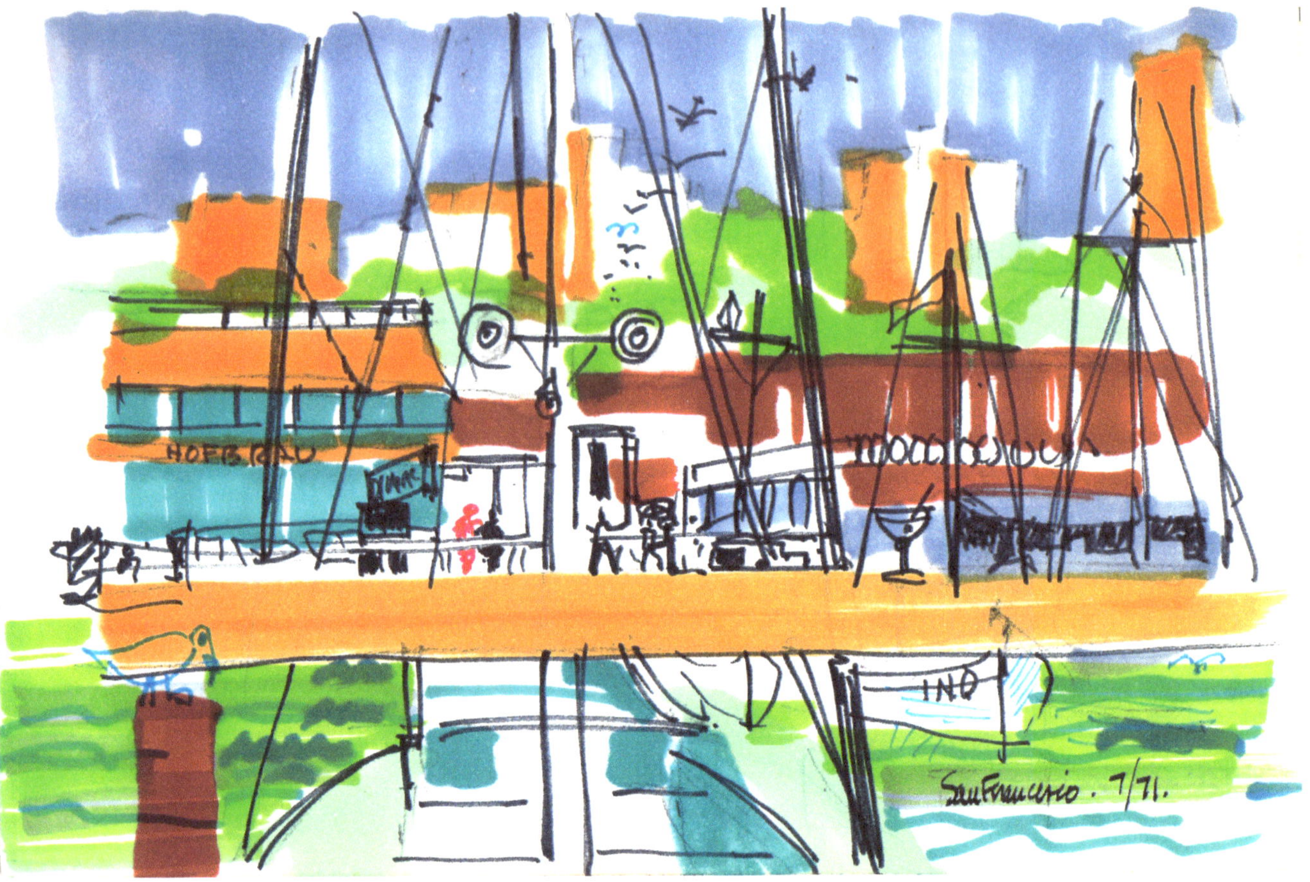

120. “San Francisco.” Watercolor with black felt tip or fiber tip pen lines on sketchbook page.

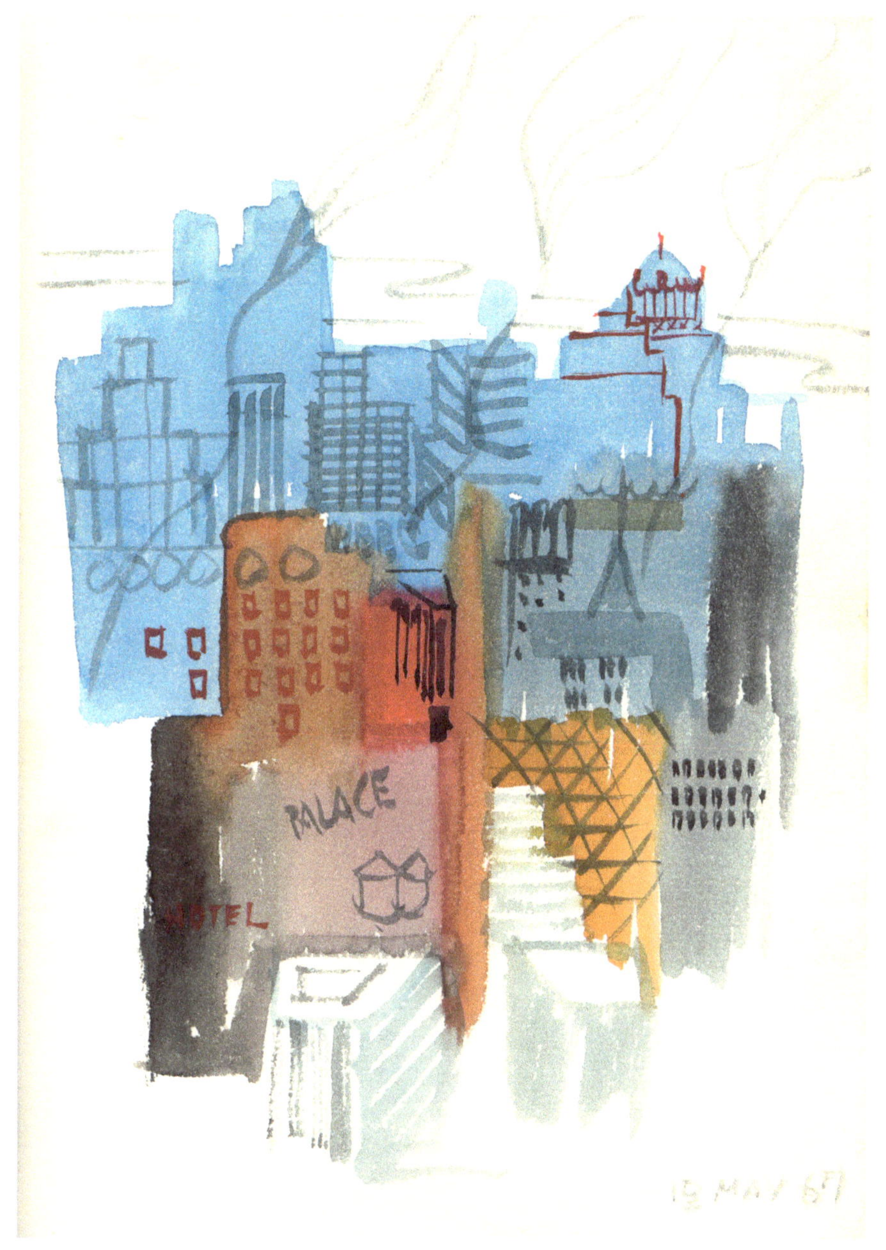

121. "15 May 67." Watercolor on sketchbook page with background wash.

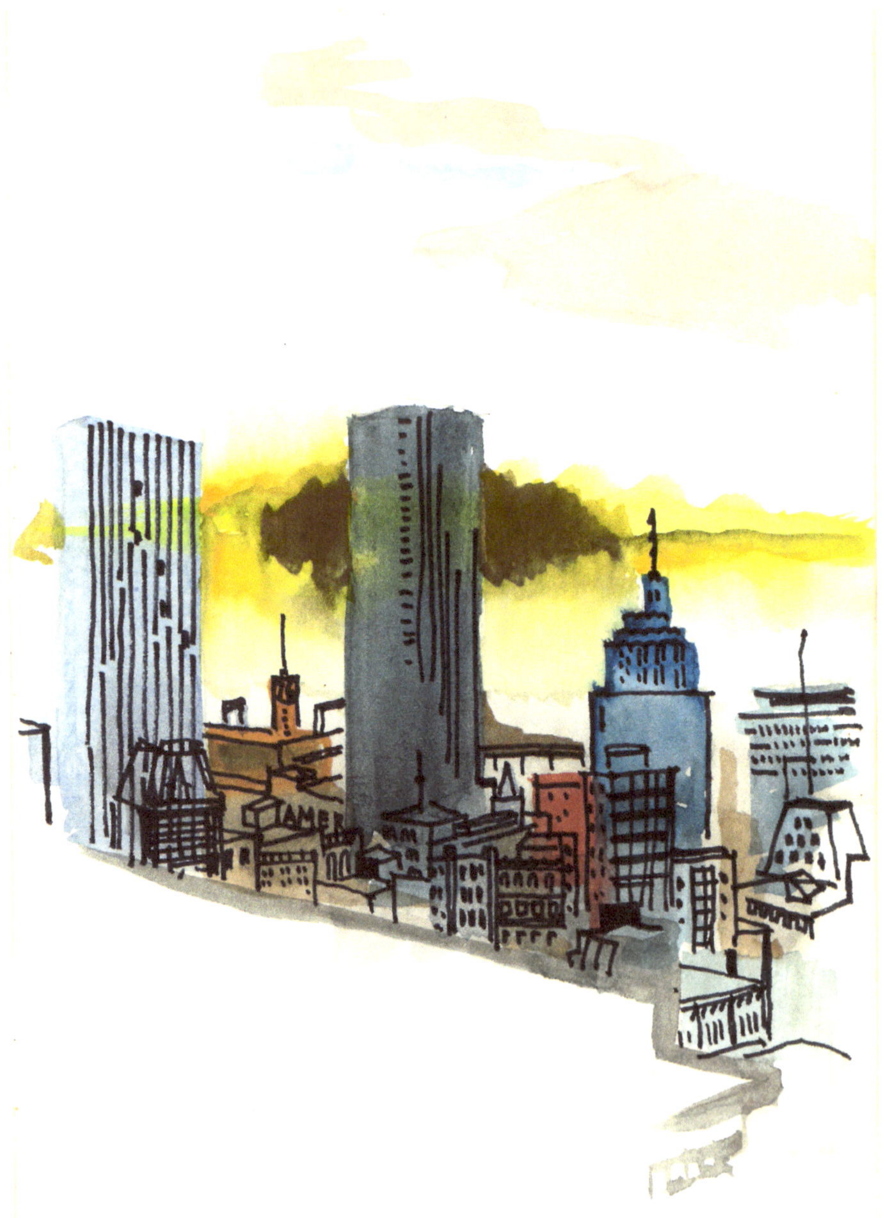

122. Unlabeled. Watercolor on sketchbook page with outlines and details in black felt tip or fiber tip pen.

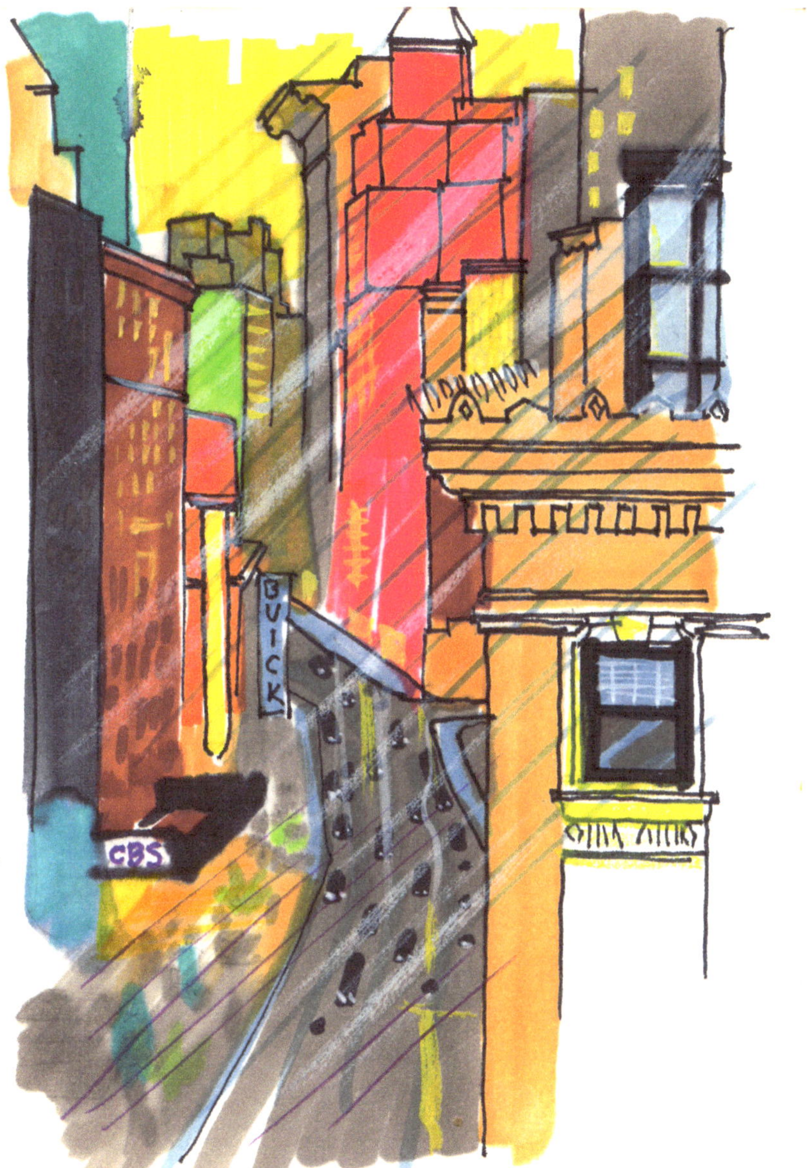

123. Urban scene. Watercolor on sketchbook page with black felt tip or fiber tip pen.

Sketch 124 is watercolor, most of which is strong in pigment. By contrast 125 employs a mix of media, including colored pencil over a background wash of transparent watercolor followed by an overlay of individual transparent watercolor tones for individual buildings. Here the transparency of the watercolor and its soft muted tones invite accents by pencil. Note that graphite pencil almost always emerges in the background as a layout technique for watercolor, but it is used in drawings such as 125 as an integral part of the expression of the sketch as well, providing surface texture and more emphatic lines than watercolor alone can provide.

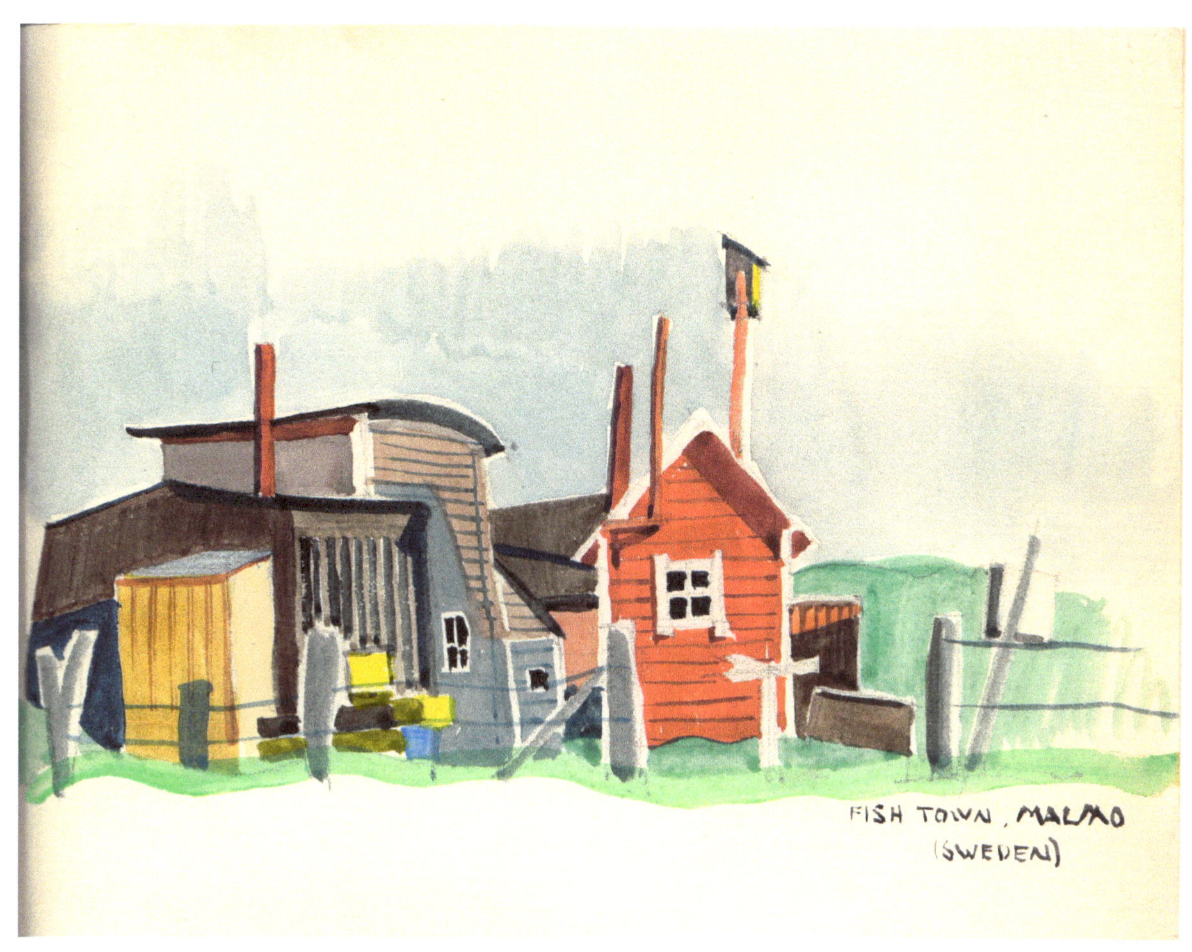

124. "Fish Town, Malmo." Watercolor on sketchbook page.

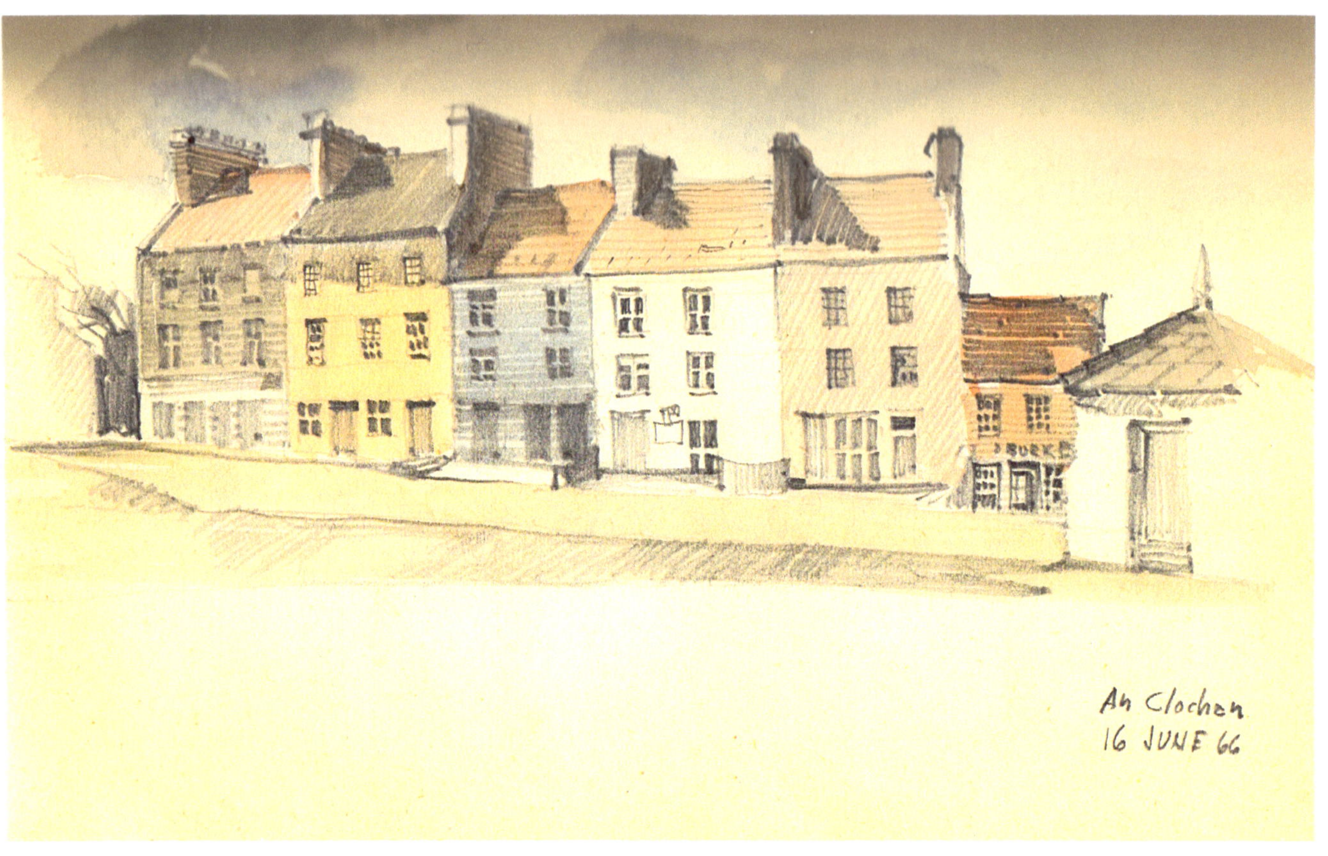

125. "Ann Clochan. 16 June 66." Watercolor wash with colored pencil and graphite pencil.

The next sketch, 126, is Conté crayon on textured sketchbook paper. The technique is essentially the same as soft graphite pencil, but the result is a stronger image, with deeper contrasts in light and dark areas. Note that the textured paper adds a special character to the drawing. This may be done as well over a background wash of watercolor in a complimentary color, although here it is rendered directly on the sketchbook page.

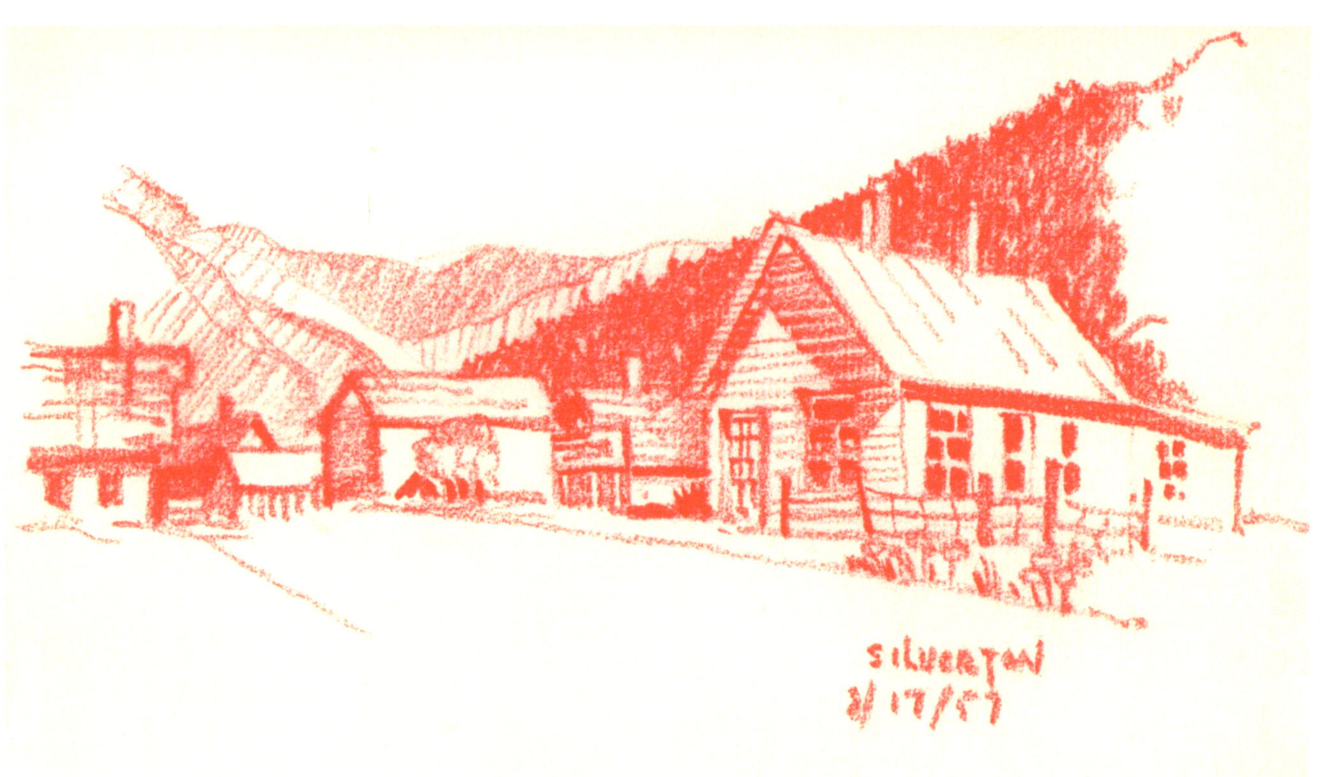

126. "Silverton. 8/17/57." Red Conté crayon on textured sketchbook page.

The final drawing in this series provides a note about detailed rendering of materials and light. Notice how the window reflects light. It is opaque in some places, while we can see through it in others. The clapboard siding is rendered by depicting the shadows it casts on itself, and details like the dentil course just under the eave of the little projecting bay window provide realism. The tiny drawing of the house above it, on the other hand, provides the illusion of detail with only a few simple strokes of a soft pencil, suggesting the textural qualities of clapboard siding, shingles, and a picket fence.

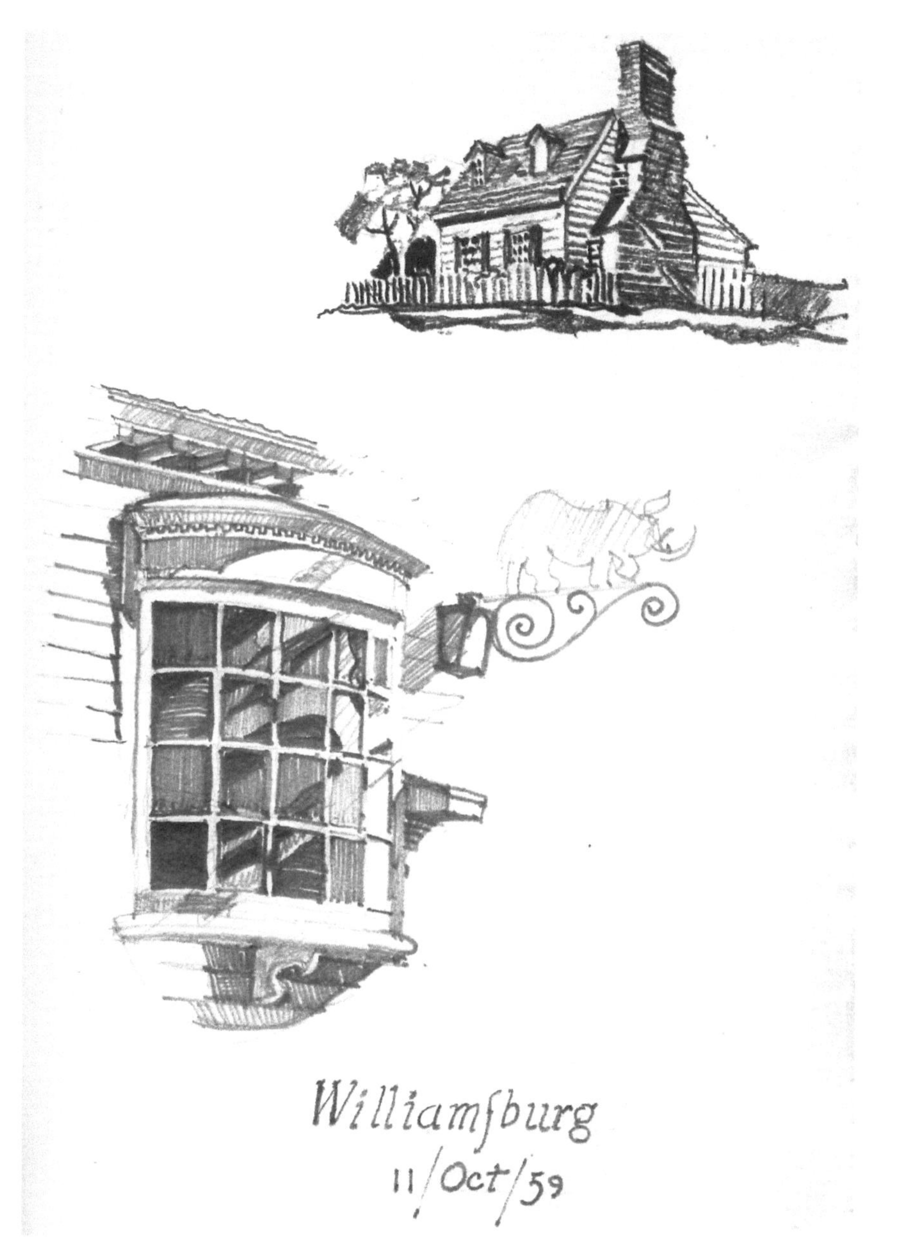

127. "Williamsburg. 11/Oct./59." Soft pencil on sketchbook page.

Chapter 3 on technique and media is included not only as a discussion of yet another way to appreciate the work presented here, but especially, to provide some encouragement to anyone who may be interested in taking up sketching. It provides a basic explanation of a few elemental techniques that can be put to the task at the onset. The next step for anyone who wants to become more involved in travel notes and sketching in general is to develop one's own style and preferences for capturing information in the field. Eventually, when sketching becomes largely intuitive, it will shift from task to enjoyment, and the results will show a spontaneity in character in contrast to the more labored drawings of one's earlier sketches.

Some Reflections 4

We may marvel at the skill that lies behind a drawing, quick sketch, or watercolor presentation in a sketchbook, but ultimately, what inspires us is something more comprehensive: the beauty of the drawing itself and a connection to the one who drew it. The source of that connection is difficult if not impossible to define. The subject of the sketch—an exotic foreign scene or a familiar place now seen in a new way—becomes entangled with what we know about the technique of producing the drawing, our response to its composition, and especially a sense of the presence of the one who made the sketch in the first place, whether it was recent or long ago. It is all these things as well as others too subtle to name that come together to inspire. For this particular collection of sketches, we expect New Mexicans in particular will find special inspiration. A large part of what we see here is one person's discovery of New Mexico as a place of distinct cultural and topographic richness. Publication of these sketches provides us with a window on that discovery as it progressed through his life. All places may be said to be unique, but we believe New Mexico to be especially unique, and we celebrate its special qualities by living here. As John McHugh came to know New Mexico, it became his center, a kind of axis mundi from which places outside New Mexico may be seen and compared. But they are always on the periphery, and like John McHugh, we always return to the center. We hope these sketches will awaken a new appreciation for, and a new intensity of interest in New Mexico as well as in the art and craft that these sketches reveal.

Appendix A

Biographical Notes: John McHugh, 1918–1995

1918: Born, Springfield, Ohio.

1924: Mother died in childbirth.
John and his sister Hazel were brought up by aunts.

1925(?): Father, an engineer, died in car crash.

1941: Graduated cum laude, University of Notre Dame.
Practiced architecture in Springfield, Illinois.
Worked as a planner in the Air Corps.

1944(?): After discharge from the military, traveled to Europe with sister Hazel before returning to Notre Dame to teach art.

1946: While on a trip across the U.S., John stopped in Santa Fe, New Mexico for car repairs, sought short-term employment in the offices of John Gaw Meem, Architect, but remained with the firm for ten years.

1953: Met Gillian Wethey, a musician and educator traveling on an exchange program from England.

1954: Married Gillian Wethey.

1956: Left John Gaw Meem's office; formed partnership with Van Dorn Hooker to start architectural firm in Santa Fe, with a branch office in Farmington, New Mexico.

1957: First Santa Fe Opera Pavilion completed.

1961: Gillian Wethey McHugh and John McHugh adopted Patricia Annette.

1963: Gillian Wethey McHugh and John McHugh adopted Colin Matthew.

1981: Received American Institute of Architects Fellowship in Design.

1982: Received award for Humane Design by New Mexico Arts Commission.

1988: Suffered stroke.

1995: Died, Santa Fe, New Mexico.

Early Architectural Commissions (listed in order of completion dates):

1957: First Methodist Church, Farmington
1957: Santa Fe Opera, Santa Fe
1960: Remodeling, Hall of Ethnology-Museum
Remodeling of Parish Hall, St. Anne's Church, Santa Fe
Elks Club, Santa Fe
1961: Immaculate Heart of Mary Seminary, Santa Fe, Chapel, Residence Hall, Dormitory
St. James Episcopal Church, Taos
Our Lady of Guadalupe, Taos (dedicated, 1962)
1962: Kearney School, Santa Fe
1963: Our Lady of the Assumption Church, Albuquerque

Selected Other Architectural Commissions (not listed in order of completion):

Restoration of San Ildefonso Church
Restoration of Isleta Mission Church
Addition and restoration, Episcopal Cathedral, Albuquerque
The Chapel to Holy Faith Church, Santa Fe
Santa Fe Animal Shelter, Cerrillos Road.

Residential Works:

Tacoma Ranch
The Greer Carson Ranch
General and Mrs. Patrick Hurley House
Artist Webb Young House

Appendix B

Notes on the Life of John Wells McHugh: A personal perspective by Gillian W. McHugh

John McHugh and I first met at his house in Santa Fe in 1953. At that time I was staying with Dr. Bertha Dutton of the Museum of New Mexico, helping her with a project which had taken us to Mexico and Guatemala on a six month's long research trip.

Immediately on my return I was swept into the Museum's hospitality program to help entertain the Director of the Turkish Opera from Ankara, his interpreter from Washington, and an Italian architect, . . . The occasion to be hosted by local architect, John McHugh on the condition that he had hostess help.

I discovered John to be a source of boundless energy, Irish charm and humor, with an all-embracing love of the good life and every aspect of it which he considered to have beauty. Architecture was his passion and he never deviated from his desire to follow that star.

[He was] orphaned by the time he was seven [sic], having lost his mother in childbirth and his engineer father to a car accident.

The children [John and his sister Hazel] were brought up by aunts in Springfield, Ohio, with very formal training and an iron hand where money was concerned. This did not prevent John from spending his paper route earnings on plants and creating a garden, as well as using his strong, fertile imagination to find ways of having a great deal of fun.

His excellent mind carried him easily through school and into the University of Notre Dame where he graduated cum laude in architecture. Strangely, although his aunt who managed the family estate allowed John to have his father's money on loan to be repaid with interest, neither family member attended the college commencement exercise to witness his success.

Although there was never any sign of bitterness, certainly this affected John's desire to put the "more important things of life" ahead of his concern for how they might be paid!

After a happy apprenticeship to an architect in Ohio and a war spent in the Air Force, but not seeing combat, he taught art at Notre Dame until his need to know the country better took over, and in an ancient Ford he traveled west. Anything that took his eye was sketchable, and in order to keep his skill sharp he would stop every hour or so and draw and/or paint anything that happened to be at hand, whether monumental building or telephone pole!

Arriving in New Mexico the long suffering Ford broke down, and while 'fixing' was taking place John called upon the illustrious architect John Gaw Meem to see if perhaps there was work to be had while waiting.

Ten years later he was one of the chief designers in the office and had purchased land from John Meem on which to build a house.

It was during his years at Meem's firm that our story began. I had returned to Santa Fe from Mexico and while still involved with working with Dr. Dutton, began to pick up my interrupted music life. This had been seriously neglected since coming to the States in 1952 as a delegate for International Scouting, but my training as a pianist was calling out and I was asked to give some programs in Santa Fe.

So what with music and museum work, I was busy, and in addition, John, I, and his wonderful Studebaker convertible (named Arabella) would travel round the State—John's sketch books becoming more filled with delightful mementos all the time—until in 1954 we were married.

Our launching (literally) into a new life began by taking a ship to England and my family there for our honeymoon.

John's amazing trust in people and experiences showed up dramatically as we arrived at the dock just as our ship's gangway was being drawn up. Undeterred by the annoyance, bags were thrown to porters, car keys to a security guard with a shouted "take care of this please, we'll be back on . . . " and the newlyweds staggered up to the moving deck accompanied by loud applause from fellow passengers lining the rails.

This was an initiation into a happy-go-lucky approach to events, which, in some extraordinary way, truly worked for John who was so often unhampered by looking at his watch.

Sketching in England was pure delight and remained so throughout the travels in many other parts of the world which we were fortunate enough to be able to experience over the years.

John was an early riser and one memory is of him returning to our hotel in Athens with quite a vocabulary of Greek words. The crowd gathered around his sketch pad and cup of coffee, and were delighted to instruct him as his pictures grew!

In 1956 John and Van Dorn Hooker opened their own architectural firm, and although times were often tremendously difficult, John reveled in all aspects of architectural design. When he was not involved in this he was exploring different forms of art.

In 1961 and 1963 we adopted our daughter Patty, and son, Colin (the best accomplishment of our lives!) and it is interesting to witness the way in which a "seeing eye" has been of importance in influencing their lives.

When a devastating right hemisphere stroke hit John in 1987 he virtually had to re-learn to function in every way.

After his stroke, St. Joseph's Hospital rehabilitation program was his salvation, along with his life-lure of working to study the arts in every imaginable form.

It was possible for family affairs to continue because of John's longing for independence: every aspect of the young peoples' development, my necessary involvement in running a music studio and giving an occasional benefit recital, my work with civic affairs and as a member of the New Mexico Arts Commission, all continued in very active form.

As John's condition gradually improved he was invited to become arts instructor at St John's College and to give a show there.

This was a wonderful addition to his life and to regaining confidence in himself.

Having survived for eight years following the stroke, working courageously to "come back" every step of the way, John died in 1995 while still able to enjoy the use of his talents in sketching the world around him.

—Gillian Wethey McHugh
February 9, 2010

Note: Gillian Wethey McHugh was named a Santa Fe Living Treasure in a ceremony on June 10, 2012.

Appendix C

Comments on John Wells McHugh by Van Dorn Hooker

John McHugh was working in the office of Meem, Zehner, Holien and Associates in Santa Fe when I joined the firm as a draftsman on July 5, 1951. Johnny, as his friends called him, was an assistant to Edward O. Holien, the chief designer in the firm. Johnny did most of the renderings of the office's projects, usually in pencil but sometimes in ink. He was extremely good at drawing and sketching.

Johnny had built an adobe house in the block of Camino del Monte Sol south of the Meem office and in it was a vacant apartment which my wife Peggy and I rented and lived there for about two years until we built a house of our own. One day in late 1955 or early 1956 Johnny asked me to join him in forming an architectural partnership. He had received a commission from his friend Lincoln O'Brien to design a printing plant for the Farmington Times. I immediately accepted his offer.

In a year or so, the office had so much work we asked Bradley P. Kidder, FAIA, to join us. Johnny would get commissions and design the projects, Brad would write specifications and take care of the business of the office, and I would run the drafting room and do a lot of inspection work during construction. It was a good office, the work was enjoyable, usually, and the three partners got along well with no arguments that I can remember.

Johnny was very proud of his Irish ancestry and a devout Catholic. He never worked on St. Patrick's Day. In the morning he would come by the office dressed in green with a green hat on his head. Then it was off to La Fonda bar for the rest of the day.

The project that got us a lot of good publicity was the design and construction of the first Santa Fe Opera Pavilion in 1957 for John Crosby. It was successful and after the finale of Madam Butterfly on opening night, there was standing applause and cries of "ARCHITECTS! ARCHITECTS!" A rare compliment.

Ours was a general practice. We did a lot of work for the Archdiocese of Santa Fe, including the chapel and other buildings at Immaculate Heart of Mary Seminary, Santa Fe; Our Lady of the Assumption Church, Albuquerque; and Our Lady of Guadalupe, Taos. Other works included residences, office buildings, and schools.

It was a good practice, but I left it for a better paying job as University Architect at the University of New Mexico. Brad died in January, 1973, and John in April, 1995, after retiring in 1989. We were the only three-member partnership in New Mexico in which all the partners were made fellows in the American Institute of Architects.

It is my great pleasure to have participated in the production of this volume of sketches by my old friend and partner John McHugh, FAIA.

—Van Dorn Hooker, FAIA

December, 2011

www.ingramcontent.com/pod-product-compliance
Lightning Source LLC
LaVergne TN
LVHW070212110826
845147LV00003B/563

9780865348950